HOLLYWOOD DREAMS
and
BIBLICAL STORIES

HOLLYWOOD DREAMS
and
BIBLICAL STORIES

Bernard Brandon Scott

Fortress Press
Minneapolis

HOLLYWOOD DREAMS AND BIBLICAL STORIES

Cover design: Nancy Eato

Library of Congress Cataloging-in-Publication Data

Scott, Bernard Brandon, 1941–
  Hollywood dreams and biblical stories / by Bernard Brandon Scott.
    p. cm.
  Includes bibliographical references and index.
  ISBN 0-8006-2753-9 (alk. paper)
    1. Motion pictures—Religious aspects.   2. Motion pictures—Religious aspects—Christianity.   I. Title
PN1995.9.R4S36   1994   93-38943
791.43'682—dc20
                                                                        CIP

The paper used in this publication meets the minimum requirements of the American National Standard for Information Sciences—Permanence of Paper for Printed Library Materials, ANSI Z329.48-1984.   (∞)^TM

Manufactured in the U.S.A.   AF 1-2753

98   97   96   2   3   4   5   6   7   8   9   10

To
Mary Caroline Marchal, S.C.
Damian Dietlein, O.S.B.
for friendship over the years

CONTENTS

PREFACE

A FEW YEARS AGO IT DAWNED ON ME THAT some of my students thought differently than I did. I mean literally that their thinking process was different. Though able to read and write, they truly came alive when discussing television shows or movies. Their powers of analysis were greater in this arena than in the traditional literary one. From that point on I increasingly sensed that my fate might parallel that of the dinosaurs. Our culture had passed over some great divide, and I was on the other side.

But I was not bereft of tools to engage this new world. Having spent many years of my life studying parables, I recognized that this new age exhibited striking similarities to that bygone era of orality. The tools I have developed as a scholar enable me perhaps to begin a conversation among myself, the ancient biblical texts, and modern American movies. I confess to feeling at times like an anthropologist in a strange village, only now the village is an electronic global one.

My goal for this conversation is both simple and ambitious. I want to begin to lay a foundation for hermeneutics in an electronic age. How will the Christian gospel find expression in this new age? I recognize the irony of writing about something that is essentially visual, but then again I'm a dinosaur. It is easy to recognize that print has already been taken over by the demands of the new media. The two largest mass-circulation magazines in North America are *Readers Digest* (16,269,637) and *TV Guide* (15,053,018). No other magazine even comes close. By contrast 100 million people watch prime-time television every night, and the average person spends over thirty hours watching television weekly. When living on the edge, between two ages, it is easy to become apocalyptic and call down damnation on the new age. Or one can fall victim to its wonders. I hope instead to begin a conversation that will allow each partner, the Bible and American movies, to appear differently in the eyes of the other or to hear different and new intonations in the other's voice.

I have tried to keep the apparatus of scholarship to a minimum, so I have dispensed with footnotes but have listed at the end of each chapter books and essays referred to in the text. The problem of biblical translations is particularly difficult because we have become too accustomed to the tyranny of a single translation. All translations are mistranslations. In an interview shortly before his death, the great American filmmaker John Huston remarked that the novel *Moby Dick* was a great book about industrialization, technology, alienation, nature, madness, ambition, capitalism, and a great many other things, but that his movie was a big fishing story. Translation involves loss. I have therefore availed myself of several modern translations, depending upon which best catches the sense of the Greek for a particular aspect or point. Unless otherwise noted, the translation is NRSV (New Revised Standard Version). I have noted the use of REB (Revised English Bible), NAB (New American Bible), and SV (Scholars Version). Sometimes I have employed my own translations.

Many people have encouraged me in this project. My two children have always enjoyed arguing with Dad about what a movie means and have frequently insisted I got it wrong. My wife has sat through many a film with me, even *Dirty Harry*, and Charlie and Martha and Sharon have helped clarify ideas over pizza. Many students over the years have contributed more than they will ever know not only in my classes on film, but in conversations that frequently begin with "Did you see . . ." or "What about . . . ?" To single some out is not to downplay the others, but some do require special notice: Gueric Debona, O.S.B., who was very helpful on the hero myth; and Margaret Dean, who read the whole manuscript, offered many helpful suggestions, and served as my research assistant. A special thanks must be extended to the late John A. Hollar, who encouraged this project from its inception. He is greatly missed. Michael West of Fortress has been most helpful and patient as an editor, and David Lott and Pat Lewis provided excellent editorial assistance. Finally, Thomas Boomershine has encouraged me and argued with me; I have stolen freely from him. I hope he will find here support for his courageous vision.

The Krichinsky family (Armin Mueller-Stahl, Joan Plowright, Elizabeth Perkins, Elijah Wood, Aidan Quinn) are engrossed in the new phenomenon of television in Barry Levinson's *Avalon* (1990). (Photo courtesy of Archive Photos/copyright © Fotos International)

1

A FLICKERING LIGHT

All life's riddles are answered in the movies.
—*Steve Martin,* Grand Canyon

SOMETIMES WE SEE AN ERA SHIFT RIGHT BE-
fore our eyes. The movie *Avalon* (1990) captures such a moment.
The story follows four immigrant brothers and their extended family.
The brothers form a kind of mutual aid society, supporting each other,
bringing other members of the family over from the old country,
providing loans to help start family businesses and enterprises, and
finally celebrating and fighting together. On the day the family's first
television set is installed, they all gather around it and stare at the
test pattern, unblinking and unspeaking. The elders think the new
contraption is silly, but the younger ones are fascinated. A new age
has been born. Previously, the extended family, spreading out in rings
from the patriarchal grandfather through the brothers and their wives,
the sisters, aunts, uncles, cousins, and assorted children, was the
center of life. Now everything revolves around the television set.
Dinner is a TV dinner, served on a TV tray. Conversation dies as
people stare instead at the screen. The extended family dies with it,
replaced by the nuclear family of husband, wife, and child sitting in
front of the television set. The mass audience for television consists
of isolated groups of two or three individuals or often just a
single person.

The old family does not survive television in *Avalon*. In the final scene the narrator as an adult takes his young son to visit his hero grandfather in a nursing home. Fittingly, the flickering TV screen is the grandfather's sole companion.

The television is a metonymy for a major shift that began in the Western world with the invention of the telegraph and photography and is now spreading to the rest of the world. We often refer to the agents of this change as "the media" and sometimes call our new era "the electronic age." Both are appropriate. *Media*, a term first used in advertising, indicates the importance of image and the visual, while *electronic* refers not only to the power (electricity, the electron) behind this change but also to its ephemeral, almost magical, character.

Coming to terms with the new media challenges all the institutions of postmodern society, including churches and religion. The electronic media form a cultural atmosphere that envelopes us as completely as the air we breathe. They affect us in incalculable ways that we never even notice.

How we come to terms with these new media, this new environment, is critical. For the most part, North American churches have responded to the changing environment in two ways. On the one hand, wholesale acceptance of the media has spawned the electronic church: the blow-dried preacher, lounging on a sofa, trying to imitate Johnny Carson or some other media creation. Ironically, the electronic church is culturally and religiously conservative, ranting and raving against the values of the very electronic media that created it. On the other hand, the more liberal, mainstream churches have adopted a studied disdain of the media, which they regard as incapable of having a critical dimension. Most of their approaches to electronic media appear to imitate educational TV. They deem television too frivolous to deal with the complexities of modern life and religion.

Neither response—acceptance or disdain—will get the job done. *Avalon* depicts the social change wrought by television, but at a deeper level the electronic media are all generating an epistemological change, a change in the way we know, in what we can know, and in the way our consciousness is formed. The electronic environment has engaged us; we have no choice about engaging it; the question is *how* we engage it. In the past the gospel has always been part of a particular culture and has undergone change as it shifted from one culture to another, although never without debate or controversy. As Paul remarks, "Jews demand signs and Greeks desire wisdom" (1 Cor. 1:22). There is no pure gospel, no essence of the gospel, separate from particular cultures. Just as the churches had to respond to the printing press with a new literacy, so we need a new "literacy" that encompasses the electronic media.

To get at this new epistemology, we need both an approach and a focus. David Tracy has suggested "conversation" as the most appropriate method or stance in this pluralistic age. In conversation, we respect and cherish our partner. Conversation also recommends itself because, as *Avalon* indicates, it was an early casualty of television. One need only observe the debasement of conversation on the "McLaughlin Group" to yearn for its restoration. For conversation partners, I have chosen the Bible and popular American movies. To provide a focus for a conversation between two such apparently disparate partners, I will concentrate on movies as examples of an American mythology. This first chapter explores the perimeters of our task. Like the blind men examining the elephant, we will investigate one aspect of the project at a time so that the effect is cumulative. Thus I will eschew as much as possible a heavy theoretical framework up front. I will examine movies as myth, indicate the place of myth in our self-understanding, and suggest how conversation provides an appropriate model for our project.

> Mythical thought always progresses from the awareness of oppositions toward their resolution.
> —*Claude Lévi-Strauss (1963)*

OUR ANCESTORS GATHERED AROUND THE camp fire while the shaman sang stories of mythical times and places. Strange though these stories may seem to us, they played an important role by encoding solutions for life's problems. They helped the listeners determine who they were, what the world around them was like, and how they were to behave. The French anthropologist Claude Lévi-Strauss captures two of myth's fundamental characteristics: They mediate the fundamental problems of life, and they think for us without our being aware of it. These two characteristics are related. All societies face conflict that threatens to disrupt social unity. Chaos is always a danger, so hero myths fortify the group against chaos. Other stories justify inequities that might threaten social cohesion by explaining our fate as the will of the gods. Where did we come from? Where will we go? Myths furnish the answers. But for these stories to work, they must mask their sleight of hand; otherwise the solution will be undone.

Now as we gather around the flickering light of the television screen and movie projector, the purpose of stories remains the same. The movies and television shows are our modern myths; through them we work out who we are and negotiate the problems of modern life. A spate of recent box-office hits highlights the shamanistic character of modern movies. These movies from 1989 through 1991 mirror the underlying conflicts of American life and prescribe how we will attempt to resolve them.

Home Alone (1990) is a children's movie that took off at the box office and did very well with adults. This movie was something of a sleeper, so why did it do so well? While the direction, acting, and writing are not spectacular, they are all competent and all the pieces work together to form a delightful ensemble. The young boy Kevin (Macauley Culkin) is engaging, although not in a league with Shirley Temple.

Raising children gives rise to a number of conflicts. The ancients recognized this, as the proverb "Spare the rod and spoil the child" testifies. Proverbs summarize myths, boiling down a community's wisdom into a succinct and memorable phrase. Parents must often discipline their child, a duty that goes against the parents' desire. The proverb reminds parents of their responsibility and exempts them from the task of determining what it entails by thinking for them. Similarly, a major reason for *Home Alone's* success was that it implicitly confronted several strong anxieties of its adult audience. Surveys consistently show that a major concern of young mothers is their children's safety. They believe we live in a dangerous world. Tales of gangs, mugging, kidnapping, and child molestation abound, and milk cartons carry pictures of missing children. The movie meets this concern. Kevin, who is regarded by his siblings as a helpless geek, is left behind, while his family flies off to Paris for Christmas. He successfully defends himself against two invading burglars who have more in common with the Three Stooges than with professional criminals. The story reassures mothers worried about their children's safety, guilty about leaving them in day-care or even home alone after school (latchkey children), that their children can take care of themselves. Even though the plot is preposterous and the assurance or comfort temporary, it has a momentary payoff. Besides, the movie reaffirms a truth that all children know—they're smarter than their parents. So everyone comes out of the movie feeling good.

Home Alone exemplifies how a myth operates. It provides a resolution to unresolved or irresolvable conflicts in the audience's experience. The deeper the conflict, the less obvious will be its resolution. Our fear of death leads us to prefer happy endings so we are assured in myth, if not in reality, of our immortality. The boy left home alone, while his mother tries frantically to get back and the rest of the family vacations in Paris, mythically parallels the abandonment of children to day-care and babysitters. The various dangers he faces parallel the perilous world in which our children must live. The boy's resolution of these dangers reassures the viewing parents of their own children's viability.

A mythical resolution also appears on the child's part. Kevin's older brother and sisters pick on him as a helpless little jerk. "Families suck," he says, wishing they would all disappear. His dream comes true when he wakes up to find them gone. First he engages in an orgy of fun and snack food; then he becomes responsible, helping an elderly neighbor reconcile with his son and finally welcoming back his own family after defeating the burglars. The movie helps a child deal with the fears and anxieties about family that plague all children. In story, the child works through the need for family, sees that the abandoning mother is not truly abandoning, and builds self-respect by overcoming the status of despised sibling.

Since the plot is ridiculous, how can it have such an effect? No one takes this movie seriously, despite its slick and professional production. Yet that is the genius and subtlety of myth. For myth to be successful, it must operate in a hidden, subterranean fashion. As soon as someone points out a myth and elevates it to consciousness, the myth appears to be empty. This is because myth has an impossible task. "The purpose of myth," says Lévi-Strauss, "is to provide a logical model capable of overcoming contradiction (an impossible achievement if, as it happens, the contradiction is real)" (Lévi-Strauss 1963,

229). For this reason—to maintain myth's masquerade—mythical movies need a happy ending. This is precisely why those who have invested highly in a myth, who see it as reality, become so defensive when the myth is exposed or, in Rudolf Bultmann's famous phrase, demythologized. In *Home Alone*, the myth hides under the guise of a child's movie, humor, and a ridiculous plot, a very effective disguise as the many people who saw the movie and liked its happy ending indicate.

The family remains a paradigm for how we relate to other people, and relationships always contain the potential for conflict. *Rain Man* (1988) approaches this problem in a distinctly American way. Charlie and Raymond are two brothers forced into a relationship after their father's death. The father's will leaves all of his estate to Raymond, who is autistic. Since Charlie was unaware of Raymond's existence, he had expected to receive all the inheritance. Feeling cheated, Charlie angrily kidnaps Raymond and begins a cross-country trip in an old car, the only thing the father left him. A road trip is a clear metaphor for a journey of self-discovery. Eventually, Charlie comes to appreciate his brother and to care for him, rather than trying to exploit him. When Charlie must finally return Raymond to the institution that has taken care of him all these years, he tries to reach the autistic Raymond, and magically, as can happen only in the movies, he does so for a moment. Raymond acknowledges his brother as his "main man."

Charlie epitomizes the young, hard-driving, scheming salesman trying to make it big. In his relations with other people, especially his girlfriend, he is metaphorically autistic. An early scene shows Charlie and his girlfriend in the car driving to the reading of the will. Absorbed in his own world, he talks past her and is unconcerned about her. He can neither relate nor reach out. He represents the great fear of an individualistic society that throughout the 1980s pursued an aggressive "me-ism." This is evident not only in the predatory, greedy tactics of *Wall Street* (1987), but in our living arrangements. We increasingly live in suburbs designed to isolate us from our neighbors. Sidewalks are disappearing, and front porches are replaced by patios and decks surrounded by a privacy fence. The house is oriented inward and no longer looks toward the street. The living area is oriented around the television set, which is often the dominating piece of furniture in the room.

Rain Man reassures the viewer that, despite our rugged individualism and isolation from each other, we too can reach out, even in impossible situations, if we wish. The shaman spins another magical incantation. Despite the breakdown in our society and our increasing social and economic isolation from each other, the magic is still there. We only need to reach out.

Race is another source of conflict and isolation in our society. *Driving Miss Daisy* (1989) draws on this situation. Well directed and acted, the movie won an Academy Award for best picture and was generally popular with the critics. Its story is set in Atlanta during the period after World War II, and the emerging civil rights movement forms a backdrop, intruding from time to time. Although the black-white relation is the movie's primary theme, another wrinkle is that Miss Daisy (Jessica Tandy) is Jewish. The plot revolves around the growing friendship between Miss Daisy and her chauffeur (Morgan Freeman), and the climax is Miss Daisy's confession that he is the only true friend she has left.

At times the movie paints a poignant picture of southern racism. In a particularly powerful and graphic image of the separation imposed by racism, Miss Daisy and the chauffeur both eat dinner, she in the dining room, he in the kitchen, mostly in silence, but occasionally exchanging a few words through the doorway. The movie addresses current racial alienation indirectly by looking back at a period when things supposedly were worse and racism was institutionalized. It shows that even then individuals could surmount the barriers. In keeping with the 1980s when we had turned away from governmental solutions, the movie implies that individual effort, not societal regulation, is the key.

The movie does depict the truly unequal relations between Miss Daisy and her chauffeur. She could and did treat him as a child, accusing him of stealing and attempting to control when he could go to the bathroom. He had no choice in the relationship; he needed the job. That cheap domestic help vanished as soon as blacks had other options in the workplace clearly indicates that such positions were hardly desirable. At the same time, the movie softens its depiction of inequality with warm light and feelings. *Driving Miss Daisy* succeeds not only because it is a well-produced movie, but also because it soothed and held out a temporary nostrum for our plague of racism. It comforted when a little more discomfort would have been desirable.

Women's struggle to achieve equal rights is a repeated theme in American life. We may well be in a time of backlash, as Susan Faludi (1991) argues in her book of the same title. Nevertheless the mass entry of women into the workplace and many families' need for two incomes continue to challenge the traditional roles of men and women. Such change is profoundly disturbing. Traditional male-female roles that have persisted for millennia do not change without exacting a heavy price.

Pretty Woman (1990) sashays into this maelstrom. Its characters are attractive; its direction, editing, and writing are sharp. The hero is another hard-driving businessman, although much more successful than Charlie in *Rain Man*. He buys corporations and then breaks them apart to sell at a profit. The heroine is the hooker with a heart of gold, made highly appealing by Julia Roberts in a strong comedic performance. As the hero remarks, they both screw people for money. While she awakens in him feelings of devotion and compassion, he sends her down Rodeo Drive on a shopping spree that proves that clothes do make the woman. She doesn't want to be a kept woman, however—she wants it all. And she gets it in an ending straight out of a fairy tale. Like a white knight disguised in a business suit, he comes riding to her rescue in a stretch limo with umbrella raised high and climbs the fire escape to the walkup flat where she waits like the princess in the tower. Like Charlie, he is somewhat autistic, but she changes him from a greedy destroyer into a builder, while he saves the "working girl" and gives her the status of his wife. The movie brings the fairy tale into the real world. At the movie's end, a black street prophet proclaims, "Everybody comes to Hollywood, where dreams come true."

Pretty Woman makes the obligatory nod to women's liberation. In retelling the fairy tale, he says the knight will save her, and she adds that she will save him back. Thus there is a hint of mutuality. But in reality this is the Pygmalion story, in which "the Wall Street tycoon . . . remakes the loud, gum-smacking hooker into his soft-spoken and genteel appendage, fit for a Ralph Lauren ad" (Faludi 1991, 136). As a measure of the deep disturbance of female and male roles in our society, this movie glances in the direction of the change but reasserts a number of old myths (the princess in the tower, Pygmalion) as well as some old clichés (clothes make the woman and, as Johnny Bench said, what every man wants is a princess in the living room and a whore in the bedroom). The movie's polish and production values hide the dangerous character of the invoked myths, which encourage women to accept enslaving roles.

The rapidly rising divorce rate in the United States since the end of World War II underscores the problematic character of these princess myths. Increasingly, divorced women are single parents with full responsibility for the children and less income than when they were married. A majority of children will spend a significant part of their childhood and adolescence in a single-parent family, and many will spend it in poverty.

Ghost (1990) indirectly meets and comforts these concerns and dislocations. The movie centers around a typical two-career couple, Sam (Patrick Swayze) and Molly (Demi Moore), who are madly in love. Sam is killed by his business partner; nevertheless, through a medium, hilariously played by Whoopi Goldberg, he continues to protect Molly until his murderer is brought to justice. In form this movie closely resembles a medieval morality play with those who still have unresolved matters to work out here on earth experiencing a purgatory-like existence after death. Apparently, purgatory is located somewhere in the vicinity of the New York subway.

If *Ghost* were as simple as its plot summary indicates, it would never have been a major box-office sensation. The movie wraps the separation and the ghostly presence of the husband in a sensualism and romanticism that mask the pain that many feel in the separation of divorce. In a society where women are often left alone, are afraid they will be left alone, and hear constant warnings of the dangers of being left alone, this movie reassures them that someone will watch over them.

Myth does not deal with conflict directly but indirectly, implicitly, at one step removed. *Driving Miss Daisy*, though set in the 1940s and 1950s, concerns the 1980s and 1990s. Likewise the "working woman" in *Pretty Woman* was meant in several senses. At the level of narrative, it signifies a prostitute, while on the mythical level it stands for the American woman as a "working woman" and implies that she is a whore. Similarly, in *Rain Man* Raymond's clinically and Charlie's metaphorically autistic behavior mythically stand for a similar pattern in our relations as a polarized and isolated society. On the surface *Ghost* is not about divorce, for no divorce occurs in the movie. It deals with a widow and her anguish. Myth operates by analogy—"this is like"—not by direction. This hidden aspect allows myth to operate without our being aware of it. The pain of separation and loss in *Ghost* serves to mediate indirectly the pain of separation and loss that divorce has created in our society. This movie reassures those who feel abandoned that they are not ultimately alone, that the princess myth still holds. Yet remove myth's façade and the movie breaks down.

A basic purpose of myth is to keep chaos at bay, to weave a web of order in story. Yet every evening the TV news quickly reminds us of the violence and mayhem that surround us. The United States leads all other industrialized nations in murders, rapes, and armed robberies, in the percentage of the population in prison, and in the number of executions. The violence in our society contradicts our belief that we are a peace-loving nation. The murder rate is higher in the United States than in the most dangerous country in Europe, Northern Ireland. We forget that our nation was born through violent revolution, that we in fact initiated the modern revolutionary age, that our Civil War was the first modern war in which machines drastically increased the slaughter of men, and that since World War II we have remained in an almost constant state of war readiness, waging a "cold" war for much of that time. Though we increasingly fear going outside our protected domains, our response to violence is more violence.

One of the most expensive and popular movies of 1991 addresses this situation. *Terminator 2* follows on the hugely successful *Terminator* (1984) but with an interesting twist. The robot model (Arnold Schwarzenegger), which was the villain in the first *Terminator*, now becomes the defender and must face a new, improved model. Both robots, the original terminator and its new version, were sent from the future. One must defend and the other must kill the future hero, now a boy, who will lead humans against the triumphant machines. The fate of humanity is at stake.

Terminator 2 asserts the inevitable happy ending. This is important because one of the first attacks on myth is the denial of the happy ending. Next a superhero meets superviolence, thus affirming our society's basic strategy in the face of increasing violence. Since a machine, an alien, inflicts the violence needed to defeat the enemy,

the violence is masked and divorced from us. The good are so protected from exercising violence that the little-boy-future-hero asks
the terminator robot not to kill anyone. The robot complies by shooting them in the knees. Mythically, we draw a line between good
violence and bad violence, thus maintaining our own innocence.

> Myths operate in men's minds without their being
> aware of the fact.
> —*Claude Lévi-Strauss (1969)*

A MOVIE MAY BE POPULAR, AND REACH A MASS
audience for a variety of complex reasons. Certainly, the media moguls cannot force us to view what we do not want to watch. Nor is
a movie's popularity a matter of a good advertising campaign, although
that is important. Many movies have failed at the box office even
though they had strong campaigns, and others have succeeded without massive advertising. Sometimes the studios are surprised. If the
moguls could decree our likes, then movie-making would not be such
a risky business. One reason a movie does well is that it intersects
with basic struggles, conflicts, or tensions within a society in such
a way that it provides a temporarily masked resolution to that conflict.
Frequently, people complain that serious movies should be entertaining and make us feel good. In other words, the movies should
live up to their mythical dimension.

Because the ancients propagated their myths in stories of the gods,
we think that myth belongs to the past and has been superseded by
Christianity and modern science. But that misunderstanding only
allows myth to remain hidden. Basically, myth is a narrative that
mediates fundamental conflicts by indirection so that we are not even
aware that it is happening. We have seen all these characteristics in
the popular movies we have just reviewed. We propagate our myths
in films and TV programs. We sit before their flickering light and
listen to this new shaman sing our songs. Yet just as these media can
be used to propagate myth, they also can be turned against myth
when they refuse to mediate the conflict, thereby making us aware
of what is really happening. When Job refuses to buy his friends'

explanation of why misfortune has befallen him—when he refuses to blame himself—he upsets the order of the universe and exposes for all time the basically unsolved problem of good and evil: how can a good God be implicated in an evil world? Likewise, when Martin Scorsese in *GoodFellas* (1990) refuses to ennoble the violence of the mobsters as other gangster movies such as *The Godfather* have, we are forced to come to terms with our own violence. The mask is removed.

Stories can be used in two ways: mythically, to mediate and hide conflicts, or nonmythically, to expose the conflict. To paraphrase Lévi-Strauss, myth's problem is doubly hard because frequently the conflict it seeks to mediate cannot be mediated. Reality constantly besieges our myths so they must work ever harder to keep their processes hidden.

As we adjust to the new epistemology of the electronic media, we must become electronically "literate." We must become aware of how the new media communicate and how they are retelling the old stories we have inherited. Since myth seeks to hide its actions, our basic strategy must be to unmask it. The new media work against this strategy by creating such a strong sense of presence that we are frequently overcome by it and placed in a radical *now*, without past or context. This sense of the now greatly facilitates the operation of myth and makes literacy, a sense of distance and objectivity, much more difficult yet more important than ever. Without learning how to "read" our myths, we will be subsumed in an ever-present now.

A basic way to achieve this distance is to objectify a story and become aware of its levels of operation. First is the surface level of the story itself, which is sometimes called the syntagmatic level on analogy with the syntax of a sentence. Just as syntax determines the order of the sentence, so the syntagmatic level of a story concerns the sequence of the story, its plot, or, in Aristotle's terms, the beginning, the middle, and the end. This is the level that is most evident to us as we watch a movie or read a book.

Another, deeper level of meaning is based not on the story's sequence but on its connections to the audience's value and meaning systems. This is called the paradigmatic level, on analogy with the paradigm of a conjugation, which sets out all the possible inflections of a word. Narratives never invoke the complete paradigm, just as a sentence never uses all available forms of the verb. Yet the paradigm or system of meaning remains. The viewer makes these connections, often subliminally or implicitly. Myth operates at this level. To become literate, aware, and objective about the new media, we must make this deeper level visible, something it resists because it communicates by masked or hidden connections, which often appear foolish when made evident.

Advertising, a product of the new media, provides a good example of the paradigmatic level at work. Cigarette manufacturers face a particularly difficult problem because their ads must include a warning that the product can kill you. The warning is always placed away from the eye's path so that it will not stand out as the eye takes in the picture. The path of the eye is predicable and can be called the syntagm of picture, or the order in which we view the picture's various elements. Tobacco ads use bright colors and show youthful, beautiful people enjoying life, sport, or conversation. These images all belong to the paradigm of a healthy life, so we associate smoking with life-giving activities, not life-threatening ones. Never do we see an emphysema victim carrying an oxygen tank.

> No clearer example of the difference between earlier and modern forms of public discourse can be found than in the contrast between the theological arguments of Jonathan Edwards and those of, say, Jerry Falwell, or Billy Graham, or Oral Roberts. The formidable content to Edwards' theology must inevitably engage the intellect; if there is such a content to the theology of the television evangelicals, they have not yet made it known.
>
> —Neil Postman (1985)

RELIGION HAS TRAFFICKED IN MYTH ALthough it has also warred against it. This interaction is inevitable since both deal with claims of ultimacy and conflict. The interaction of religious traditions, and in particular the Bible, with the new media has already begun with the televangelists; and the prospects are not encouraging, as Neil Postman has forcibly argued. The media seem to have a much greater influence on the televangelists than the Bible is having on the media. As noted before, they look more like updated versions of Johnny Carson than prophets dressed in sackcloth and ashes (Postman 1985). In fact, prospects are so discouraging that they have driven many to despair of any attempt to engage the Bible and the new media. For many mainline Protestants this is understandable. Their tradition is so wedded to—indeed was birthed by—the printing press and their commitment to literacy so strong that the new media seem almost blasphemous.

But we cannot run from the new media. They surround us, and we are influenced by them even when we try to deny their power. We need a method whereby we can engage the new media, and as I noted earlier, conversation appears to be the most appropriate model. The advantage of conversation is that as metaphor it suggests mutuality, a common seeking for truth while recognizing the ambiguity and plurality of our situation. As David Tracy says, conversation "is not a confrontation. It is not a debate. It is not an exam. It is questioning itself. It is a willingness to follow the question wherever it may go. It is dialogue" (Tracy 1987, 18). When a conversation is created between two different realities or situations, they both appear in a new configuration in the horizon of the other conversation partner. In conversation, Tracy continues, "we notice that to attend to the other as other, the different as different, is also to understand the different *as* possible" (20). Thus conversation allows a dialogue in which each is mutually enlightened by the other's horizon. Because we are engaging in a conversation, we can learn both to hear and to speak in different ways. Thus, as part of the rules of conversation, we outlaw the Bible's standing in judgment on postmodern culture or our culture's standing in judgment on the Bible. Too often there is no conversation because each partner makes claims of ultimacy and takes a judgmental stance. This is especially true of religious folk. Believing that God is on one's side can stop the conversation very fast, whether the believer be from "right" or "left." We have gone to war over what we take to be ultimate principles, when conversation would be more fitting. Tracy puts it well: "If one demands certainty, one is assured of failure. We can never possess absolute certainty. But we can achieve a good—that is, a relatively adequate—interpretation: relative to the power of disclosure and concealment of the text, relative to the skills and attentiveness of the interpreter, relative to the kind of conversation possible for the interpreter in a particular culture at a particular time" (22:23).

This reminds us that we also must be aware of our situation as interpreters. My own education gives me a high investment in the values of the printing press and the Enlightenment and therefore a negative impression of the new media. Tracy's model of conversation is a helpful corrective because it sets judgment aside and asks both sides to be open.

To pursue this conversation, I have picked two partners. To represent our current situation, I have chosen a group of recent popular American films. In this interconnected world, it is sometimes difficult to determine what constitutes "made in America." I have taken this to mean that the movie was developed and supported by an American studio and designed primarily for the American market. The emphasis on recent movies will ensure that we arc viewing the latest trends. I have violated this criterion on occasion and examined some earlier films because I wanted to take a developmental view of a particular mythological aspect. Since myth is conservative and tends to be stable, this procedure is justifiable. Most important, I have dealt with popular movies, that is, movies that did well at the box office. This ensures that they will represent popular mythology. Thus, I discuss many movies whose artistic contribution may leave much to be desired. Few films of our great directors, like Woody Allen and Martin Scorsese, receive attention. This is not because I don't like or appreciate these directors. In many ways I would have preferred to write a book about them, but such directors tend to make antimythical movies that subvert the myth. My concern is with the myth that thinks for us without our being aware of it. Only by making ourselves aware of the myth can we begin to develop a hermeneutic of the new electronic media. Many may deride these popular films as not worthy of serious attention. But their very popularity demands explanation, and attributing their appeal to the audience's lowbrow taste is not sufficient. By not taking popular movies seriously, we allow myth to triumph and do our thinking for us.

The order of the chapters is obvious. Initially, we will consider the effect of media on our consciousness; without such a broad understanding of our situation, the significance of the project will fail. The chapters on the movies themselves follow a thematic outline that surveys many of the primary conflicts in our society, beginning with the hero and then following a predictable sequence. The same method is used in each chapter. We are not interested in the director or stars, nor even particularly in the movie's plot. We are searching out those oppositions and conflicts that myth attempts to resolve. Thus we are seeking scenes that typify the myth—where it comes to the surface, so to speak. Myth works its magic by constantly repeating the same patterns over and over. Repetition is myth's handmaid.

Doubtless other themes and movies deserve attention, but limits of space and method consigned many films I would have liked to include to the cutting-room floor. This book is an experiment in that it tries to develop a conversation between partners who have not been properly introduced. As an experimenter, I beg the reader's patience. But I remain convinced of the project's importance. If we do not develop an awareness, literacy, and objectivity about our new media, understand their epistemology, and formulate a hermeneutics of Bible translation in the new media, then religion will become entertainment. Neil Postman charges that this is already well under way: "What is preached on television is not anything like the Sermon on the Mount. Religious programs are filled with good cheer. They celebrate affluence. Their featured players become celebrities" (Postman 1985, 121). Without a major effort to come to critical terms with the new media, the prophetic voice of religion will be choked in the electronic polyester of television evangelism.

WORKS NOTED

FALUDI, Susan. 1991.
   Backlash: The undeclared war against American women. New York:
   Crown Publishers.

LÉVI-STRAUSS, Claude. 1963.
   The structural study of myth. In *Structural anthropology,* 202–31. New
   York: Harper & Row.

————. 1969.
   The raw and the cooked: Introduction to a science of mythology. Vol. 1.
   Translated by John Weightman and Doreen Weightman. New York:
   Harper & Row.

POSTMAN, Neil. 1985.
   Amusing ourselves to death: Public discourse in the age of show business.
   New York: Penguin Books.

TRACY, David. 1987.
   Plurality and ambiguity: Hermeneutics, religion, hope. San Francisco:
   Harper & Row.

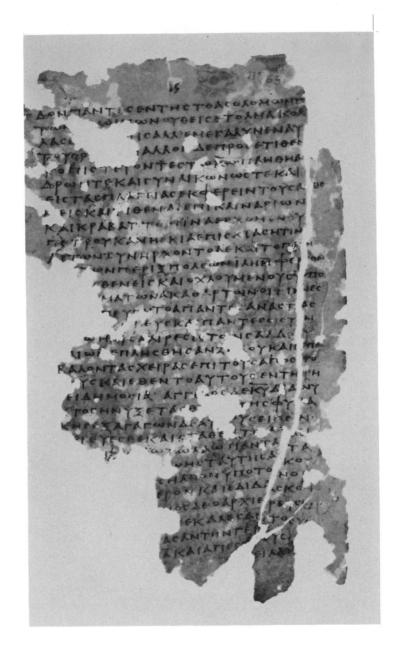

The reverse side of uncial manuscript 0189, contains Acts 5:12-21, the oldest parchment manuscript of the New Testament, dating in the 2d/3d century. (State Museum, Berlin, P11765; used by permission)

2 FROM GRAVEN IMAGE TO DREAM FACTORY

> In a culture like ours, long accustomed to splitting and
> dividing all things as a means of control, it is
> sometimes a bit of a shock to be reminded that, in
> operational and practical fact, the medium is the
> message. This is merely to say that the personal and
> social consequences of any medium—that is, of any
> extension of ourselves—result from the new scale that
> is introduced into our affairs by each extension of
> ourselves, or by any new technology.
> —*Marshall McLuhan (1966)*

THE INVENTION OF PHOTOGRAPHY MARKS
only the tip of an iceberg in the communications revolution that is
shaping or, depending upon your perspective, distorting our world.
Photography and the telegraph, its companion invention, did not just
make communications easier—they changed the way people perceive
the world. The technology we use to store knowledge and the way
we think are intrinsically related. Indeed, Walter Ong, a great student
of oral literature, says boldly that the way we store our information
determines consciousness (Ong 1982, 33). Marshall McLuhan captured the same idea in his famous slogan, "the medium is the message." Carrying this idea even further, we might say that the technology employed to store and manipulate knowledge is a primary
determinant of the shape of a civilization. In the history of humanity
four technologies have served as the primary receptacles for storing
knowledge: the brain, the pen, the printing press, and the electronic
media. Each technology led to a different way of looking at the world.

In exploring this thesis, I need to set a number of caveats. I am
claiming only that the technology we employ to preserve knowledge
is *an* agent that shapes consciousness or creates change, not *the*
agent, much less the only agent. Without this caveat my exposition

will appear excessive, exclusionistic, and ridiculous. Perspective is another problem. When viewing a long sweep of history, one is always impressed with the continuity: there is nothing new under the sun, as the proverb has it. But on closer examination of a particular period, sometimes revolutionary movement is afoot. What I am proposing here is a model for understanding a revolutionary change, or what Thomas Kuhn has called a paradigm shift. Proving a model is very difficult, as the various receptions of Kuhn's own model illustrate. We live in an age of methodological fragmentation and the accusation of totalizing is damning.

> How could you ever call back to mind what you had so laboriously worked out? The only answer is: Think memorable thoughts.
> —*Walter Ong (1982)*

THE OLDEST AND THE MOST COMMON MEANS of storing knowledge is the human brain. We still depend highly on it and are always looking for new ways to reinforce it, as witness the ubiquitous Post It™ notes. Oral cultures must remember everything they desire to know, but their knowledge is limited by the brain's capacity to remember. Thus, the challenge of oral cultures, as Ong notes, is to think memorable thoughts. This mnemonic demand results in the copious production of proverbs, which are memorable storage units of a society's hard-earned wisdom. Proverbs and aphorisms summarize human experience. While the epic poems of oral cultures seem to us stupendous feats of memory, Albert Lord (1960) has shown in the case of the *Iliad* and the *Odyssey* that rhythm and rhyme as well as the constantly recurring formulas all aid memory.

Forgetfulness is the great threat in such a culture—to remember is to be alive. At the conclusion of Jesus' eucharistic blessing as recorded in 1 Cor. 11:25 he says, "Do this in memory of me." This undoubtedly reflects the eucharistic practice of an early Christian community and demonstrates its oral character. In an oral culture the act of remembering creates real presence. At the end of the book of Nehemiah, after recounting the good deeds he has done for God's people, Nehemiah pleads, "Remember me, O my God, for good." What makes this plea so plaintive is that as a Persian official he was probably a eunuch and so had no children to remember him. Without a strong belief in life after death, Nehemiah depended on God to keep his memory, that is, himself, alive (Frost 1972).

The family and its extension, the tribe, constitute the basic social organization of an oral culture. People are known by their relations, by where they come from. Behavior is often explained by relationship—she is like her mother or aunt, or no prophet is to rise from Galilee (John 7:52)—in what anthropologists call stereotypical thinking. But the family and tribe are not simply genetic or racial groups. What ultimately makes a group of individuals a family or tribe is a common stock of stories that instruct them about who they are. The current eruption of "nationalism" in Eastern Europe following the crumbling of the Russian Empire reflects orality's prevailing power. Never bought into the new Soviet Russian story, these cultures maintained their own stories underground and within the family and now are reemerging to seek their identity.

Oral peoples think concretely; they are closely connected to the concrete world about them. In a famous test, the Russian psychologist A. R. Luria asked illiterates to select the three items that belong together from the following list: hammer, axe, log, saw. We literates, who think abstractly and not concretely, immediately see the "correct" answer as hammer, axe, and saw because they are all tools, the abstract category that ties them together and excludes "log." Luria's illiterate subjects, however, would choose particular objects, for example, the hammer, saw, and log because they could be used to build something. The subjects didn't select the axe because it was dull. So concrete was the illiterates' thinking that they envisaged a particular hammer, axe, and so on (Ong 1982, 49-57).

In oral cultures the mnemonic and concrete figure prominently in proverbs and stories, the dominant literary forms for wisdom. When Jesus is asked about the kingdom of God, he does not provide an abstract definition that would satisfy a Greek philosopher or a modern theologian. Instead he tells a parable—a concrete image that the tradition has tried ever since to reduce to abstract truth. In an oral culture truth is based on the ability of the story to explain concrete experience. While the world of Homer's *Iliad* and *Odyssey* may seem remote to us today, to the ancients these stories were powerful explanations of the reality about them. Today, television and movies perform much of this same function. The flickering light is no longer a camp fire illuminating the face of the shaman or storyteller, but the glow coming from a TV set.

The concreteness of the stories serves the value of presence. Sometimes modern literary studies describe this as realism, but as any reader of Homer or the Gospels can tell you, they are not realistic in the modern sense. The proverb and the story are true because they can bring the audience into the presence of reality by creating an insight into the community's experience. The story creates a bridge or correspondence between the community and the hearer's reality. Plato, living in the early generations of literate Greeks, had a mixed mind about orality. On the one hand, he distrusted the poets (that is, the singers of oral tales) and thought they should be banished from the city because they charm and lead astray (*The Republic*, 607b). On the other hand, he was not sure that writing could be trusted either. One could lie in writing; without being able to look the writer in the eye, the reader would have no way of knowing whether the truth was being told. In *Phaedrus*, Plato has Socrates argue that a speaker can be asked to explain a statement, but a writer cannot. To this day, our legal system preserves this ambivalence by requiring the accuser to confront the accused face to face (Havelock 1963).

Other traits of oral culture also persist today. Gossip is an abiding form of orality. Why do social stereotypes retain their power (as witness the effectiveness of the Willie Horton advertisement in the 1988 presidential campaign) despite attempts by literate evidence to demonstrate their unreliability? We believe these stereotypes because they make sense of our experience. Paradoxically, a special type of orality persists among poets and novelists. We keep these great practitioners of the written word in some kind of national park called literature like other nearly extinct species, afraid that their tales may be accurate descriptions of reality. We invest our great poets and novelists with a shamanistic power.

> The only phenomenon with which writing has always
> been concomitant is the creation of cities and empires,
> that is the integration of large numbers of individuals
> into a political system, and their grading into castes or
> classes. . . . It seems to have favoured the exploitation
> of human beings rather than their enlightenment. . . .
> My hypothesis, if correct, would oblige us to recognize
> the fact that the primary function of written
> communication is to facilitate slavery.
> —*Claude Lévi-Strauss (1968)*

> As language became separated visually from the person
> who uttered it, so also the person, the source of
> language, came into sharper focus and the concept of
> the selfhood was born. . . . Achilles may have had a
> "self" in our sense of the word, but he was not aware
> of it. . . . The "self" was a Socratic discovery or,
> perhaps we should say, an invention of the Socratic
> vocabulary.
> —*Eric Alfred Havelock (1986)*

THE ABILITY TO STORE KNOWLEDGE IN WRIT-
ing was a great technological advance over storing knowledge only
in the brain. Yet writing does more than aid memory; it gives rise to
abstraction and logical organization. Those who write have the great
luxury of forgetting, because they can always look up the answer.
With forgetting comes experimentation.

In picture writing a single pictograph or character represents a
single word or concept. To be literate, one must memorize or know
a huge number of characters, as in Chinese. Despite the complexity
of their pictographic writing system, Chinese bureaucrats found that
it provided a way to unify their empire, which included many peoples
speaking a variety of languages. Because a pictograph represents a
concept and not the sound of a word, both Mandarin and Cantonese
speakers, for example, could use the same pictographs to communicate in writing even though they could not understand each other's
spoken words.

Even a pictograph is an abstraction. It is a representation, not an
exact copy, of the reality. It maintains a pictorial relation to the word
or concept. An alphabet is quite different. The relation between the

word and the concept is purely arbitrary. The very use of an alphabet requires a level of abstraction never demanded, nor even possible, in an oral culture. In orality data are organized by key words or similarities. For example, the Sermon on the Mount obviously is organized not by logical or abstract principles, but by sound, by the repetition of similar sounding phrases: "Blessed are. . . ." "You have heard it said, but I say. . . ." The alphabet begins to impose an abstract order on reality. The alphabet has its own order—the alphabetic order—by which all reality can be organized in libraries and encyclopedias, although this feature was not exploited until the invention of the printing press. Not only does the alphabet make the recording of data more precise and easier, but it also provides a built-in method of retrieval, alphabetical order. An index is unimaginable in an oral society (Logan 1986).

The ability to read and write creates an elite who can control access to this skill, and the social organization of manuscript cultures reflects this—they are ruled by elites. William Harris (1989, 328) estimates that only about 5 percent of the total adult population of classical Athens was literate, a percentage that probably marked the high point of literacy in the ancient world and was not exceeded until the sixteenth century. The birth of empires in Mesopotamia and China coincided with the invention of writing. Writing gave rise to governing elites who by reading and writing could record and control taxes, count harvests, and observe the stars and weather, while the rest of society remained illiterate (from the perspective of the manuscript culture) or oral in nature. The earliest writings still extant, the Sumerian cuneiform tablets developed in the fourth millennium B.C.E., are tax records.

The hierarchical structure of these societies is replicated in the way they construe truth. Again Plato is a good example. In the "Myth of the Cave" in *The Republic*, he uses the image reflected on the cave wall as a model of the divine or absolute truth as reflected in human understanding. This sets the stage for the allegorical understanding of truth, which dominated the manuscript culture. Earthly reality is always a poor reflection of the true, immaterial, divine reality above. Likewise, even though he was raised in democratic Athens, in his political theory, Plato opts for an authoritarian king who has the right and knowledge to rule. He distrusts the *hoi polloi*, Greek for "the many" (Stone 1988).

The parable chapter in Mark 4 exhibits both oral stories and an allegorical (literate) mindset. The parables in that chapter are the products of an oral culture. They are concrete and draw their truth from the everyday. Farming activities furnish the material images for the parables. Yet when these oral parables become part of a written gospel, they undergo a subtle change. The earthy images are no longer the real truth; behind them is a secret to be revealed. Like the reflection in Plato's cave, the parable reflects the real, secret, heavenly truth that must be revealed, so Jesus explains the parable to his disciples in secret. In Mark 4, we see a manuscript culture remaking an oral form into a reflection of an empire culture, a culture that is dualistic and in which secrets are given to elites.

One can hear at times in the Hebrew Bible the debate between a tribal, oral religion and an imperial, manuscript society. Temple and monarchy enter Israelite life at the same time. Even though Solomon built the first temple in Jerusalem, the editor of 2 Samuel needs to explain why David did not build the temple. "Here I am living in a house of cedar, while the Ark of God is housed in a tent!" (2 Sam. 7:2 REB). While Nathan the court prophet initially assures David that God is on his side, later in a dream God indicates otherwise: "Go, tell my servant David, 'Thus says the LORD: Should you build me a house to dwell in? I have not dwelt in a house from the day on which I led the Israelites out of Egypt to the present, but I have been going about in a tent under cloth. In all my wandering everywhere among the Israelites, did I ever utter a word to any one of the judges whom I charged to tend my people Israel, to ask: Why have you not built me a house of cedar?' " (2 Sam. 7:3-7 RSV). Yahweh in Nathan's dream recalls and rejoices in being the wandering God of the tribe.

Rabbinic Judaism, which evolved into medieval and modern Judaism, likewise exhibits the earmarks of a manuscript culture. Unlike Roman Catholicism, it does not manifest the structure of a political empire, nor like the kingdom of David and his successors is its national life built around a temple. Nevertheless, the manuscript was a strong influence in its development. Both the Mishnah (third century C.E.) and the Talmuds (fourth to fifth centuries C.E.) reflect a continuing interest in the codification of the Bible as a text that can reflect hidden truths. A sacred book, not an organizational structure nor a temple, typifies rabbinic Judaism. The rabbi, the teacher, grants access to the mysteries in the Hebrew Bible, which are in its words, even at times in its very letters.

Catholicism, born in a manuscript culture, carries its marks to this day. It replicated Caesar's empire, establishing a hierarchical order that resembles Roman organization with the pope (father) taking many of the titles of a head of state. In a manuscript culture, priests are among the elites. Finally, classical theology acquired its canonical form in a manuscript or empire culture. As that culture has died away, the theology has become more problematic. The attack of feminists on the patriarchal structure of theology and church is but one signal of this problem.

> Every written text occupies physical space and at the same time generates a conceptual space in the minds of writers and readers. The organization of writing, the style of writing, the expectations of the reader—all these are affected by the physical space the text occupies.
> —*Jay David Bolter (1991)*

WE SELDOM REFLECT ON THE CORRELATION between the physical space required for writing and the conceptual space it generates in the minds of writers and readers. The space for orality falls between storyteller and audience. In a literate society, the page furnishes the space, and for film, computer, or television, the space is electronic. This correlation between physical space and conceptual space has a profound effect on the conversation we are seeking to open. Christianity reveres an oral Jesus, but the New Testament was born in a manuscript space. Finally, the printing press made possible both the development of Protestantism and historical criticism, still the dominant model for understanding the Bible.

Between the oral storyteller and the audience is a transitory, impermanent space without physical limit. The storyteller's abilities and the audience's patience and interest, not the physical environment, determine the length of the story.

Oral storytellers, like the Homeric poets, use traditional formulas and patterns so that in a sense the audience always already knows the story. Achilles is swift-footed, divine Achilles. The poet invokes a series of well-established networks that are rearranged over and over in ever novel patterns. For this reason, oral storytellers often start *in medias res* (in the middle of things) rather than at the beginning. Again Homer provides the classic example. The *Iliad* begins not with Helen's abduction from Greece, which precipitated the Trojan War, but with the Achaeans' swift ships encamped at Troy. The poet invokes an already known network, and no physical space defines the story. The space is the audience's expectation.

The story has no canonical order; the network can be aligned in an almost infinite pattern of relations. The well-known Trojan horse episode, for example, does not occur at all in the *Iliad* and appears only indirectly in the *Odyssey*. The wooden horse tale forms part of a series of stories associated with Troy, only a small selection of which has been preserved in Homer. As Bolter observes, the Homeric poet improvises like a jazz musician. The melody is there, the phrases are traditional, but the poet or musician freely remakes the material with each performance.

The invention of writing changed the space for storytelling by giving it a physical boundary. That boundary has in turn shifted as the technology of writing has changed. The papyrus scroll was about twenty-five feet long and in many ways imitated orality in a different medium. Ancient scribes had few typographic conventions. They ran words together with no space in between, provided little punctuation, and did not indicate paragraph divisions. Lines arbitrarily ran about twenty characters (the width of a sheet of papyrus), and sometimes at the end of a line the scribe started back in the opposite direction (called *boustrophedon,* "as the ox turns"). Few readers of scrolls could read by sight. One had to prepare to read, beginning with finding the breaks between words.

The linearity of scrolls projected a linear canonical order onto stories. The reader had to follow the author's order. In the Hellenistic period, authors began to write to fit the length of a scroll. Scrolls are difficult to consult because one must unroll and find one's place without the aid of page divisions or typographic conventions. Since no two scrolls are identical, referring back to something is also difficult, which explains why the ancients frequently misquote—they are quoting from memory. Likewise the scroll poorly suggests closure, and as a result many ancient texts have weak endings. Oral storytellers tended to start in the middle of things, so the scroll establishes a firm beginning but a less satisfying ending. The Gospel of Mark, which opens decisively with the coming of John the Baptist but ends abruptly at 16:8, is a good example of this phenomenon.

With the introduction of the codex, technology once again shifted the understanding of writing's conceptual space. The codex is an early form of book in which small sheets of cut material are bound together. The early Christians were among the first to adopt the codex. The earliest extant New Testament papyrus, $\mathfrak{P}$ [52], dated around 125 C.E., comes from a codex, and only four of the eighty-four extant papyrus manuscripts are scrolls. Even today the Hebrew canon and the Christian Bible reflect their different origins on scroll and codex. For liturgical purposes, the Hebrew canon is preserved on a scroll, while the Christian Bible is a book. Following the expected model of a scroll, the Hebrew Bible has no definite ending and in a sense has remained open by the constant commenting of the rabbis that resulted in the Mishnah and the Talmuds. The Torah is oral, whereas the Christian Bible adopts the scroll's definite beginning in Genesis and adds a conclusion, the Apocalypse, with its tales of the end of the world. Thus, the book begins to enclose the whole world.

The codex can hold in a manageable way more material than a scroll and is much easier to consult, although the problem of referencing was not solved until the printing press set the book in a definitive, repeatable form. A codex frequently held more than one "book," and the new work would begin wherever the first left off, not necessarily at the top of a page. For example, in codex Vaticanus, one of the earliest and best manuscripts of the New Testament, Luke ends at the bottom of one column and John begins in the next (see Aland and Aland 1987, 15). Likewise these early codices contained more than we recognize as the New Testament, frequently including one or more texts of the so-called Apostolic Fathers. In our days of cheap books, the expense of a codex can be shocking. The Alands have estimated that a New Testament codex made from parchment required the hides of fifty to sixty sheep. Add to this the cost of preparation and of a scribe to do the copying, and you have invested a small fortune. Again we see why writing belongs to the elites. As the Alands note, complete manuscripts of the Bible "must have been commissioned by persons of the upper classes who could afford to ignore the expense" (Aland and Aland 1987, 77).

The codex reached its apex with the illuminated manuscripts of the High Middle Ages. By this time silent reading had developed so that the monk or scholar could use a book in a library without having to read it aloud. But the illuminated manuscript became an object of art, not utility. It has a multimedia dimension, and scribes began to write in the margins, building up glosses on the text. Illumination not only demonstrates the importance of the codex, but once again underlines its elite character.

> Opening the window of his cell, he pointed to the immense church of Notre Dame, which, with its twin towers, stone walls, and monstrous cupola forming a black silhouette against the starry sky, resembled an enormous two-headed sphinx seated in the middle of the city. The archdeacon pondered the giant edifice for a few minutes in silence, then with a sigh he stretched his right hand toward the printed book that lay open on his table and his left hand toward Notre Dame and turned a sad eye from the book to the church.
> "Alas!" he said, "This will destroy that."
> —*Victor Hugo,* Notre-Dame de Paris *(1831)*

SINCE THE EARLY MESOPOTAMIANS MADE their first scratchings on clay tablets, many technological advances had occurred—ink, papyrus rolls, the codex, and finally paper—but all of these simply enhanced manuscript culture. The invention of the printing press had a more profound impact. Although early printers imitated the art of the scriptorium, as the beauty of Gutenberg's Bible testifies, the printing press turned out to be not just a refinement of manuscript culture, but its replacement. The printing press precipitated the Industrial Revolution, the age of science, the Enlightenment, and the modern world, which many proclaim is now passing away (Eisenstein 1979).

On a surface level, the printing press brought to the masses the benefits that the elites of the manuscript culture had enjoyed for almost four millennia. We reflect this attitude when we insist that education is the road to upward mobility. But the printing press did much more than that. On the one hand, the elites lost their reason for being elite, and on the other, since everyone could read, a public,

social interpretation was no longer needed. Interpretation, like reading, now became private and individual, not public and common.

The effects of the printing press are so ubiquitous today that we
seldom notice them. Even without the aid of a computer, a modern
scholar could peruse more and different books than most medieval
scholars could peruse in a lifetime of wandering. When the printing
press was invented around 1450, probably some 200,000 manuscripts
were in existence in Western Europe. By 1500 over 9 million books
had been printed.

The most obvious physical advantage of the printing press is its
ability to produce an almost limitless number of identical copies. No
two scribes, much less a roomful, could reproduce a manuscript
exactly by either sight copying or dictation. The classical manuscript
tradition was corrupted during the medieval period. A correction at
best affected only a few manuscripts. The press made corrections
easier because it turned out improved identical editions on a
mass scale.

A more subtle and less obvious shift created by this communications revolution is summed up in Elizabeth Eisenstein's often-
repeated aphorism, "Learning to read is different from reading to
learn" (1979, 1:65, among other places). Eisenstein sees this difference
as the primary distinction between manuscript and print cultures.
For her reading rather than printing marks the real difference. In a
manuscript culture, the major effort is expended on producing a
manuscript rather than on using it. The illuminated manuscript graphically illustrates this tendency. The manuscript is beautiful to look
at, but not easy to read. Learning for the most part took place outside
or apart from reading in apprenticeships or in the debates of the
rabbis or the scholastics. In a print culture, learning takes place
primarily through reading: students are taught to read, not so they
can reproduce manuscripts, but so they can learn from reading books.
This difference lies at the heart of the shift from manuscript to print.

Eisenstein has identified five major results of the printing press
that constitute a communications revolution. They derive both from
the physical aspects of the printing process and from its impact on
reading and learning. Not only do these factors define the hidden
agenda that we literates take for granted as the way the world should
be, but they represent a major part of our value standards.

1. Widespread Dissemination.   The printing press created a mass culture. Not only were many more books produced in the first fifty years of the printing press than had been turned out by all the scribes in Western Europe since the death of Constantine, but the variety of subjects also exploded geometrically. The price of books declined dramatically so that they were no longer the preserve of the wealthy, and as books became more readily available, demands for literacy and universal education increased.

Books are handled very differently in print and manuscript cultures. The medieval scholar was a wanderer, traveling from library to library to consult manuscript collections. The mass production of books made possible the ready comparison of different texts. Among the first efforts in biblical scholarship made possible by the press were the polyglot Bibles that printed the Hebrew, Greek, and Latin texts side by side for easy comparison. In the Catholic world Cardinal Ximenes's *Computensian Polyglot* appeared in 1517–1522, and in the Protestant world Platin's *Antwerp Polyglot* in 1569–1572. Because the texts now could easily be compared, both contradictions and differing traditions became much more evident.

2. Standardization.   The benefits of standardization are hard to imagine because it is so prevalent today that we are often not aware of its effects.

The first effect of standardization was correction or purification of the manuscript tradition. That tradition was subject to a vast number of corruptions and errors, as anyone who looks at the bottom of the page of Nestle-Aland's twenty-sixth edition of the Greek New Testament can testify. Medical manuscripts were so corrupted that their prescriptions were dangerous. In science the purification of the manuscript tradition led to the testing and frequent rejection of the older science on the basis of a comparison with the book of nature, as they called it. In this way experimentation became the foundation of science.

Standardization and mass culture led to similar and shared views of the world. For example, the ability to print maps led not only to their correction by use, but also allowed everyone to have a common imagination of what the world looked like, where cities were located, and so on. In religion, catechisms were published and the dogmatic tradition was purified. As a result, religion became less tolerant. Once

printed, positions become fixed and known, and differences or de-
viances were easier to detect and less readily tolerated.

3. Reorganization. The typographical needs of printing led to
the reorganization both of texts and data and of the way we think
about texts. This is perhaps nowhere more evident in Bible studies
than the division into verses that resulted from Robert Estienne's
Greek New Testament of 1551. The typological division of the Bible
into verses not only made it easy to reference and cross-reference,
but also led to the Bible being allocated in an extremely piecemeal
way, both in popular piety and in scholarship.

We have already noted the revolutionary effect of the alphabet.
The alphabet created an abstract order that theoretically allowed the
ordering of all reality, but this inherent possibility was not exploited
until the invention of the printing press. Although medieval scribes
sometimes prepared indexes for their own use, they were idiosyn-
cratic. Printers however, had to follow typographic conventions and
devise organizational systems that could be used by a mass audience.
The encyclopedia movement of the sixteenth century was a direct
result of the reorganization of texts and data made possible by the
press. "Ever since the sixteenth century, memorizing a fixed sequence
of discrete letters represented by meaningless symbols and sounds
has been the gateway to book learning for all children in the West"
(Eisenstein 1979, 1:89).

4. Data Collection. Through standardization and mass marketing,
the printing of books created a "feedback" system whereby corrections and emendations could be added over successive editions of a
text as scholars communicated with each other. More scholars would
see a printed work than had ever seen a manuscript. This feedback
process was at the heart of the communications revolution created
by the printing press.

5. Preservation. Type creates immortality in a way the anonymous scribe could never envision. Although faceless monks in monastic scriptoria struggled to preserve the heritage of the West and
the ancient world, much was lost. Yet the press preserves, if only by
making a multitude of copies. The persistence of the story of the
Woman Taken in Adultery illustrates this tendency. People frequently
quote this episode as typical of Jesus, yet textual critics have attempted to remove it from the printed text or devalue it because it

does not occur in any of the early manuscripts. But once printed at John 7:52, it has remained fixed there. The power of the press to preserve also led to the view of the past as something to save and thus to museums.

The printing press created a new kind of audience, as the hearing "audience" was transformed into a reading public. To communicate, individuals no longer needed to be within voice range; they needed only to read. Not only could one person communicate with more people, but communication also began to take place more often in private. Even public debate initiated a written form. Although the Lincoln-Douglas debates were given orally, they look like written speeches.

With the printing press, empires and kings began to fall. The dominant form of social organization became the nation-state, based not on the tribe or the family, but on the geography of printed languages. Maps defined reality. Linguistic traditions were preserved through the publication of Bibles in the vernacular and the establishment of a printed literature (as distinguished from an oral tradition). Languages that disappeared did so because they failed to achieve a printed literature. We can now see that the Soviet Union was an immensely conservative effort to preserve the Russian Empire, and as such it stopped history and prevented the development of various nation-states. With the empire's collapse, the evolution of nation-states in Eastern Europe has continued with a vengeance. Not only have vernacular linguistic traditions supported nationalist movements, but the division of Latin Christendom into various vernacular traditions in the sixteenth century has proved permanent (Eisenstein 1979, 1:118).

Private reading and mass production of Bibles gave rise to private interpretation. Once individuals could read for themselves, the masses no longer needed a member of the elite to interpret for them. This aspect of the communications revolution influenced many nation-states and contributed to the birth of democracies—the first being the United States. The Declaration of Independence in 1776 and the U.S. Constitution and Bill of Rights reflect the print culture. They emphasize individual freedoms, and one of the first rights guaranteed in the Bill of Rights was freedom of the press. Thomas Jefferson, James Madison, and other founding fathers saw religion as the reflection of a bygone age and identified it with monarchy. In various ways they attempted to build a wall between the state and religion, so that the divisive claims of religion would not destroy the freedoms guaranteed by the state. Yet if the press favored democracies, it also facilitated propaganda and thereby made possible mass control and the modern totalitarian state.

The evaluation of truth radically changed under the printing press. In a manuscript culture the primary method for determining the truth was deductive reasoning, whereas in a print culture induction became the primary method. Deduction reflects a dualist, hierarchical culture. From generalized, ultimate truths, subsidiary truths are deduced. In the West the ultimate truth was, of course, revelation. From the truths of revelation, one could deduce all other truths. This method led not only to the brilliance of Thomas Aquinas's *Summa Theologiae*, but also to the Inquisition. The printing press allowed and rewarded the collection and comparison of data. One of the earliest tasks of printers and scholars was the purification of the manuscript tradition. To do so, they collected data, compared them, and drew conclusions. In the scientific area, this process led to the development of the scientific method based on experimentation and the testing of hypotheses. In the liberal arts, it led to the development of historical method and its characteristic hermeneutics of suspicion. In history as in the empirical sciences, the gathering and comparison of data led to the observation of differences and then to the development of a hypothesis about what really happened.

A somewhat humorous illustration of the difference between manuscript and print cultures is the medieval logical problem posed by Baalam's ass. According to the logic of the day, an ass placed between two identical stacks of feed would starve to death because it was governed by instinct and not by reason. Even conducting an empirical test by actually putting an ass in such a predicament would not have solved the problem, since in the medieval mindset answers were determined by deduction, not by experiment. A more serious example is Galileo's clash with the Roman church, which can stand as an icon of the clash between print and manuscript cultures. The officials of the church were wedded to Aristotle and the Bible as their first truths. Subverting or ignoring these authorities would destroy their world. Galileo committed himself to the new science in which observation led to a hypothesis. Although Galileo lost the battle, the church increasingly lost the war.

Both the possibility of universal education and the necessity for universal literacy are results of the printing press. Some people in ancient Greece argued for universal education, but it never developed because producing books was so laborious. The printing of many books created a need for a reading public, however, so schools produced students to meet this demand.

Martin Luther referred to printing as "God's highest and extremest act of grace, whereby the business of the Gospel is driven forward." We have already seen how printing encourages private interpretation. Now the university professor was transmuted into the priest, as witnessed by the number of reformers who were university professors. Enshrined in the Protestant pulpit is the Bible, the book. It is not the book of the manuscript culture, however, but the printed Bible that each and every one could interpret. The church building was stripped of its elaborate decoration, carvings, paintings, and stained glass. The plastic arts were eliminated so the congregation could give total concentration to the Bible as print (Goethals 1990). At this time churches abandoned the free form of medieval cathedrals and began to be ordered by pews, lined up like type on a page. Despite the advantages of the printed Bible, one of its results has plagued Protestantism—private interpretation and individual integrity as the standard of truth inevitably give rise to fragmentation.

> Vernacular Bible translation . . . led to the typical
> Protestant amalgam of biblical fundamentalism and
> insular patriotism.
> —*Elizabeth L. Eisenstein (1979)*

PRINTING WAS ESSENTIALLY A GERMAN INVENtion and initially had its greatest impact in that country. It turned Luther's protest into a mass movement. Although vernacular Bibles were already in circulation in Germany prior to the Reformation, ordaining the printed vernacular Bible as the center helped determine the course of the Reformation. Knowledge of the Bible (biblical literacy) among the laity and the clergy exceeded anything in scribal culture. In the Middle Ages most Bible knowledge came from sermons, popular storytelling, stained-glass windows, and carvings of salvation history around the altarpiece. With the Reformation, for the very first time a majority of (Protestant) Christians could read and re-read the Bible. This private reading and re-reading led to an interiority, a turning inward toward individual piety and a consequent loss of a corporate meaning for the Bible. It became *my* story more than *our* story. Furthermore, the vernacular translations reinforced the fragmentation of Christendom into competing linguistic camps.

While printers initially produced Vulgate Bibles—St. Jerome's Latin translation—they soon began looking for larger markets since the demand for a printed Latin Bible was rather small. In 1460 an enterprising German printer, Johann Mentelin, produced a cheaper and, more importantly, a more desirable Bible: His Bible was in German. The search for mass markets was under way. But to produce translations, printers needed scholars who could read Latin, Greek, and Hebrew, and these scholars had their own needs. Thus, the printer became the broker between the demands of the scholar and the needs of the laity.

Translations made the Bible transparent to the lay reader—the Bible was in his or her language. This transparency is the real power of the vernacular translations. To read the Bible in one's own language must have been a powerful experience in the sixteenth century: for the first time people could read the whole text and interpret it for themselves without having to receive it through an intermediary. Yet translation also had a down side. A translation's transparency hides the differences between our culture and language and those of the Bible. It speaks directly, in the reader's own language. Because the Bible was apparently transparent, it "had an inordinately strong influence on half-educated men of this kind because they read little else" (Delany, *British Autobiography*, 29, quoted by Eisenstein 1979, 1:366). Fundamentalism and the Bible Belt are direct by-products of the printing of a vernacular Bible.

If open books led at times to closed minds because of the transparency effect of translations, what might be called the Erasmian influence of the printing press had the opposite effect. The humanist scholarship of the Renaissance was accelerated by the printing press and eventually produced the Enlightenment.

In the printing press's early stages, as we have seen, the effort to purify the textual tradition was paramount. The printers' need for an ever better text turned the printing shop into a scholarly workshop. The production of trilingual Bibles created a pluralistic humanist society that was not necessarily divided between Catholic and Protestant, or Christian and Jew; it was very different from the societies created by the reading of the Bible in the vernacular.

Moreover, the trajectories of these two uses of the Bible veered off in different directions. On the one hand, readers of the vernacular translations treated the Bible as a transparent and authoritative guide. On the other hand, as scholars tried to purify the text, their work became more and more complex. In textual criticism the discovery and collation of more manuscripts led not to the recovery of the original, but to a thicket of textual data printed at the bottom of the page. Furthermore, in the effort to find out what really happened, historical criticism not only gave rise to many competing theories but erected an even higher wall between the vernacular readers with their transparent text and the scholars with their theories.

In the long term, readers of vernacular Bibles and Erasmian scholars were opposed to each other. Both in effect were seeking the pure text, but this plain, original text, whether of the Bible itself or its simple meaning, is an illusion of the press. The very permanence and uniformity of the printed book create the illusion that behind all diversity must lie a single, simple text. Because vernacular translations created the illusion of obviousness, readers believed they could gain by the act of reading the simple truth. Meanwhile, the scholars' efforts to recover the plain or original text were only uncovering more problems. Moreover, the readers of vernacular translations and scholars belonged to different communities. Scholars formed the academy, or as they called it in the early period, the Republic of Letters. Increasingly, the academy became pluralistic, humanistic, and driven by science. In contrast, the readers of vernacular Bibles were drawn toward biblical fundamentalism, insular patriotism, and denominationalism. These disparate drives have persisted to this day.

It is a principal characteristic of the electric age that it
establishes a global network that has much of the
character of our central nervous system. Our central
nervous system is not merely an electric network, but it
constitutes a single unified field of experience.
                                    —*Marshall McLuhan (1966)*

EVEN THOUGH A NEW AGE IS NOW OBVIOUSLY
dawning, describing the future is still difficult—prophecy is always
hard and is certainly not my gift, since as a historian I stare into the
past. Yet we are compelled to consider the future because in many
ways it has been with us at least since the invention of the telegraph
and photograph in the last century. You can tell that the tectonic
plates of Western culture are shifting because the forces of reaction
are so outraged. Alan Bloom's *The Closing of the American Mind*
(1987) is a noteworthy example. Bloom would have us go back to
Aristotle and Plato—the manuscript culture. That is why he is so
fond of elites and cries out in agony as blacks, women, scientists,
and social scientists, all with agendas quite different from his, invade
his precious intellectual ghetto.

What are the characteristics of this electronic or graphic culture?
The very difficulty of identifying the dominant technology indicates
our problem. In an oral culture, the dominant technology is the brain;
in manuscript and print cultures, the technology has given its name
to the culture. But what is the dominant technology of the new age?
Sometimes the generic term *media* is used and it is not unworkable.
Advertising people originally used the term in a positive sense to
indicate that they had to work in more than one medium, for example,
newspapers, magazines, radio, and television. The advantage of describing this as the media age is that the name reflects the importance
of the various methods we now use to store, retrieve, and convey
knowledge. Others call this the information age from the information
explosion that has occurred as computers have gathered ever more
data. Managing that information is a critical problem. But information
represents only one aspect of the post–printing press age. Still others
have referred to this period as the electronic age to indicate the
technology that we now use to store, manipulate, and generate knowledge. For this reason I prefer this term. Like electricity itself, the
term *electronic* lacks the solidity and specification of manuscripts

and the printing press. Electronic is a serviceable metaphor and reflects the chief characteristics of the emerging age.

Marshall McLuhan, a very early prophet of the new age, christened it the global village. By this metaphor McLuhan wanted to signal that the world was shrinking into a single village and was no longer a group of isolated nations. Even more, to him "village" signaled the similarities between electronic media and orality. In fact, some theorists have described the characteristics of the new age as secondary orality. The abstraction and distance of reading are giving way to the presence of electronics. Electronic communications have striven to wire the world together, shrinking the time it takes for messages to travel around the earth. First came the telegraph, wiring continents together and bridging the chasm between the Americas and Europe with an underwater telegraph cable. Since 1962 satellites have overlooked the whole world and together with cellular phones may enable developing nations to avoid the prohibitive cost of stringing cable.

Because the world is increasingly "wired together," by satellites if not physically, our relations with other peoples and nations are increasingly interdependent. We know almost immediately what is happening elsewhere in the world. The invasion of a small Middle Eastern state not only draws the United States into war, but we follow the events on television, almost as though the war is a video game or a sporting event with anchor persons substituting for play-by-play announcers and ex-generals (ex-players) providing color commentary. Perhaps the real symbol of the global village is tourism, one of the largest industries in the world.

A primary difference between an oral culture and the emerging electronic culture is the importance of the graphic image, or what Daniel Boorstin has called the "graphic revolution." The plastic arts have always been important in the repertoire of human expression. The wonderful, abstract, almost modern cave drawings at Lucerne testify to the importance of images to our ancestors. Yet photography introduced a new type of image into our midst. Daguerre, one of the inventors of the new medium, advertised, "The daguerreotype is not merely an instrument which serves to draw nature . . . [it] gives her the power to reproduce herself" (quoted in Postman 1985, 71). Until this point the plastic arts had never been able to reproduce nature, only to represent it. There was a distance between nature and the representation. But with photography all that changed. The photo-graph is extremely concrete; its verisimilitude is so high that we accept what the camera presents as the real world, as Susan Sontag has noticed. Thus, there is no arguing with the photograph—its very concreteness is the assertion of its trustworthiness. The image threat-ens to replace print as our way of representing reality. Simply observe how images have gradually replaced print in advertising over the past fifty years, or the dominance of the thirty-second sound bite—per-haps more accurately graphic/sound bite—in our political discussion.

Neil Postman has worried and warned us about the disastrous consequences of the loss of a print culture, and his warnings should be taken seriously. The subtitle of his recent *Amusing Ourselves to Death* (1985) underscores his concern: "Public Discourse in the Age of Show Business." For Postman the dominant metaphor in the elec-tronic age is show business or entertainment. As a result, serious discourse and serious learning are becoming increasingly difficult, if not almost impossible. Yet, as he admits, the new media are here and we cannot go back. So what are we to make of the future?

Other theorists have posited a much richer future (Bolter 1991). Soon giant, centralized databases will allow people in the most remote parts of the world to engage in research that until recently could only be pursued in the major universities and research labs of the industrialized nations. Control of and access to this data will be a critical ethical issue in the future. These giant databases are not some futuristic dream, but are already in place in many cases. With this enormous accumulation of data, priority will be given not to collecting more new data, but to understanding the interrelations among data. Model theory is replacing logic as the basic tool for organizing data. In addition, knowledge is becoming increasingly segmented as we all turn into specialists. In the future the key will be collaboration.

Even the nature of the book and its concomitant writing space are changing. The electronic medium undermines the fixity of the printing press, for the very essence of the computer is electronic fluidity. The computer also encourages a more active participation on the part of the reader/computer user. Hyperbooks are already coming onto the market. One of the earliest, *Afternoon* (1987) by Michael Joyce, offers the reader multiple paths through its text seg-ments. Though the basic plot remains the same, the reader can choose among different plot options and time lines and can view the story from the perspective of various characters. Thus, the fixity of the book, as a canonical order that must be followed, is gone. The author and reader now interact as "co-learners or co-authors, as it were, fellow-travelers in the mapping and remapping of textual (and visual, kinetic and aural) components, not all of which are provided by what used to be called the author" (Coover 1992, 23). Some regard the new technology as promise, not threat. The printing press evoked similar reactions—some saw it as a boon to humans, while others regarded it as the devil's workshop.

The availability and sharing of information, knowledge, and images on an undreamed-of scale pose real challenges to the nation-state. Paradoxically, while computers make the vast centralization of data possible, they also facilitate its instant dispersal. That is why those who want to control access to knowledge find personal computers so threatening. Historians will long debate the many reasons for the collapse of the Russian Empire, but a few points might be mentioned here. Maintaining an empire in which the masses are ruled by an elite (the Communist party) required a degree of control not possible in a world wired together by modern technology. Television broadcasts pictures of the rest of the world, while fax machines, photocopying equipment, and personal computers all create a degree of freedom incompatible with an empire. Several images come vividly to mind. Several years ago, even before Mikhail Gorbachev came to power, the announcer on National Public Radio was simply dialing direct to Russia and speaking with the man-on-the-street about events in that country. Direct dialing to Russia surely punched a huge hole in the iron curtain. Likewise, when the repressive government in Romania fell, the phone system was still entirely manual, so the state secret police could control it. An automated phone system makes observation and control much more difficult. Finally, during the brutal repression of the student demonstrations in Tianamen Square in Beijing, fax machines and television transmissions kept the students' cause alive and the world informed. The government literally had to pull the plug to regain control. Electronic signals are the new spirit, blowing where they will.

The social organizations that will develop in the electronic culture will be global and less hierarchical. To date, the most viable social organization that has emerged is the multinational corporation, which is increasingly making the nation-state less relevant. The old hierarchical model, à la General Motors, is remaking itself into a much more decentralized organization that emphasizes team building and decision making at the middle management level. More and more organizations and institutions in our culture find themselves under pressure to remake themselves in the image of the corporation. This is particularly evident in the churches. The minister is becoming a CEO, responsible to and hired by a board. Frequently, the minister is a type of religious entrepreneur. The activities of the church are divided into a series of ministries, for example, youth, married with children, single parents, senior citizens, and so on. These are the church's clients, and they consume the specialized products (ministries) of the MacChurch or megaChurch. Thus, the church is gradually being remade on the consumerist/corporation model.

As we leave the Gutenberg galaxy to enter this brave new world in a new galaxy whose name we know not yet, our consciousness is undergoing a massive change. We should not expect a utopia that will solve the ills of the postmodern age. Transitions in consciousness are dangerous times, and we should be concerned about what might happen. The rise of the alphabet brought with it brutal empires, oftentimes celebrated and romanticized by historians. The empires were the winners in history's game, so they wrote the story. But the Pax Romana was only Pax if you were the Romani; if you were the Judae, Britanni, or Germani, it was oppression. The printing press brought totalitarianism and the atomic bomb. The triumph of image in the electronic age could bring even greater horrors. But the reactionaries are wrong—we have no choice but to go forward.

To go forward in an intelligent fashion, we need to become "literate," aware, and objective in the new media that create the noetic environment in which we live. Just as the invention of writing demanded new criteria and epistemology, as exemplified by Plato, and the emergence of the printing press threatened old ways of knowing (deduction) and created new (the scientific method), so too these powerful new media will force us to adapt.

This book is a small effort in this new literacy or rhetoric. But to gain objectivity about the new media, we must subvert and overcome their powerful sense of presence. To achieve this, I propose to narrow my focus to movies, only one of the media, but one with a powerful effect. Yet I will not focus on this medium from its point of view, that is, the directors, stars, or studios, all of which hide what is really going on. In Postman's phrase, these are ways of amusing or entertaining us so we don't see what is really happening. Rather I propose to examine the movies as mythologies. Like an anthropologist visiting a native village, I am examining our popular stories as the most direct reflection of who we are. As a way of giving depth to these stories, I propose to open a conversation with New Testament stories and themes. I open this conversation not so much to stand in judgment on the movies, but to gain leverage from our past storytelling.

WORKS NOTED

ALAND, Kurt, and Barbara Aland. 1987.
The text of the New Testament: An introduction to the critical editions and to the theory and practice of modern textual criticism. Translated by Erroll F. Rhodes. Grand Rapids: Eerdmans.

BLOOM, Alan. 1987.
The closing of the American mind. New York: Simon & Schuster.

BOLTER, Jay David. 1991.
Writing space: The computer, hypertext, and the history of writing. Hillsdale, N.J.: Lawrence Erlbaum Associates.

BOORSTIN, Daniel J. 1962.
The image, or What happened to the American dream. New York: Atheneum.

COOVER, Robert. 1992.
The end of books. *The New York Times Book Review*, June 21, 1, 23–25.

EISENSTEIN, Elizabeth L. 1979.
The printing press as an agent of change: Communications and cultural transformations in early modern Europe. 2 vols. New York: Cambridge University Press.

FROST, Stanley Brice. 1972.
The memorial of the childless man: A study in Hebrew thought on immortality. *Interpretation* 26:437–50.

GOETHALS, Gregor T. 1990.
The electronic golden calf. Cambridge, Mass.: Cowley.

HARRIS, William V. 1989.
Ancient literacy. Cambridge, Mass.: Harvard University Press.

HAVELOCK, Eric Alfred. 1963.
Preface to Plato. Cambridge, Mass.: Harvard University Press.

————. 1986.
The muse learns to write: Reflections on orality and literacy from antiquity to the present. New Haven: Yale University Press.

KUHN, Thomas S. 1970.
The structure of scientific revolutions. 2d ed., International Encyclopedia of Unified Science. Vol. 2, no. 2. Chicago: University of Chicago Press.

LÉVI-STRAUSS, Claude. 1968.
Tristes tropiques. Translated by John Russell. New York: Atheneum.

LOGAN, Robert K. 1986.
The alphabet effect: The impact of the phonetic alphabet on the development of Western civilization. New York: William Morrow.

LORD, Albert B. 1960.
The singer of tales. Harvard Studies in Comparative Literature 24. Cambridge, Mass.: Harvard University Press.

MCLUHAN, Marshall. 1966.
Understanding media: The extensions of man. New York: Signet Books.
————. 1967.
The medium is the message. New York: Bantam Books.

ONG, Walter J. 1970.
The presence of the word: Some prolegomena for cultural and religious history. New York: Clarion Books.
————. 1982.
Orality and literacy: The technologizing of the word. New Accents, edited by Terence Hawkes. London and New York: Methuen.

POSTMAN, Neil. 1985.
Amusing ourselves to death: Public discourse in the age of show business. New York: Penguin Books.

SONTAG, Susan. 1977.
On photography. New York: Farrar, Straus & Giroux.

STONE, I. F. 1988.
The trial of Socrates. Boston: Little, Brown & Co.

Shifts in Media-Culture

	Oral	Manuscript	Printing	Electronic
Technology	Brain Memory	Writing Scribe	Printing Press Book	Computer Graphic Image Mass Media
Social Structure	Family Tribe	Empire	Nation-States Democracy	Corporation
Truth	Presence	Dualism The Real	Science History	Credibility Model Theory
Genre	Story Proverb Myth	Allegory	Novel History	Photography Advertising Films
Religion	Primitive Religions Israel Jesus	Judaism Catholicism Islam	Protestantism	TV Evangelists? Performer/CEO Charismatic
Church Architecture	House	Temple Basilica Cathedral	Pews	TV Studio Performance

Shane (Alan Ladd) teaches Joey (Brandon De Wilde) to use a gun as Marian (Jean Arthur) looks on in George Stevens' *Shane* (1953). (Photo courtesy of Archive Photos)

3 THE HERO

My Heroes Have Always Been Cowboys.

—Willie Nelson

EVERYONE HAS A FAVORITE NOTION OF WHAT makes us different from the rest of the animal world. For my part, humans are animals that tell stories about themselves and everything else. Shakespeare said all the world was a stage, but on that stage the actors were acting out a story. The power of story surrounds us. Television is a continuous set of stories—maybe the same story over and over. In the afternoon Americans watch soap operas and in the evening "L.A. Law" and "Northern Exposure." The titles change, but the story goes on. In our heads we carry about our own private version of our life story by which we make sense of our experience. Some may call this daydreaming, but it is a continuous mental rewriting of our own story. Frequently, counseling includes helping people change their script or story about themselves.

Just as we write our own story, we constantly transform the events around us into a story, complete with plot and destiny. A baseball game is not a single game but a story. At its beginning two teams contest for the victory. The home team is the protagonist while the visitors are the antagonists. The announcer is the story's narrator in disguise. At the climax one team wins, and finally the game is revealed to be part of the wider story of a pennant race. The metaphor of

47

game as story is beginning to dominate large segments of our public life. Politics is now a sport, with winner and losers and most importantly the big MO (momentum). Some believe that the wide swings in public opinion polls are due in part to people wanting to be on the winning side.

Why do we tell all these stories? Why do we tell stories about the past (history and myth), the present (the news), and the future (science fiction)? We tell these stories because they are about the most fascinating thing in the universe, us. Stories renew our self-interest, something that never bores us. Homeostasis is the ability of stories to update themselves constantly and remain forever in the present, even if they are about the past or the future. New Testament scholars refer to a saying's *Sitz im Leben*, the context in which the community preserved it. No saying of Jesus was preserved out of an antiquarian or historical interest. The early communities remembered Jesus' past sayings because they spoke to the communities' present. The historian studies the past to throw light on the present, and science fiction frequently issues an apocalyptic warning not to squander the present.

Storytelling stands at the heart of the Judaeo-Christian tradition. Not only is the Hebrew Bible largely narrative (only a small part is law in the technical sense), but so also are the gospels. They are narratives about Jesus and Jesus himself was a story (parable) teller. Because he was a storyteller and not a learned lawyer in Torah, some consider his parables to be simple stories for simple people. Yet simplicity can be deceiving—it is also a sign of genius and exposes the arrogance of modernity. Jesus' parables resemble many other rabbinic parables. They lack depth and psychological drama, rely on stock plots, and are peopled by stock characters who are frequently stereotypes. Yet the use of stereotyped, stock characters in Jesus' stories is not a fault. I am increasingly convinced that there are only a few basic stories with infinite variations. Understand how a society tells its stories and you understand that society and, even more, the options for existence imagined in that society. Ultimately, this is what stories reveal. They allow the teller and hearer to experiment with options for existence. They allow us to undergo a life experience without risk. We can seek in story to overcome death without dying and return to everyday life all the wiser for having learned our options from story. But stories are also inherently dangerous in that they select what they reveal. They manipulate what we see and thus hide other options for existence.

Every culture has hero stories. The *Epic of Gilgamesh*, preserved in Akkadian, is one of the earliest stories we have. Gilgamesh, a king and city builder, enlists the help of Enkidu, a wild man, and the pair set out on an odyssey to find the secret of avoiding death. Through a culture's hero stories, we can see how a society envisions the struggle against chaos—how it attempts to bring order out of chaos. Since threats to life are part of the human experience, the solutions a culture incorporates into its stories are clues on how to live everyday life.

The Western is a major vehicle for the American hero-myth, and the movie *Shane* (1953) is a classic representation of the genre. Recently, two other movies have made allusions to *Shane*. Clint Eastwood's *Pale Rider* (1985) is a remake of *Shane*, and Peter Weir's *Witness* (1985) takes up many of *Shane*'s major themes.

Progress is our most important product.
—*General Electric slogan*

The highest expression of this aestheticizing tendency is in George Stevens' *Shane*, where the legend of the West is virtually reduced to its essentials and then fixed in the dreamy clarity of a fairy tale.
—*Richard A. Maynard (1974)*

CRITICS ALMOST IMMEDIATELY RECOGNIZED George Stevens' *Shane* (1953) as a classic of its genre. The movie is set sometime after the Civil War in the great American West. Its plot is simple and straightforward. A group of pig farmers attempt to establish farms for their families but are resisted by the cattle ranchers and their cowboys, who need an open range. Alan Ladd plays the hero Shane who comes to the farmers' aid. He is a man of mystery with an unknown past and a no-name name: Shane. Shane befriends the Starretts, who happen to look like the all-American 1950s family: a husband (Van Heflin), his blonde wife Marian (Jean Arthur), and their young boy Joey (Brandon De Wilde).

The opening scene sets the story's mythical context. A lone horse-man quietly rides out of the mountains into a peaceful valley. The camera's eye shifts until it appears to be sighting down the barrel of a gun at a young deer grazing in a wetlands with a cabin in the background. But the gun is unloaded, it's a toy, and the young boy aiming it is only playacting. The opening scene invokes powerful mythical images from the past. The mountains are the place of the gods, and a new godlike wild man, another Enkidu, rides into the valley. The valley itself is another Eden, an idyllic place of water and gardens with no violence or only play violence. The protection of this Eden is the story's goal.

At the center of this Eden is a log cabin with garden, stream, and outbuildings. In many ways the cabin resembles a Levittown tract home. The house is Marian's space, female space, and the land outside is the male world. The cabin door is a Dutch door, and Marian is frequently pictured looking out through the top half but fenced into the house by the bottom half. At the barnyard's center lies an enor-mous tree trunk. Since the valley is basically treeless, this is somewhat puzzling, but the tree trunk has a mythological function as the navel of the universe, the tree of paradise. Together Shane and Starrett remove the trunk by the sweat of their brows—they refuse to use dynamite. The feat is both an act of male bonding and, more impor-tantly, one of several signs of the bonding of the outsider Shane to Starrett's family.

When Shane rides into the valley, he is wearing buckskins, but as long as he remains among the farmers, he wears store-bought jeans. Furthermore, he no longer wears his gun but hides it. He renounces his former ways and takes up those of the farmer. Joey openly idolizes Shane, even comparing his father negatively with the newcomer. The boy admires Shane's prowess with a gun, which he contrasts with his own impotency. He's always asking for bullets. When Shane gets into a fight in the saloon with the cowboys, Joey peers underneath the swinging doors to watch and cheers for Shane.

The story develops a triangular relation among Shane, Starrett, and Marian. The movie code of the 1950s placed strict limits on relationships, leading at times to the ridiculous. When Shane departs and a kiss would be appropriate, they shake hands because the code forbade an unmarried man to kiss a married woman. Yet paradoxi-cally, the reticence made the relationship more implicit and powerful.

For example, during the farmers' Fourth of July celebration, Shane dances with Marian, who is wearing a wedding dress, while Starrett is both literally and metaphorically fenced out. Despite the triangle there is no competition between Shane and Starrett over Marian. Relationships and boundaries are respected. When Starrett contemplates facing a hired killer and almost certain death, he remarks that he is not blind and knows that Marian would be cared for.

Sexual roles in this movie are so stable they can replicate and thus resolve the conflict between cowboys and farmers. Marian, Starrett's wife, represents the female world just as her husband, together with Shane and the cowboy opponents, belongs to the male world. Honor undergirds the male world, which is violent, chaotic, open, and without fences. Her world is a home and garden, fenced off from the range. No violence intrudes on this peaceful, pastoral world. In this movie females are off-limits to the male world. The cowboys inhabit a saloon in town, except when they are threatening the farmers. Apparently, they no longer ride the range. The American mythological map casts the saloon as a place of evil because of its associations with drinking. To some extent the positive males in this movie become feminized. The farmers stay out of the saloon and are accused of traveling with their women folk for protection. One farmer who always threatens to pull out at the first sign of trouble personifies this overfeminization of the male. Since he has only daughters, he is surrounded by women. At the Fourth of July celebration, Starrett acknowledges that Marian has roped and tied him. In this movie the female and her family represent the future. They are what the farmers are struggling for, and the male world of the cowboy, the world of the lone rugged individual, is past and must be abandoned.

Even though the female represents the future, she has no part in the salvific event. As the plot reaches its climax, it becomes evident that unless the farmers resort to violence, the cowboys are going to run them off the range. Starrett arms himself to go into town to kill the chief cowboy bully. Marian pleads with him not to go. She says that the farm is not worth dying for and that he is going only because of his foolish male pride. He responds that his honor is at stake and that he is doing it for her and for Joey, their son. He rejects her pacifist vision out of hand in favor of his concept of male honor. She must be protected because she represents the future—but she will be protected by violence. This theme is remarkably similar to one of the points of conflict in another Western made the year before *Shane*. In *High Noon* (1952, Fred Zinnemann, director; Stanley Kramer, producer) a murderer returns to town to kill the sheriff (Gary Cooper) who sent him to prison. The sheriff's new bride (Grace Kelly) is a Quaker, and she opposes his plan to fight the murderer. Like Marian she argues that violence must stop somewhere, and that there must be another way. But he insists that he must fight, even though the town has abandoned him and he stands alone. Again like Marian, in the end she comes to his side.

In the end Shane alone, dressed again in buckskins, goes into town to destroy the cowboy villains. Shane is purified violence. He is celibate but he loves. He is not from the valley but from the mountain, the place of the gods.

The young boy Joey mediates between the story's various conflicts. As a child, he belongs to the woman's world, but is becoming a man. He loves both Shane (the past) and his father (the future). In one of the movie's most important scenes, Shane initiates Joey into the ritual of the gun. While Shane has lived within the family, his gun has remained hidden. But Joey confesses to Shane that he has broken the taboo and seen the gun, and he asks Shane to show him how to use it. When Shane shoots the gun, in one of the most technically perfect scenes ever shot in a movie, Joey at first recoils in horror and then breaks out in a grin of ecstatic joy. He expresses perfectly what Rudolf Otto calls the awe and joy in encountering the sacred. At the gun's explosion his mother Marian rushes out of the house in her wedding gown. Thus, the violence and death of the gun, the male organ, are in sharp contrast to her virgin fertility as the mother-goddess. She lectures Shane, telling him that the gun is evil and that the valley would be better off without any guns, even Shane's. But Shane responds that the gun is not evil. "It's only a tool," he says. "It's men who are good or evil." His pragmatic defense echoes a standard American justification for violence. The boy mediates between his mother's vision of peace and the necessity of violence to defend that peace.

Shane is a retelling of a basic element of the American myth. As a product of the 1950s, the movie and the country celebrate the virtues of domesticity and family. The country had just emerged from the Great Depression of the 1930s, World War II, and the Korean conflict; now it was engaged in a "cold war" to defend the world yet again.

Most importantly, the country was becoming an urban nation. Between 1930 and 1955, the rural sector of the population had declined from 82 percent to 16 percent, the most massive population shift in U.S. history. *Shane* mythically argues that, just as the Indian gave way to the cowboy and the cowboy to the farmer, so now the farmer must give way to the urban/suburban dweller. In one of the movie's most moving scenes, the villain Ryker pleads his case. He has offered to call off the range war if Starrett will join him. Without Starrett the others will leave. After Starrett rejects the offer, Ryker turns to Joey and asks if he doesn't want to join up with him and ride the range, every little boy's dream. He recounts how he and others have fought and died to settle this wild country. They fought the Indians and made the range safe. Now the farmers want to fence in the range and drive them off. The power of Ryker's speech emerges from his offer to Joey, which represents what every little boy wants—to grow up to be a cowboy, not a farmer.

The conflict in *Shane* revolves around how to justify progress in the face of individual rights and freedoms. Some, like the Indians, cowboys, and now rural America will lose or die in the name of progress. Because the conflict between progress and individual rights is irresolvable, a savior-hero mediates the opposition. The film defends and justifies progress as life and condemns the failure to progress as death. Violence is the agent of change because without it those past values would be lost. Shane is the pure cowboy who represents the pure values of the past that are handed on to Joey. In the movie's final scene, Shane tells Joey to take care of his mother and father.

Our view of ourselves as peace loving and our history of violence create a permanent schism in the American mythical landscape. Marian's female values are the true values, yet they would be lost without a gun to defend them. This conflict is resolved by having a purified savior destroy the enemy. Our villains must be morally evil so that we may be morally pure and our violence justified. While celebrating female values of peace and family, we believe they cannot survive on their own against the outside evil that threatens them.

> I saw, and behold, a pale horse, and its rider's name
> was Death.
>
> —*Revelation 6:7*

CLINT EASTWOOD HAS ACKNOWLEDGED THE dependence of his film *Pale Rider* (1985) on *Shane*. As a result, *Pale Rider* is a good example of how our culture's view of the hero has shifted since the 1950s when *Shane* was made. It illustrates homeostasis, a story/myth updating itself.

Though the plot remains the same, the characters have been significantly transformed. The conflict now involves two groups of miners rather than cowboys and farmers. One group, to which the Pale Rider attaches himself, are poor gold prospectors, simple miners who work within the confines of the ecosystem, while the others are corporate miners who rape the land (and attempt to rape the young girl who is Joey's counterpart). This movie asks whether progress has gone too far; in fact, the Pale Rider explicitly raises the question. The opposition is not the cowboy who must give way to the farmer (and by implication the farmer who must give way to the urban dweller). Now the opposition is the corporation that in its greed threatens to destroy the earth.

This shift in structure accounts for the movie's apocalyptic temper. As a result, the tone of this movie's opening scene differs dramatically from *Shane*. A group of riders come roaring out of the mountains with the hooves of their horses pounding the earth. They tear into the miners' camp and begin to destroy it, pulling down tents and shacks. Then the camera shifts from the mayhem to a young girl praying in the woods, reciting a psalm: "If *you* [God] exist, I would like more of this life. I need a miracle."

The name Pale Rider comes from the scene in which he first approaches the mining camp:

> And when he had opened the fourth seal, I heard the voice of the fourth beast say, Come and see. And I looked, and behold a pale horse: and his name that sat on him was Death, and Hell followed with him. And power was given unto them over the fourth of the earth, to kill with sword and with hunger and with the beasts of the earth. (Rev. 6:7-8 KJV)

He comes from no place and has a mysterious, unexplained past. Signs abound that he may even be a supernatural character or a ghost. When he takes his shirt off in one scene, the camera focuses on his back where six bullet wounds form a pattern that suggests that survival was highly unlikely. At odd moments he simply disappears, like a ghost. He is the answer to the young girl's prayer, "I need a miracle." Sometimes the miners address the Pale Rider as "preacher," and he arrives in the camp wearing a clerical collar. Shane was human, and his heroism was underplayed by the restrained performance of Alan Ladd. Now the hero is a superhero who destroys the opposition in apocalyptic superviolence. All those Saturday morning cartoons with their superheroes have now become part of the mythic landscape.

Whereas the family in *Shane* had furnished a stable undergirding on which to build a mythological bridge to resolve other conflicts, now the family is in disarray. Joey has become a teenage girl, Megan (Sydney Penny), who falls in love with the Pale Rider. Film critic Pauline Kael found this a bit unseemly for a man of Clint Eastwood's age (Kael 1985, 64), but she allowed her animus for Eastwood to prevent her from seeing what is really happening. By changing Joey's mythical role into a girl's and then transforming Joey's hero worship of Shane into her sexual attraction to the hero, the movie demonstrates both the importance of sex as a primary way of symbolizing bonding between two people and the breakdown of rigid sexual roles in our society. The sexual bonding aspect is evident in other transformations. The tree trunk mutates into a huge rock blocking the middle of the stream. Barret (Starrett's counterpart) daily attacks the rock with his sledgehammer. The Pale Rider joins him in a bonding scene. Yet when the son of LaHood, the powerful corporate miner (Ryker's substitute), comes to the camp with his protector (Richard Kiel, a giant featured in the James Bond movies), the Pale Rider attacks the bodyguard by hitting him in the groin with a sledgehammer. The bonding scene turns into a dirty joke.

The family is likewise broken. The new Marian, Sarah Wheeler (Carrie Snodgress), and her daughter live with Barret. Despite Barret's proposals of marriage, she is reluctant. Where the attraction between Shane and Marian was implicit, now it is open and consummated.

Even the contest between the two groups of miners has a sexual overtone. LaHood's miners use a hydraulic method of mining in which water under pressure is shot out the end of a nozzle to blast the earth away; then the pulverized earth is washed through sieves exposing the nuggets of gold. The sexual metaphor is obvious. When Megan ventures into their camp, LaHood's son attempts to rape her, and she is saved only by the preacher.

While many would argue that the more explicit sexuality in *Pale Rider* indicates the effects or ravages of the 1960s, more important from a mythical point of view is the loss of stable male and female roles as a basis on which to build symbolic values and mythical resolutions. Instead, the instability and confusion of sexual roles now reflect the general chaos of society and demand their own mythical solution.

In *Shane* Starrett euglogizes one of the farmers killed by Ryker's hired gun. The eulogy rallies the demoralized farmers. Starrett summarizes their hope for the valley by saying "someday there will be a church." Though the valley is still uncivilized and lacks the accoutrements of sheriff and church, this should not be interpreted to mean that God is absent from the valley. God fundamentally sustains Shane because of the assumption that good will triumph in the end. The eschatology is progressive and drives the movie forward, guaranteeing that good will win out in the end.

In *Pale Rider* theodicy receives primary attention. Megan in her midrash on Psalm 128, which opens the movie, says, "If You exist, I need a miracle," and the preacher/Pale Rider arrives as the answer. Sarah even questions him, "Who are you?" and he answers, "It really doesn't matter," although he is clearly a superhero. The movie even hints that he has risen from the dead. Not only does he have those bullet holes in his back, but in the climactic final scene, when he confronts the corrupt hired lawman-killer, the lawman remarks, "I thought you were dead." God is not the presupposition of the world of *Pale Rider*. In fact, one can say that, for Hollywood, God died sometime between *Shane* and *Pale Rider*. The Pale Rider comes from outside and does not become part of the miners' world. Furthermore, the end is by no means assured. The loss of God is a loss of the future. The mythical succession pattern demonstrates this aspect. In *Shane* the pattern of succession was Indians, cowboys, farmers, suburbanites—a clear progression, an eschatological pattern of replacement. In *Pale Rider* the succession pattern disappears. The miners who represent the good are from an earlier, more primitive time and are threatened by the corporate miners, who are both evil and their successors. Therefore the future itself becomes evil. The movie ends with the Pale Rider eliminating LaHood in an explosion of violence. But what comes next? Will there ever be a church in the valley?

> This gun of the hand is for the taking of human life.
> —*Eli Rapp,* Witness

DIRECTOR PETER WEIR'S *WITNESS* (1985) OFfers a variation on the themes we have pursued. The symmetry of characters is familiar from *Shane*, and the mutations are similar to those in *Pale Rider*. A grandfather who is the family patriarch and a suitor (Alexander Godunov) serve as substitutes since the movie opens with the funeral of the Starrett character. The rest of the equation is straightforward. The Shane stand-in is Detective John Book (Harrison Ford), Marian is Rachel (Kelly McGillis), a young Amish widow, and her son Samuel (Lukas Haas), the witness, is Joey's counterpart. Once again the family is broken, but not in the social sense as in *Pale Rider*.

The plot is set in motion when the young Amish widow takes her son on a trip to Baltimore. During a stopover in a Philadelphia train station, he witnesses a murder in the men's restroom. The investigating detective John Book soon discovers that the chief of police and other high-ranking officers are involved in the murder to cover up their drug dealing and that he, the widow, and her son are all in danger. After he is seriously wounded by one of the officers, they all flee to an Amish farm for cover.

At the plot's *denouement*, the corrupt police discover where the detective is hiding and come to the Amish farm to kill him. Three heavily armed policemen trap the unarmed Book in the barn, and a highly imaginative chase scene ensues. After Book eventually manages to kill two of the policemen, only the police chief remains. But instead of ending with a final catastrophic scene of violence in which all the bad guys are eliminated, the movie has the young boy summon the neighbors by ringing the warning bell, a fixture on every Amish farm. The Amish come running over the fields in great numbers and surround the armed police chief. He must now kill them all or surrender. He surrenders—and for one of the few times in an American movie, peace triumphs without the final act of violence. Peace, not violence, is the way. Marian's option finally has an advocate.

Peter Weir has almost constructed an antimyth. From a marginal fragment of American life, he suggests another possible way of being. Unfortunately, he does not seem to believe in his own story. Many reviewers of this movie, while praising its cinematography and direction, did not find the story line plausible. Perhaps the Australian point of view or the marginal character of Amish life struck these reviewers as untrue. Peace goes against the grain of the American myth.

Book's gun is a primary character in this movie, its presence or absence a strong symbol. Just as Shane dressed in a farmer's jeans and hid his gun while among them, Book wears plain clothes while among the Amish and his gun is hidden. Rachel carries it to the kitchen cabinet as though she were holding a rat by the tail. She puts the bullets in the flour tin, which leads Book to remark that it's a good thing she didn't put them in the marmalade. When Samuel finds the gun, it does not lead to an initiation scene as in *Shane*; but Rachel like Marian recoils in loathing and lectures Book about respecting the ways of the Amish. Unlike Shane, he has no comeback but lowers his head shamefaced. Eli the patriarch takes Samuel on his lap and explains the ways of the Amish: "This gun of the hand is for the taking of human life." He cuts directly to the issue and unlike Shane does not divorce the gun from human behavior. From the patriarch's point of view, the taking of life is only for God. Yet the grandfather understands the conflict between good and evil and the appeal of the gun as a means of repulsing evil: "Many times wars have come and people have said to us, 'You must fight; you must kill; it is the only way to preserve the good.' But, Samuel, there's never only one way." This "never only one way" is the Amish protest against war and violence. They represent another way. The price they must pay is the separateness of Amish life.

When the grandfather asks Samuel if he would kill a man, the boy replies that he would only kill a bad man. And how would he know who was bad? "You can look into their hearts and see this badness?" the grandfather asks. Samuel replies that he can see and has seen what they can do, referring to his experience in the city. Now, as the camera focuses on the gun, the grandfather drives home the Amish choice: "What you take into your hands, you take into your heart.

Wherefore come out from among them and be ye separate, says the Lord, and touch not the unclean thing." Jacob takes exactly the opposite point of view as Shane. The gun is violent and to touch it is to take it into your heart. Therefore they must separate themselves from violence to avoid taking it into their hearts. Herein lies both the courage and problem of the Amish other way. To protect their purity, they must maintain their borders.

The appearance and maintenance of boundaries are a strong feature of this movie. Its setting is divided into two nonconversing, opposing worlds—the world of the Amish and that of the English as the Amish refer to them. The pastoral Amish world contrasts vividly with the urban world of Philadelphia. The Amish world is peaceful, ordered, and communitarian. The opening scenes of fields of waving grain, the burial of Rachel's husband, and the communal meal graphically set the pace for this world. Ironically, the City of Brotherly Love stands in strong contrast. The initial scenes in Philadelphia are pictured through Samuel's eyes. The train station appears large and foreboding. As the boy wanders around the station, he finds strangers eyeing him with suspicion. The center of the station is dominated by a statue depicting brotherly love, a type of *pietà* that ironically underlines the violence of the city. The murder that the boy witnesses in the train station is the primary symbol of the city's violence.

The contrasts extend to eating. In the city people eat on the run—unhealthily, as Rachel remarks. While living among the Amish, Book has to be taught how to eat. At the hardy, predawn breakfast that begins the farm day, Book only wants coffee and tries to make a joke that draws on a TV ad. The joke falls flat because the Amish have no electricity, much less televisions. At the barn-raising scene the communal feast becomes the center of the action. The barn-raising itself is a strong contrast to the city. The Amish world is one of cooperation and community. Philadelphia is a place of competition, suspicion, and betrayal. Amish families are whole and extended, secure in their place in the world. All the Philadelphia families in the movie are broken except that of the police chief. He lives in an ideal suburb, with wife, daughter, and barbecue, but is corrupt at the core. In a final difference between the worlds, the Amish have no telephones, and the police are therefore unable to locate Book while he is hiding. As the local policeman asks, how do you call around in Amish Land?

The law is another boundary transgressed in the film. The purpose of the law is to regulate violence, to demarcate "good violence" from "bad violence," and to sanction violence to control violence. In this movie the threat—indeed the terror—is that the law itself is lawless. It has turned to bad violence. In such a state one is defenseless. In Shane there had been no law in the valley, but the valley was not lawless. Both sides were fighting for their version of the law and for what they thought was right. Ryker broke that boundary when he brought in a hired gun from the outside to enforce his version of what was right. He unmasked how the law hides violence and as a consequence was cast as the villain. But the unmasking was precisely what allowed Shane to engage in lawful, pure violence. Although the Pale Rider's violence is justified by his "supernatural" status, that movie has an interesting twist. LaHood's hired guns are lawmen, a sheriff and his deputies. Here the law is for hire, and once again the violence is unmasked but rehidden by the Pale Rider in his justified and lawful attack. In *Witness* the law itself is corrupt and lawless, so the contrast with the nonviolent Amish is starker. At the film's end Book leaves the Amish farm, even though he has fallen in love with the young widow. The message is clear: Shane is still the only real option. Only in the fairyland world of the Amish is nonviolence a possible option. In Philadelphia, the gun will be needed.

> In the same way the chief priests, along with the scribes, were also mocking him among themselves and saying, "He saved others; he cannot save himself. Let the Messiah, the King of Israel, come down from the cross now, so that we may see and believe."
> —*Mark 15:31-32*

MYTH'S POWER DERIVES FROM ITS CONSTANT repetition. Because we hear it over and over, we become unaware of its presence and so it quietly thinks for us. We need to understand American stories because they provide the matrix in which and out of which we live. They provide the options for our existence. Like myths of yore, they not only tell us who we are without our ever asking, but also indicate how we will perceive and behave toward the rest of the world. Any indigenous American theology must understand its story tradition.

The myth embodied in *Shane* did not originate with the American Western or in the 1950s. As we have indicated, it bears a striking similarity to the earliest story we have, the *Epic of Gilgamesh*. Jesus himself told a version of this same story, the parable of the Good Samaritan (Luke 10:29-37). A disguised version of the hero story occurs in the parable of the Prodigal Son (Luke 15:11-32).

A conversation demands give and take on both sides. Each party must listen to the other and be open to discovering oneself in that other person. Such openness is especially necessary in dealing with ancient texts because they cannot talk back. We restore them to life. Since the stories we tell about ourselves affect the way we hear other stories, we must be very careful to listen to the ancient story and not impose ourselves upon it. Listening to parables is doubly difficult because we have heard them so often that we have become deaf. We believe they are simple, and in keeping with the perspective of manuscript and print culture, we reduce each parable to an abstract point. Yet as stories become more and more important in the electronic age, we need to appreciate the parable as story. A further problem with Jesus' parables is that much like a Woody Allen film they play against the expectations of the conventional story. Therefore we must take special care not to impose our expectations on the parable, but let it speak to us.

Since Luke's time, the parable of the Good Samaritan has been classified as a hero/savior story and viewed from a Gentile perspective. But when Jesus told the parable, the effect was different. His Jewish audience did not view the Samaritan as good nor as a hail-fellow-well-met. To them he was a mortal enemy.

As a famous Jewish scholar once remarked, in Judaism the triad priest-Levite-Samaritan is as odd as the triad bishop-priest-Frenchman is in English (Montefiore 1909, 2:467). In English the expected triad is bishop-priest-layperson, and in Hebrew it is priest-Levite-Israelite, where "Israelite" means layperson. This triad appears frequently in rabbinic literature. One example from the Mishnah will make the point:

> A priest precedes a Levite, a Levite an Israelite, an Israelite a bastard, a bastard a Nathin, a Nathin a proselyte, and a proselyte a freed slave.

This applies when all are otherwise equal. But if a bastard is learned
in the Law and a high priest is ignorant of the Law, the bastard that
is learned in the Law precedes the high priest that is ignorant in the
Law. (*Horayoth* 3.8, quoted in Scott 1989, 198)

In this example, the threefold formula of priest, Levite, and Israelite
marks out the divisions of respectable Jewish society, yet an ignorant
high priest is less than a learned bastard. The comparison is illuminating because it highlights the importance of point of view. From
the point of view of the writers of the Mishnah, the rabbis, the comparison is at the expense of the priests. The rabbis are the Israelites.

In the expectation of the first-century Jewish telling of the hero/
savior story the third character, the hero, was supposed to be an
Israelite, a Jewish layman. Instead in Jesus' story the hero turned
out to be his mortal enemy, the Samaritan. When the Samaritan came
down that road and had compassion on the half-dead man in the
ditch, the parable was no longer a hero story but an antihero story.
The audience had three options: (1) To identify with the Samaritan.
In this option, to remain the hero, listeners would have to become
their hated, mortal enemy, not a very likely identification process.
(2) To leave the story, an option that most in Jesus' audience probably
chose. It's only a story, and in real life things don't happen that way.
Samaritans cannot be trusted to behave compassionately. (3) To become the man in the ditch. Instead of playing hero/savior, the listener
becomes victim. Thus, to enter the kingdom of God, to experience
God's ruling activity, one must become victim. This is not much of
an option for those awaiting God's Messiah to bring an apocalyptic
vengeance upon their enemies. But in story, that is, within the kingdom, it is the only option. Just as many critics rejected the movie
Witness as unreal, few have considered with Jesus the option of
rejecting the hero myth. To reject the hero/savior myth is to face
life's chaos without a mythical guarantee of rescue. One would have
to side with the Amish and against Shane.

We have often understood the parable of the Prodigal Son as a
hero/savior myth in which the father, a stand-in for God, saves the
younger repentant son and avenges the self-righteous elder brother.
The younger son was lost and found, was dead and is now alive. The
father restores him to life and banishes the elder brother for refusing
to come into the party and rejoice in the father's reclaiming of his

younger son. The parable represents a perfect example of God's free grace at repentance. It fulfills our most narcissistic wish—restoration to innocence after sin. In identifying with the younger son, we play, in the phrase of Krister Stendahl, honorary sinners. Not only are we forgiven, but that forgiveness is reinforced by the rejection of the unloving elder son. Such is the reading of the parable from the point of view of the hero/savior myth. But does the parable offer up other clues that compel us to listen to it in another vein?

The parable's construction clearly leads to an identification with the younger son. A two-sons tradition, in which the sons play stereotyped roles, the younger being a rogue and the elder self-righteous, sets up the identification. In Israel's stories about itself in the Pentateuch, the line of inheritance is through the younger son at the expense of the elder—Cain and Abel, Ishmael and Isaac, Esau and Jacob, Jacob's favorite son Joseph and, after his supposed death at the hands of his brothers, Benjamin. Over and over again the stories of the patriarchs feature younger and elder brothers who play stereotyped roles. As a rabbinic parable has it:

> God has set the love of little children in their father's hearts. For example, there was a king who had two sons, one grown up, the other a little one. The grown-up one was scrubbed clean, and the little one was covered with dirt, but the king loved the little one more than he loved the grown-up one. (*Midrash on Psalms* 9.1, as quoted in Scott 1989, 112)

While Gentiles also identify with the younger son, they assume that Jewish listeners would see themselves as the elder son. Only the supersessionist mindset, which sees Christianity replacing Judaism, can justify such a reading. Jewish listeners likewise would identify with the younger son. After all, Israel considers itself the youngest among the nations.

Supersessionism is only the first thing amiss with the standard reading of the parable. Jewish law and custom looked askance at what the younger son requests and what the father does. For a father to surrender his property before his death is foolishness because it leaves him vulnerable in his old age. As a rabbinic proverb has it, among the three who cry out to God and are not answered is "he who transfers his property to his children in his lifetime" (Scott 1989, 110). Although other needs frequently prevent us from seeing it, as in many of Jesus' parables the father in the parable is a fool; the younger son by asking for an early division in effect kills his father. The Greek text makes this point evident. The son asks for his share of property, and the narrator reports that the father divided his "life" between them.

The younger son's adventures in a foreign land are a disaster. He even commits apostasy by feeding pigs, for he is a Jew. Further, he comes to his senses not because he sees what is right but because he is starving—he wants bread. It is a soup-kitchen conversion. The parable depicts the son's deprivation in images of hunger, though it could have pictured his need in many other ways. For example, he began by asking for money, so his lack could have been pictured as a lack of money. But hunger and its binary nourishment imply the female.

When the son returns home, the father runs immediately to him and kisses him. Many have objected to this behavior because running offends the dignity of an Oriental man. Even more, he demands no proof of repentance from the son. The son is in no way punished or tested. Most scandalously, the father kisses the young son. The Greek word, *katēphilēsen*, has overtones of an affectionate kiss of the type exchanged by husbands and wives. Many try to avoid this connotation, but the father here behaves like a mother. This father abandons male honor for female shame.

The elder son refuses to come in and in anger lashes out at the father:

> See here, all these years I slaved for you. I never once disobeyed any of your orders; yet you never once provided me with a kid goat so I could celebrate with my friends. But when this son of yours shows up, the one who has squandered your estate (Greek "life") with pros-titutes—for him you slaughter the fat calf. (Luke 15:29-30 SV)

The elder son has played by male rules and now expects to be rewarded. Curiously, the hearers also play by male rules and expect him to be punished for not rejoicing in the younger son's welcomed return. But the father does not punish; instead he replies, "My child, you are always at my side. Everything that's mine is yours" (Luke 15:31 SV). Throughout the parable the characters have been described in male terms: sons, elder and younger, father, hired hands, and servants. Now at the parable's climax the father uses not "son," but "baby" or "child," although many translations avoid this terminology. The father's voice is that of the mother, using the mother's word. Furthermore, if the elder is rejected, how can the father say that everything is his and that he, the father, is always at his side?

Not only are both sons prodigal, but so is the father who behaves shamefully like a woman. The parable was deeply offensive to Mediterranean values of honor and shame. The father does not behave like a god punishing the wicked and unjust. He is a fool. "You want my property before I die? Take it. You want to come back? Here, come back, let's have a party. You don't want to come in to the party? I'll come out. You feel abandoned and unwanted? You're always with me." Whatever the children want he gives them. By modern standards the family is dysfunctional.

Most significantly, in the parable the younger son neither achieves forgiveness nor is vindicated at the expense of the elder's rejection. The expected rejection is a projection from the point of view of the savior myth. In the actual story, the elder son has everything and is always at the father's side, even when he doesn't think so. The father in the parable is not a judge who rights wrongs or even forgives. He foolishly spoils his children.

By truly listening to the parable, we hear another story, one that undercuts the assumptions of the hero/savior myth. This parable points up graphically a major problem in the Western tradition—the elimination of the female. This story about a family is deeply embedded in Mediterranean family values, yet the existence of an important member of the family, the mother, is only implied and is invisible in the hero/savior interpretation. Just as in *Shane*, which rejects Marian's option, the traditional hero/savior reading of this parable has no mother. It is a very male world in which males forgive males and banish other males to warrant that forgiveness. But in the parable as Jesus told it, if we really listen, the father takes up female roles—abandons his honor for female shame—to provide a radically different image of both God and humanity.

Stories are not real life; they are fictions. As Franz Kafka once wrote, "All these parables really set out to say merely that the incomprehensible is incomprehensible, and we know that already. But the cares we have to struggle with every day: that is a different matter" (Kafka 1946, 11). The saddest thing about *Shane*, *Pale Rider*, and even *Witness* is that no conversion takes place in these movies. The logic of the hero myth is inevitable. Violence is the only way to a solution. The wild man Enkidu in all his incarnations must come to the aid of threatened civilization. Evil is too overwhelming. For a brief moment, *Witness* seems to offer another option, as the Amish stand in witness against the violence from Philadelphia. But that experience is too marginal for Americans to accept. Only in an Amish world, the movie seems to say, not the real world, will this option work—only in parable, not in reality.

If the biblical texts are to speak to American life or, through Christian churches, help Americans to understand their place in the world, we must understand how our stories shape our perception of and behavior toward the rest of the world. When President Reagan said that he needed a Rambo in Lebanon, he was trying to make his stories come true. In the end, those stories do not work because they demand the apocalyptic destruction of the other. And we can no longer afford that option.

It may be that the parables are the only option left. The savior is not some outside supernatural hero who rides into the valley and destroys our enemies. In Mark's death scene the priests and scribes jeer at Jesus to come down from the cross—to play the hero's role and bring the apocalyptic remedy. Instead, Jesus dies on the cross despairing, "My God, my God, why have you abandoned me?" (Mark 15:34). The centurion who put him to death confesses that he was God's son. What are we to make of this jarring juxtaposition of jeering challenge, despair, and confession? How are we to hear this death scene? Surely not from the point of view of those who challenged Jesus to play the hero! Now we can begin to play out the conversation. With Jesus as movie producer, when Shane entered the saloon, instead of destroying his enemies, they would have put him to death, and that would not have been a tragedy but a moment of conversation that leads to a new vision of God. Had Jesus written *Witness*, Book would have found a way to go back to Philadelphia without a gun. Had he written *Pale Rider*, . . . well, we have a hard time imagining these stories without the myth of the hero/savior. Where is a Samaritan when you need one?

WORKS NOTED

KAEL, Pauline. 1985.
  The current cinema: Pop mystics. *The New Yorker*, August 12, 64–69.

KAFKA, Franz. 1946.
  Parables and paradoxes. New York: Schocken Books.

MAYNARD, Richard A. 1974.
  The American West on film: Myth and reality. Rochelle Park, N.J.: Hayden
  Book Co.

MONTEFIORE, Claude. 1909.
  The synoptic gospels. 3 vols. London: Macmillan & Co.

SCOTT, Bernard Brandon. 1989.
  Hear then the parable: A commentary on the parables of Jesus. Minneapolis: Fortress Press.

John "The Duke" Wayne shoots 'em up in Howard Hawks'
Rio Bravo (1950). (Photo courtesy of Archive Photos)

4 THE DUKE

Other people, so I have read, treasure memorable moments in their lives: the time one climbed the Parthenon at sunrise. . . . What I remember is the time John Wayne killed three men with a carbine as he was falling to the dusty street in *Stagecoach*.

—*Walker Percy (1962)*

JOHN WAYNE LOOMS LARGE IN THE AMERICAN psyche, especially its male version. Striding down a western street in battered hat and dusty jeans, Winchester in hand with an engaging smile, he was the real thing. The Marlboro man pales in comparison. From *Stagecoach* (1939) to *The Shootist* (1976), John Wayne defined the American cowboy over a period of almost forty years of movie-making, during which the Western became the dominant form of a distinctive American mythology.

Throughout the period of the classic movie Western, John Wayne was its leading star, appearing in the top ten box-office draws more frequently and consistently than any other actor. Wayne was not a character actor who experimented with different roles and developed a large range, as, for example, Robert DeNiro does today. Instead, throughout his more than one hundred films, Wayne retained the distinctive persona of the Duke, which was easily recognized, expected, and accepted by audiences. The very sameness of the persona was part of its attraction. Regardless of what else might change, John Wayne was John Wayne. The constant repetition also made the persona a great vehicle for myth because myth needs repetition. Ironically, the sameness of Wayne's movie persona and its identification

69

with his real self caused his acting ability to be overlooked while directors like Howard Hawkes and John Ford got the credit for the movies. Recognition came slowly, with an Academy Award for his portrayal of Rooster Cogburn in *True Grit* (1969).

Marion Morrison was born in Winterset, Iowa, in 1907. The place and name certainly do not conjure up the image of John Wayne, his screen name, or the Duke, his nickname. Among his friends, he used Marion Morrison throughout his life, occasionally remarking that using the name Wayne made him feel like an imposter. It was not the persona that made him uncomfortable but the name. He acquired it with his first significant role, in the film *The Big Trail* (1930), an early Western talkie; the director changed Morrison to John Wayne, choosing "John" because it sounded American and "Wayne" from the surname of the famous revolutionary war hero General Anthony Wayne. He got his nickname in high school when some firemen friends began to call him "Duke" after the dog who always accompanied him.

Wayne spent his first ten years in small towns in the Midwest, but in 1917 his family moved to California, eventually settling in Glendale where he graduated from high school. His father imbued in the boy the spirit and values of the late nineteenth century: "Clyde Morrison gave his son a personal philosophy that is directly connected to the unique development of the American frontier: keep your word, never insult someone unintentionally, and do not look for trouble but if it comes do not quit" (McDonald 1987, 111). This philosophy is at the heart of the Wayne persona, and as a summary of the frontier spirit, it allowed John Wayne to stand for a major element in the national spirit. He himself described Rooster Cogburn, the quintessential John Wayne character, as someone "who's been around long enough to know for sure that you don't mess with outlaws, but use every trick in the book, fair or foul, to bring them to justice" (Tuska 1976, 576). Wayne provided a bridge between the world of the frontier and the new alien culture of the city. He was in many ways the first urban cowboy.

The Wayne persona differed from the prevailing movie cowboy image. He eschewed the white hat, the good guy's symbol, in favor of a battered campaign hat. When he got in a fight, his hat went flying, unlike Roy Rogers who never lost his. His clothes were not the fancy duds of a dude ranch; he wore faded jeans, worn shirts, and a sweaty bandanna around his neck. Though not truly realistic, his Westerns do exhibit greater realism than previous forms of the genre. Even more they presented Wayne as a low mimetic rather than high mimetic character with whom the audience could readily identify. The high mimetic hero has few flaws, is the perfect hero, while the low mimetic hero is flawed. The John Wayne persona was not a superhero or a god.

In keeping with the low mimetic nature of his persona, his character frequently was a little on the shady side, certainly not the cowboy in white. In his first major role, he played the Ringo Kid who escaped from prison and married a woman of dubious virtue. His characters were often irascible. When the judge in *Rooster Cogburn* sums up Rooster's career as a marshal by saying that in eight years he had shot sixty-five men and broken the law, not aided and abetted it, Rooster responds that he had only killed sixty and they all deserved it.

Wayne's characters avoided the shootout in the street, the easy mythological image of good versus evil. They never emphasized the quick draw, but preferred his trademark Winchester or shotgun. They tried to outsmart the opponent rather than force a one-on-one confrontation. McDonald gives a nice summary of a typical Wayne encounter:

> In *Tall in the Saddle* (1944), he cooled an adversary by simply stating "Touch that gun and I'll kill you." The villain's hesitation earned him a blow on the head from Wayne's weapon rather than a bullet. And when a female bystander exclaimed "Why, you hit him!" he grimly replied, "Yes, ma'am, just as hard as I could." (McDonald 1987, 122)

A recurring theme in his later Westerns, beginning with *The Cowboys* (1972), the first movie in which he was killed, revolves around handing on this tradition, usually to a young boy. In *Rooster Cogburn* he promises to help a young Indian boy, Wolf, become a U.S. marshall. This promise is particularly significant in view of the animosity between cowboys and Indians that underlies the Western genre and Wayne's famous trilogy of U.S. cavalry movies in which Indians were the antagonists. In his final movie, *The Shootist*, his character J. B. Books gives probably the best summary of the Duke persona as he attempts to help a young boy adjust to adult values: "I won't be wronged. I won't be insulted. I won't be laid a hand on. I don't do these things to other people and I require the same of them." Thus, the Duke tradition is passed on to the next generation of Americans.

Wayne personified, and perhaps still does personify, those ancestral values from another time that tamed the frontier, united a continent, and determined who we were. Duke, the low mimetic hero, did not represent a god but America. "Wayne is America; not ordinary America, but super-America" (McDonald 1987, 109). He was what we would like to be as a nation, and Ronald Reagan's America, sitting tall in the saddle, strode along in the manner of the Duke.

Since the Duke sums up an aspect of the frontier experience, and that experience forms an important element in our myth of origins, we need to pay attention to how the events of our past were formed into an American myth of Genesis. Only in this way can we understand how the myth forms our national character. The two primordial events that furnished the raw material for the American myth of origins are the Declaration of Independence and the nation's rebirth in the cauldron of the Civil War. Though both events are historical, they have become mythological in popular imagination. Consider, for example, the way popular memory has collapsed the span of time surrounding these events. We forget that when the colonists revolted, Virginia had been a colony for 169 years, almost double the time between the Constitution and the Civil War. Though we tend to think of the revolutionaries as newcomers in an untamed land, their families had been here for many generations, and a visit to Jefferson's mansion at Monticello will quickly dispel the notion of the colonies as a wilderness.

The Civil War and its aftermath became a second defining moment. Before the war the United States was customarily treated as plural: "These United States are. . . ." But afterward the nation had become singular: "The United States is. . . ." As Lincoln himself proclaimed, "This nation shall have a new birth of freedom."

Accordingly, after the war, this reborn country could once again view itself as a new Israel, a promised land, with a "Manifest Destiny" all its own. A large part of that destiny, of course, was the westward drive to settle the frontier. All of these elements would be incorporated into the American myth. The period after the Civil War became the idyllic time in which our values were formed and to which we nostalgically look back to discover who we are. Similarly, the Western became one of the major literary genres by which we learned about our genesis. The Western met "a natural and normal hunger for a heroic past" (Sonnichsen 1978, 16). Though the genre may be on the wane, it still retains its vitality as Clint Eastwood's *Unforgiven* (1992) and its metamorphosis into the *Star Wars* trilogy demonstrate (Gallagher, 208).

Douglas Pye in an essay on the Western genre traces its conventions back to James Fenimore Cooper's Leatherstocking tales. Employing the categories of the literary critic Northrop Frye, Pye classifies the Western as a romance; that is, the hero is superior to other men and his environment, but is not a god as in epic myth. He does marvelous things, but represents the spirit of his time. Frye classifies this type of romance as "elegiac." At the other pole is what he calls the "idyllic" romance, which idealizes a simple pastoral life. According to Pye, the Western's strength and vitality come from combining both aspects of romance. This is already exemplified in Cooper's Leatherstocking tales. The tales follow the life of the scout Natty Bumppo, which parallels the nation's westward expansion. While his talents clearly set him apart, what is most telling about Natty is his "infallible moral sense—he has the ability to know good from evil" (Pye 1986, 147). The narrator in *The Deerslayer* describes Natty's expression as his most striking feature: "This expression was simply that of guileless truth, sustained by an earnestness of purpose, and a sincerity of feeling, that rendered it remarkable" (Cooper 1954, 44). Natty lives in harmony with the natural world, at one with its rhythms. He identifies with the wilderness on which urban civilization is encroaching. This conflict between the corrupt, ungodly city and the pristine wilderness frequently underlies or drives the plot. "Characteristically, the tales end with the genteel heroes and heroines, the army officers and their ladies, the kidnapped aristocratic girls, being reintegrated into society . . . while Natty remains estranged from it, a movement into isolation that evokes the elegiac mood, the inevitable passing of an ideal order" (Pye 1986, 147).

This dualism extends to the very idea of the West, which has always had contradictory meanings in American life. It can be the garden of Eden or the great American desert. The wildness of wilderness can bless or threaten. It can be ennobling as in "close to nature" or savage as in "far from civilization." Rousseau's oxymoron of the noble savage captures the concept's implicit dualism. Civilization can likewise be a blessing and a curse. As the future, it will destroy the wilderness.

According to Pye, this very dualism gives the Western its great power in American thought and imagery, and I would add that it also makes the Western a powerful mythical vehicle for resolving American conflicts. Duke updates Natty Bumppo for twentieth-century America.

I cannot begin to deal adequately with a career as productive as John Wayne's, and unfortunately no one has undertaken a full-length critical treatment of his career. He tended to work with the same group of actors over the years and had his own production company, so his work developed a repertory quality. Especially in the Westerns, he was also fortunate to work with a series of gifted directors, notably John Ford and Howard Hawkes, who have received critical treatment (Gallagher 1986a; Stowell 1986). I am going to examine Wayne's first major picture, *Stagecoach*, where the Duke persona first appears. Two films from the latter part of his career exhibit the mature persona. *Rooster Cogburn*, which also stars Katharine Hepburn, brings the Duke persona into conflict with a strong female, and *The Shootist*, the last movie he made, envisions the death of the persona.

> Well, they're safe from the blessings of civilization.
> —*Doctor Josiah Boone,* Stagecoach

AFTER TOILING FOR ALMOST TEN YEARS IN B movies and serials, John Wayne got his big break when John Ford cast him in the role of the Ringo Kid in *Stagecoach* (1939). This film was the first to be shot in the spectacular scenery of Monument Valley (an area not associated with the iconography of the West), pioneered some very interesting camera techniques and is one of the finest Westerns ever made. The Duke persona emerges in this movie already fully developed.

The story bears a strong similarity to Chaucer's *Canterbury Tales*. The pilgrims gather in town, are introduced, and set out on a journey telling their stories as they go. In the *Canterbury Tales* the pilgrimage represents the human journey from earth to heaven, but in *Stagecoach* the journey has a different goal, the escape of the wild man, the true man, from encroaching evil civilization. As Peter Stowell (1986, 28) argues, "the mythic function of the stagecoach's journey" is as a "return to the wilderness for a new rite of passage and a rebirth of American civilization."

As the passengers gather for the stage to Lordsburg, they form contrasting pairs representing conflicts within society. The recurrence and number of these conflicts symbolize the deep divisions in society that the movie as myth attempts to mediate. Since myth seeks to resolve conflict, a scene in which characters represent conflicts shows the myth coming to the surface. The disheveled whiskey-drinking Doc Boone (Thomas Mitchell) and the neat, courteous gambler, Hatfield (John Carradine), are a Yankee and Southerner, respectively. This contrast between Yankee and Southerner is frequent in Westerns where the hero is often of Southern descent, for example, Shane and Rooster Cogburn. The animosity of the war has faded for the movie audience, but its representation in the story suggests that other conflicts are also reconcilable. Though Doc and the gambler are failures, society's discards, they both come through in the end for the same lady, Mrs. Mallory (Louise Platt). The pregnant wife of a cavalry commander, she stands in sharp contrast with Dallas (Claire Trevor), a woman of ill repute whom the ladies of the Law and Order League escort to the stage and out of the town. The line between proper and improper ladies is sharply drawn. As Dallas gets into the stage, she is warned that Geronimo is on the warpath. The camera cuts to the stern visages of the ladies of the Law and Order League, as Dallas says, "there are worse things than Apaches." The Ringo Kid (John Wayne), who has recently escaped from prison, is contrasted with the banker, Gatewood (Berton Churchill), the establishment's representative. Peacock (Donald Meek), a whiskey salesman, and Curly (George Bancroft), the marshall, are mediators between these two worlds. The passengers call the whiskey salesman "preacher" because he is a quiet and shy family man who addresses everyone as "brother" or "sister." Yet as a whiskey salesman, he plies a somewhat disreputable trade. The marshall, like most Western law officers, is part law, part outlaw. The travelers are indeed a diverse bunch, but they basically divide into two groups, the respectable (civilized) and the nonrespectable (wild).

The first image of the Ringo Kid in the movie has become a vintage John Wayne icon. The stage is on the road when a shot suddenly rings out. Up ahead appears a lone man, standing in the middle of the road, with his legs apart; he is twirling his Winchester in the air, while his saddle dangles from his hip. His clothes are ambivalent—battered hat, jeans, and worn boots.

This trip is taking place during an Indian uprising. Since the cavalry is out chasing Geronimo, the stage has to make a portion of the trip without an escort, and at each stop the escort fails to show. As a result, tension mounts in expectation of an Indian attack. A second major plot twist concerns the Ringo Kid's escape from prison and his expected confrontation in Lordsburg with the Plummer brothers, who killed his father and brother and framed him.

The trip unveils the character of the travelers and functionally sorts out the relationships. Mrs. Mallory and Hatfield, the failed southern gentleman turned gambler, pair up immediately. Dallas appalls Mrs. Mallory who would surely belong to the Law and Order League that escorted Dallas out of town. Hatfield shows Mrs. Mallory every courtesy, defers to her, and maintains her status in the group. While this deference is ironic given his own fallen character, it is a remembrance of times past. It turns out that he had served in her father's regiment during the Civil War. During the Indian attack, he is mortally wounded trying to defend her and is preparing to kill her to prevent her capture by the Indians, when the bugle sounding a cavalry charge is heard. He dies telling her, "If you see Judge Greenfield [her father], then tell him. . . ." He has purchased his redemption and recovered his past dignity by saving her.

The relation between Dallas and Ringo provides the movie's centerpiece. The classic stereotype of the Hollywood prostitute, Dallas has a heart of gold and a will to serve. Despite her snubbing by Mrs. Mallory, Dallas and Doc Boone later come to the rescue and help deliver Mrs. Mallory's child. Early in the film, after the marshall makes a disparaging remark about Dallas's profession, Ringo shows her deference, just as Hatfield does to Mrs. Mallory. The reason for Ringo's attitude toward others is revealed in a remark about himself. When asked why he had gotten into trouble with the law, he replies, "I used to be a good guy, but things happen." Even though he is on the wrong side of the law, Ringo like Cooper's Natty Bumppo knows good from evil and is the film's moral compass. After the birth of Mrs. Mallory's baby, Dallas and Ringo discover that they have much in common and draw closer together. Both are without family and are cut off in a sense from civilization. His father and brother were killed by the Plummer brothers, which is why he wants to go to Lordsburg, and she lost her family in an Indian massacre. When he proposes to her, she responds that he doesn't know her and implies that if he did he would not want to marry her. "I know all I need to know," he replies, but she does not answer. When Dallas asks Doc if it's all right to marry Ringo, he argues that in Lordsburg Ringo will go to prison and he'll find out all about her. So civilization's law puts the mythological quest of the journey in jeopardy. As their relation grows, Dallas seeks to prevent Ringo's coming shootout with the Plummer brothers. His response is in the classic mode of the Duke persona: "There are some things a man can't run away from."

When the stage arrives in Lordsburg, the confrontation is set up. Civilization determines the fate of the two main characters. As Dallas and Ringo pass a bawdy house, she remarks, "Well Kid, I told you not to follow me." Now she thinks her fate is sealed. She is no Mrs. Mallory and entertains no dream of escape. Always true to his word, Ringo replies that he asked her to marry him. Now, however, his own fate intervenes. His code demands that he face the Plummer brothers and after that the marshall will return him to prison. Civilization will conspire to keep Ringo and Dallas apart.

The shootout between Ringo and the three Plummer brothers builds dramatically and deviates somewhat from the classic confrontation in the street. A poker hand reveals the brothers' ultimate fate. Luke Plummer draws two aces and two eights, a dead man's hand. The actual shootout takes place out of camera range. The streets are dark and full of shadows. Since Ringo only has three bullets for three brothers, the odds are long. Breaking the hero's code of the Hollywood Western but in keeping with the take-no-chances code of the Duke persona, Ringo shoots first and falls to the ground. The camera fades. In the next scene, Luke Plummer walks through the saloon door and falls down dead, mortally wounded. In the movie's final scene, the marshall relents and lets Ringo and Dallas ride off into the sunset, as Doc announces, "Well, they're safe from the blessings of civilization."

The corrupting effect of civilization is a primary, though ambivalent theme throughout the movie. The banker Gatewood represents the new business culture that is civilizing the western frontier. He preaches several sermons on the benefits of business and advocates an end to government regulation, lower taxes, and abolition of the national debt. For a movie set in the nineteenth century and made in 1939, the themes sound very contemporary. Yet this hero and booster of civilization turns out to be corrupt. When the stage gets to Lordsburg, he is arrested for absconding with the bank's funds. Thus, in the person of the banker, civilization turns out to be bankrupt. Yet Mrs. Mallory is also a symbol of civilization. She redeems the gambler, a member of a fallen southern civilization; her husband heads the cavalry, which is "civilizing" the frontier; and her child represents the future. Furthermore, the stage travels between two cities with wilderness in between. The magnificent wilderness, framed by the towering mesas of Monument Valley, is clearly a place of the gods. Yet "savages" beset this place of the gods, and only civilization can save the valley.

Ringo the hero, like Natty, stands apart from civilization. With his pure moral code and ability to distinguish good from evil, he is a law unto himself. Unlike traditional heroes, such as Achilles, Moses, and Shane, he does not save the people or the world. In its many forms, the hero myth deals with the various types of chaos that threaten our world. But the American hero myth is ambiguous as to whether the cause of that chaos is civilization or the wilderness. As we noticed earlier, at least since James Fenimore Cooper, Americans have been ambivalent about their symbols. In the Duke version of this myth, the hero is a loner like Shane; he even resembles Achilles, off brooding alone by his ships, or Moses, alone on the mountain betrayed by his people. But the wilderness is a place both of threat (Indians) and of pure moral insight. The city (civilization) threatens to overwhelm and corrupt that purity of insight. As the system threatens to destroy and overwhelm the individual, the hero must struggle against it. This myth stems from the alienating experience that characterizes modern urban living. The Duke hero paves the way for civilization, but civilization is also a source of corruption, so he must always retreat back to the wilderness to protect his pure moral insight. Alone with Dallas he escapes, without the so-called blessings of civilization, as Doc ironically observes. Ringo remains an outlaw and she a woman with a reputation. The chaos remains in force, and the individual struggles alone. It is as though Shane never joined the farmers, Achilles never left his ships, or Moses never came down from the mountain.

Even after Wayne's death, variations on the Duke persona have maintained a strong currency. One version, Duke in the City, will appear in the next chapter in the Dirty Harry movies. The Rocky series with Sylvester Stallone offers another interesting view of this hero. One might in fact entitle the whole cycle of Rocky movies "the apotheosis of a hero," for Rocky undergoes a remarkable transformation. The very first *Rocky* (1976) is a cross between Cinderella and *Marty* (1955). Rocky is a down-on-his-luck, nearly punch-drunk boxing loser, who is redeemed by the love of a good woman and a manager who makes him believe in himself. He gets his big break when the champion decides to fight a certifiable loser for his next championship bout. The movie has its charms and won Academy Awards for best picture and best director. By the fourth picture (1985), Rocky is changed. Physically, Stallone has so reshaped his body that he resembles a body builder rather than a punchy fighter from Philadelphia. His body has become armor. A corresponding mythical transformation has occurred. The enemy now is a machine-like giant, a product of Soviet physical fitness labs. The contest is between East and West, evil and good, the dehumanized machine and the natural American. Themes only innocently broached in *Stagecoach* have now responded to the impact of an even more modern and alienating civilization. As the chaos threatening the individual escalates, so does the status of the hero. The more the culture fears the encroaching chaos, the greater the need for a superhero and the less acceptable the low mimetic hero. The logical extension is the superhero of the *Terminator* movies.

In the Western society has always implicitly been an enemy. . . . The screen Western especially, where we cannot help drawing our own conclusions from the town on the one hand and space on the other, tends to be unequivocal about this reminding us that one of the things the hero is up against is monolithic, conformist, hierarchical society.

—*Jenni Calder (1975)*

THOUGH *ROOSTER COGBURN* (1975) WAS NOT one of John Wayne's better movies, it raises an intriguing mythical issue because of Katharine Hepburn's appearance as Eula Goodnight.

A sequel to *True Grit* (1969), the movie unfortunately tries to shoe-horn in the plot of *The African Queen* (1951). Yet in line with Hollywood advertising, two titans engage in a mythical conflict in which the Duke persona must confront and accommodate a strong woman.

The plot is simple. Marshall Rooster Cogburn, the essence of the lone hero who shoots first and asks questions later, doesn't fit in with the new way of doing things, so the judge retires him. Yet when a particularly despicable desperado steals a load of nitroglycerin from the army, who must come to the rescue but Rooster Cogburn? The bad guys attack an Indian mission run by Miss Goodnight and her father and kill him. She and a young Indian boy, Wolf (Richard Romancito), join up with Marshall Cogburn over his strenuous protest, and they all go off in pursuit of the outlaws and the stolen nitroglycerin. Eventually, the marshall manages to retrieve the nitroglycerin, so now the outlaws pursue the marshall, Miss Goodnight, and the Indian boy. At this point *The African Queen* intrudes as the group attempts to escape downriver on a raft. The final shootout, in typical John Wayne style, is a face-off not in the street, but in the shallows of the river. Rooster has floated the nitroglycerin downriver ahead of the raft, and as it approaches the outlaws stretched across the river, he rises from his hiding place and detonates the cases with his Winchester. Obviously, what interests us is not the plot, but the conflict between Rooster and Miss Goodnight.

Rooster's view of women is the traditional one from *Shane*. He thinks that a woman's place is in the home with Marian and that they definitely do not belong in his world. When Rooster first encounters Miss Goodnight in the wreckage of the mission, he is courteous but patronizing. When she tries to come along with him to pursue her father's killers, he forbids her and rides off without her. She insists on coming and gets her way. After an early encounter with Miss Goodnight, whom he frequently calls "sister," Rooster tells Wolf, "If they ever giv'em the vote, God help us."

She demonstrates her courage in her initial scenes. When the sinister leader of the outlaws attempts to scare her by shooting at her feet, she recites Psalm 121. When he runs out of ammunition, she turns with dignity and walks away, still reciting the psalm. Later, in a shootout with the outlaws, she turns out to be a very good shot. Thus, Miss Goodnight does not conform to the image of the weak, defenseless woman.

Two exchanges illustrate the intermingling of these two images. When Miss Goodnight asks why he is called Rooster, he replies, "In the old days I was cocky, a kinda strutting bird." His response confirms that he hasn't changed much, as he continues to strut around. Then she abruptly brings up the subject that most divides them—religion— and asks, "Is your name written in the Lamb's book of life?" His strenuous objection to this type of talk signals the deep divide between the female's world of formal religion and the male's natural religion. In *Shane* the church stands for the world of the woman, the home, and the family; its coming stands for a future time when the village will be civilized.

The conversation then turns to her Yankee accent, which marks another divide because he served in the Confederate Army. We have already seen the easy mediation of this conflict in *Stagecoach*. Rooster also comments on the difference between her citified eastern accent and her physical appearance, which he describes as "more like a prairie bird, bony and tough." She admits that she has become more aggressive than a woman should. "Amen, Amen," he says. "You're praying," she says, "the first step on the road to conversion." As usual, she has the last word, thus maintaining the image of the aggressive, talkative woman, preying on the strong, silent man of the wilderness. The principal male-female boundaries remain in place. Women are talkative and women who impinge on the male world are aggressive. Religion, which symbolizes the fundamental division between wilderness and civilization, cannot be overcome as easily as the division between Yankee and Southerner. Insofar as male and female reach a rapprochement, it is because she gains equality and becomes a male; thus, the male point of view remains the governing one.

In another exchange, Rooster and Miss Goodnight go through a pseudo marriage proposal. A lasting relationship is unlikely, however, because both are life-long loners, whose efforts at companionship have failed. His first wife left him, and Miss Goodnight says she scared off her beaux. Again equality is on male terms, as defined by the wild man. He proceeds to ask a series of questions designed to determine her attributes, in much the same way as he might look over a horse at a sale. When he asks how old she is, she responds, "It's already struck midnight." Next, he asks how much she weighs, remarking that he is not opposed to scrawny women. Then he turns to her finances. She retorts, "I take it you're on the scout for a rich widow?"

He concludes that she probably doesn't have any money and can't cook. She grumbles, "I guess I don't measure up?" but she doesn't seem all that concerned about her failure to meet the mythical standard of the female. Yet he replies in terms of another standard, "You got more backbone than femaleness. Out in the territory, we prize a dead shot more than we do a lady's charm." She questions whether a new standard is in place, "You mean in the West the men do not mind if their women can outshoot and outsmart them?" Here may be the beginning of an accommodation, but it is still exclusively on male terms. "If they're quiet about it," he retorts. The old female myth reasserts itself. She may not really outshine a male, and her place is to provide silent support. "Out here we value a spirited woman almost as much as we value a spirited horse." The horse image finally comes to the surface, although it has been implied throughout the dialogue. A woman is still property, valued for what she can contribute to the affairs of men. "Almost as much, you say," Miss Goodnight replies. "Almost, but not quite," he says. Although said with good humor, his final comment still significantly devalues her.

The final scene of this film poses a formal problem for the Western genre. Frequently, though not always, the genre employs a threesome, as in *Shane*, so the hero can ride into the sunset. This movie has a twosome with no permanent bond contemplated. Moreover, she has invaded the male world and taken on certain significant aspects of that role. Myth creates order out of chaos by seeking a balance, as in the happy ending that rounds off all the various strands of a story. Given the inevitable separation of the two main characters and the disturbance Miss Goodnight has created for the Duke persona, how can the movie reach mythical balance in its final scene? First, in proper female fashion, she rides off with the boy, even though the boy has confessed that he would like to be a marshall like Rooster. As they ride away, she abruptly turns back and says, "Ruben [his Christian name, which only she uses], I have to say it. Living with you has been an adventure any woman would relish for the rest of time." The reference to adventure acknowledges the wild man against civilization and makes her a representative woman, a role she has eschewed throughout the movie. "Ah, I look at you with your burnt-out face, your big belly and bear-like paws, and your shining eye. And I have to say you're a credit to the whole male sex and I'm proud to have you as my friend." Her description of him is accurate and certainly not Adonis-like. Yet she acknowledges that he epitomizes the male, who has stood alone and successfully fought the encroachment of civilization with his pure moral insight. Then she rides away. Stunned, Rooster finally stammers, "I'll be damned if she didn't get the last word in again! Ah, well. . . ." Despite the advertised confrontation between the strong-willed independent Katharine Hepburn and John Wayne the Duke, in the end the Duke is intact, and the female has had to acknowledge his greatness. She may get the last word, but not really, because his last word acknowledges the wily ways of women and their tolerance ("Ah, well . . .") by men. The myth has sustained attack; no new way for men and women to relate is envisioned.

> Eastern Women take no part in *public life*. This was true of Judaism in the time of Jesus, in all cases where Jewish families faithfully observed the Law. When the Jewess of Jerusalem left her house, her face was hidden by an arrangement of two head veils, a headband on the forehead with bands to the chin, and a hair net with ribbons and knots, so that her features could not be recognized. It was said that once, for example, a chief priest in Jerusalem did not recognize his own mother when he had to carry out against her the prescribed process for a woman suspected of adultery.
> —Joachim Jeremias (1969)

> Now the woman was a Gentile, of Syrophoenician origin. She begged him to cast the demon out of her daughter. He said to her, "Let the children be fed first, for it is not fair to take the children's food and throw it to the dogs." But she answered him, "Sir, even the dogs under the table eat the children's food."
> —Mark 7:26-29

THE DUKE PERSONA IS A FIXED POINT THAT sums up an aspect of the American mythology of the hero. Jesus likewise is a fixed point in our religious mythology. Strange though it may seem, the Jesus and Duke personas are interlaced. To the extent that our image of Jesus both partakes of the hero myth and has been one of its greatest archetypes in the West, the Duke reflects Jesus. And since the Duke implicitly shapes our understanding of the hero, he influences our understanding of Jesus. In a conversation, it is important to take stock of this interlacing because it happens without our being aware of it. Otherwise we dismiss the interlacing because we focus on the differences: Jesus is God and John Wayne is a movie star. But that misses the point. We unwittingly use our notion of the hero to understand Jesus. Both have many aspects in common. We associate Jesus and the Duke with the wilderness; Jesus wars with the city of Jerusalem and the Duke disparages the eastern cities; both have a pure moral insight that sets them apart. Increasingly, in our society we view Jesus as our personal savior, a solo savior on the model of the Duke.

The story of the Woman at the Well (John 4) not only offers an interesting conversation partner for some of the aspects of the Duke myth that we have highlighted but also challenges our accepted persona for Jesus. The story plays on several conflicts, some obvious and others less so. That Samaritans and Jews hated one another was a commonplace in the ancient world. We have already seen that animosity at play in the parable of the man on the road from Jerusalem to Jericho or, as the goyim tradition prefers, "The Good Samaritan." In this story, when Jesus asks for a drink, the woman asks how he, a Jewish male, can request a drink from a Samaritan female. The narrator remarks parenthetically, "Jews do not share things in common with Samaritans" (4:9). The woman is troubled by two sets of boundaries: that he is a Jew and she a Samaritan and that she is a female. The double barriers of national religion (or as we might call it race) and sex exist between them. This story breaks down both of these fundamental barriers, which are often seen to have their roots in the divine.

Jesus ignores the woman's reservations about religion and sex; instead, he dares her to see both the gift of God and who is addressing her. He does not even allude to the supposed barriers between them. He offers her *living* water. As is usual in a Johannine dialogue, the term *living* has a double sense. The commonsense understanding would be flowing water or the cool, sweet water from a deep desert well. The uncommon sense demands of the woman and reader a "spiritual sense," a figurative sense of living. Even so the woman is not sure the barrier should be so easily broached. She asks if he is greater than Jacob, our father, "who gave us the well and drank from it himself, his sons, and his cattle" (4:10). Her question harks back to patrimony. Jacob is a father and those who drink from the well are father, sons, and cattle. Women are omitted from the triad, indication that she puts herself somewhere after the cattle. She tests Jesus to see where he will erect the barrier. He continues to invite her to drink—to drink a water that will quench all thirst. The woman now requests this great gift. She has pasted the first test and seen that the gift of God overwhelms and eliminates human need. In its presence one can abide forever.

She has not yet seen who is addressing her. Jesus asks her to get her husband. This again raises a sexual barrier. Her husband will serve as a barrier between her and this other male, Jesus. With a husband present, the other male would be safe from the intruding uncleanliness and shame of a female. But rather than retreat to her husband's protection, she confesses that she has no husband, and Jesus agrees with the remarkable assertion that she has had five husbands and the current one is not a true husband. To this she responds that he must truly be a prophet. On the surface, this exchange is confusing; its real point will not emerge until later. The ancient world did not use divorce as a way of engaging in serial marriages, as we do. In Jewish society, a man divorced the woman; she had no choice in the matter and could not divorce him. Is the woman perhaps the village prostitute? Most likely not, for when she goes and calls the villagers to see the prophet, they do not shun her (Schnackenburg 1968, 1:433). Nor does Jesus demand repentance from her, although that is not as telling as one might suppose, since Jesus seldom demands repentance. More to the point, she has no man to protect her from Jesus. The sexual barrier has fallen away. Jesus and the woman face each other without shame like Adam and Eve in the garden. The religious barrier falls away even more easily. For while salvation comes through the Jews, God is no longer worshiped on any mountain or in any temple. The woman has experienced in Jesus the breakdown of two of the most powerful barriers of her day, national religion and sex. In Jesus, God breaks down all barriers. "The word became flesh" marks the breakdown of the ultimate barrier between God and humanity. God is not on that mountain or this mountain, in that temple or this temple. Like the wandering God of ancient Israel, God is in no place.

What does it mean to worship God in spirit and truth? The truth in this story is obvious—the destruction of barriers. God is not a barrier: not a he or she or a thing of any kind, but spirit. Spirit or wind (the Greek word *pneuma* has both senses) blows where it will (3:8), breathing on what it wants.

In the dialogue between the woman and Jesus, she moves to faith and insight. The story moves from a thirsty Jew to a giver of living water, to prophet, Messiah, and finally, "I who speak to you am he." For the woman, barriers are broken down. When the disciples return, however, they wonder that Jesus is talking to a woman. For them, the barriers remain intact. The disciples try to persuade Jesus to eat, but he responds that he has food of which they do not know. His food, of course, is doing the will of God. As she drank the living water, he has eaten the Father's food. As God breaks down barriers between national religions (races) and sexes, so also God provides food and water. The harvest awaits for it has already been sown.

The story of the Samaritan woman ends on two remarkable notes. First, she is a missionary who brings others to faith—and not just to faith but to Jesus himself. There is a curious parallel between this story and the preceding one about Nicodemus who is Jewish, male, and a Pharisee and thus supposedly knowledgeable in the things of God. Yet he comes in the middle of the night and becomes only a secret disciple of Jesus. But a Samaritan woman, with five husbands and no religious advantage, comes in the middle of the day and becomes a witness. Just as remarkable is that Jesus is first confessed as Savior of the world in Samaria, a foreign land, a competing tradition with Judaism (John 4:42). Ironically, this magnificent, imperial, universalist christological title was first proclaimed in a Samaritan village brought to faith by an unclean woman.

The story has one more subtle and ironical scandal for those who listen carefully. Indeed, this may have been its greatest scandal in the original telling. The background of this story is extremely detailed and carefully constructed. The Pharisees are jealous of Jesus for creating so many disciples. So now he will make a disciple out of a Samaritan woman. Furthermore, Jesus is in a foreign land, Samaria, sitting by a well, but this is not just any well. It is the well of Jacob. Later in the story the woman reminds Jesus that this is Jacob's well, even though this is unattested in the Hebrew Bible (Brown 1966, 169). The story's form is well known from the Hebrew Bible where it was told about Abraham, Isaac, Jacob, and Moses. When a hero encounters his future wife, the meeting usually takes place in a foreign land; the hero says or does something characteristic of his role in the story; one of them draws water; and the maiden rushes home to prepare for the man's coming to meet her father and eat with them. A wedding will follow. Here the form of an older hero story is being used to help an ancient reader understand the way Jesus is a hero.

All the form's elements appear in the Johannine story, although ironically. Indeed, some are emphasized: the foreign country (Samaria), the well (Jacob's well), and the maiden coming to draw water. Yet the irony becomes extreme: the well water is never drawn, and she leaves her jar at the well when the disciples approach. Drinking does take place, and is so deep and satisfying that she will never again need her jar to draw water. She is not a maiden but the wife of five husbands, but now she has no husband. So she is marriageable. Further, although there is no meal with the future father-in-law, the disciples talk about feeding Jesus. A type of marriage does take place. The woman is Jesus' witness, giving birth to the faith of her village. At a deep level John attacks the barriers that divide us from each other and from God by marrying Jesus and the Samaritan woman. In a woman's shame John finds the witness for Jesus as Savior of the world.

In the contest between Miss Goodnight and the Duke persona, despite all the jousting, Miss Goodnight must adjust to the Duke persona in the end. In the Johannine story, one would assume that the Jesus persona is fixed, but that is not the case. In fact, there is a christological motion in the story so that the woman gradually sees more and more who he is: first, a Jewish male, then a prophet, the Messiah, and Savior of the world. The function of these titles is not simply to further the self-revelation of Jesus, but to accommodate the various barriers between the woman and Jesus so that the final title, Savior of the world, eliminates the ultimate barriers within the Roman Empire. Jesus is not the savior of the Jews alone, or of a Samaritan woman, but of the whole world. In the Roman Empire, such a title places Jesus in sharp contrast to the Roman emperor, who also claims the same title. That empire is extremely hierarchical and based on power. Jesus' dialogue with the woman explicitly rejects the hierarchical model of empire in favor of a world without barriers, and in his trial before Pilate, Jesus rejects a kingdom upheld by power (John 18:36-37). In *Rooster Cogburn* Rooster and Miss Goodnight reach a grudging accommodation, but in the end she has to acknowledge the greatness of his maleness; the boundaries are not truly broken down. Even more, as a hero the Duke persona represents the rugged individual in flight from civilization and society. This model has insidiously inflicted modern belief with the idea of Jesus as my personal savior, a notion supported by the Duke persona but at odds with the Johannine story. "My personal savior" reinstitutes the barriers. In fact, at the end of the Johannine story is an explicit warning against such an interpretation. The townsfolk approach the woman and implicitly rebuke her: "It is no longer because of what you said that we believe, for we have heard for ourselves, and we know that this is truly the savior of the world" (4:42). Apparently, she was becoming a barrier between Jesus and the townsfolk, and John quickly rejects such a possibility.

A man's death is about the most private thing.
—*J. B. Books,* The Shootist

THE SHOOTIST (1976) WAS JOHN WAYNE'S LAST movie, and many consider it one of his finest. The film has a quiet almost eloquent beauty. In his discussion of the romantic hero as part of the Western genre, Douglas Pye captures the spirit of *The Shootist*, although his piece was written the year before its release: "When such a [romantic] hero dies, it creates the sense of a spirit passing out of nature, coupled with a melancholy sense of the passing of time, the old order changing and giving way to the new" (Pye 1986, 147).

The year is 1901 and the newspaper announces the death of Queen Victoria. The Victorian age is passing and the twentieth century is at hand. If Rooster Cogburn was out of step in the Indian Territory of the 1880s, J. B. Books is positively a dinosaur in modernizing Carson City, a town caught between the old west with shootouts in the saloon and the automobiles and trolley beginning to ply the streets. The sense that an age is passing pervades the movie, but it is also concerned with how the values of that age will be handed on.

J. B. Books, described by a newspaper man as "the most celebrated shootist extant," has killed more than thirty men. He comes to Carson City to have his old friend Doc Hostetler (James Stewart) confirm a diagnosis of cancer and then to die. What makes this movie even more poignant is that John Wayne himself was dying of cancer during the film's production. So not only does this movie mark the end of an age, but the Duke persona must deal with his own death. Death is especially revealing in myth, for as a primary human conflict it is one of myth's abiding themes.

On the surface *The Shootist* closely resembles *Shane*, which also dealt with the passing of one age and the inauguration of another, as well as with the justification of progress. Mrs. Bond Rogers (Lauren Bacall) plays the Marian role and represents the female values that come into conflict with the chaos represented by J. B. Books. Joey, the young initiate into the values of Shane, becomes Gillom (Ron Howard), a teenager passing into manhood. As in *Shane* the young man receives an explicit initiation into the rite of the gun. Perhaps the greatest contrast between the two movies is the main character. Shane was a quiet hero who dressed like the farmers and kept his gun hidden. Books is a bull in a china shop. His very presence is a threat, causing the sheriff to tremble until he realizes that Books is dying. Then he dances a jig to celebrate.

But the greatest difference is the gun. It is always a presence in this movie, ever at Books's side ready for use, whereas in *Shane* it was implied and hidden away. Twice the film reveals Books's motto, and as we noted earlier, this is also the philosophy of the Duke persona (as well as of John Wayne personally). As the movie begins, director Don Siegel, who also includes *Dirty Harry* among his credits, presents a flashback of Books's career by using black and white clips from previous John Wayne movies, thus emphasizing that Books is the Wayne persona. During this reprise, a narrator repeats Books's motto: "I won't be wronged. I won't be insulted. I won't be laid a hand on. I don't do these things to other people and I require the same of them." The words are repeated during Gillom's initiation to the gun.

Although Books tells Gillom "there's more to being a man than handling a gun," a shooting lesson functions as Gillom's initiation. In

Shane the actual firing of the gun furnished the dramatic focal point, but here that is secondary, nothing more than target practice. Instead, the emphasis is on the lesson where Books hands on the tradition of what it means to be a man. Gillom's mother worries that he has fallen in with bad company, but Books reassures her that the youth's underlying soundness will see him through this difficult period. As Gillom and Books are looking for a suitable place for a shooting lesson, Gillom asks how he happened to kill so many men. Books replies with his motto. Like Natty Bumppo, Books represents a pure moral sense developed by life on the frontier. Thus, killing was not something he sought, but it happened as the inevitable result of his integrity. At one point when Mrs. Rogers questions him about his reputation as a killer, he remarks, "I never killed a man who didn't deserve it." To which she replies, "Surely, only God can judge that." But her point is ignored; no one else ever questions the logic of his motto and its outcome. But if this motto were universally adopted, would everyone have to kill thirty men? After all, the motto allows no compromise. Like the revolutionary motto "Don't tread on me," it offers no way out. And as Eli, the voice of protest in *Witness*, tells his grandson, "There's always more than one way."

Since such a motto inevitably leads to conflict, Gillom wonders how Books always came out on top. Books observes that most men are unwilling to kill. So they blink or do something else that gives them away. To kill one must never hesitate to take advantage of the other man's weakness, that is, his unwillingness to kill. But, as he also observes, with what turns out to be prophecy, "It's usually some red-eyed amateur that gets you."

Bond Rogers is Marian with her house in a city, not on the emerging frontier. She represents the values not only of the woman but also of civilization and the coming new century. When Gillom asks for a shooting lesson, before Books agrees, he asks if Gillom will have to tell his mother about it. The gun is outside her world, which is threatened by the chaos and violence of J. B. Books. When she finds out who he is, she asks him to leave because as a widow she must protect her reputation or lose her boarders. Books confesses that he can't leave because he is going to die, but he promises not to be a burden. The solo savior myth remains intact; the male must be independent. But as the disease progresses, he finds he cannot take care of himself and becomes dependent on Rogers: "I've been too proud to take help from anyone. I guess I'll have to learn." Mrs. Rogers tries to persuade him to go to church or see her minister. As in *Shane*, church embodies female values. He refuses, arguing in the tradition of James Fenimore Cooper that his cathedral is the open air. Even more, he rejects the church's (that is, civilization's) interest in his death, "A man's death is about the most private thing." Yet he confesses that he's "a dying man scared of the dark."

Though Mrs. Rogers and Books come to respect each other, they never quite meet, and much always remains unsaid and unasked between them. Late in the movie, when she notices that he is running low on the narcotic laudanum used to kill the cancer's pain, she offers to order some more, and he says that it won't be necessary. When she deduces that he is getting ready to do something, his only reply is "no tears." Even in death the male and female worlds must remain separate, for death is a private thing. When he leaves the boarding house for the saloon at the movie's end, she compliments him on how fine he looks in his suit. He tells her it's his birthday and remarks on what a beautiful day it is. She replies, "It's what we call a false spring." The false spring is clearly a reference to his own situation: as good as he looks, the winter of death is coming. Even in this final moment he cannot accept her offer of compassion. With dignity he merely replies, "Good-bye, Mrs. Rogers." "Goodbye Mr. Books." Even in death, the lone hero remains alone and private.

After describing the terrible death facing his friend Books, Doc Hostetler says, "I would not die a death like I just described . . . not if I had your courage." The implication of suicide is clear. With his courage Books should arrange to die some other way. Thereupon Books sets about planning meticulously for his own death. It takes him eight days, one more than the week of Genesis. During this period, he reads the entire newspaper, prepares his tombstone, gets a hair cut, gives his horse to Gillom, gets his clothes cleaned, and puts his affairs in order. He plans for his death by inviting three men to meet him at the saloon—the mean-spirited brother (Richard Boone) of a man he had killed, a bully that Gillom has been associating with, and a slick faro dealer (Hugh O'Brian) whose gun determines the fairness of the deal. Books calculates that one of these will kill him. In typical John Wayne fashion, the shootout involves cunning, not a one-on-one confrontation in the street. Books takes up a position behind the bar and shoots it out with each invited guest in turn. Though wounded and surrounded, he triumphs.

At the shooting's end, Gillom bursts into the saloon to find Books wounded. Just then the bartender approaches from behind and shoots Books in the back with a shotgun, fulfilling Books's prophecy about the red-eyed amateur. Gillom grabs Books's gun and shoots the bartender. In disgust he throws the gun away, and Books with his last dying gesture nods in approval, apparently at the throwing away of the gun. Gillom covers him and walks out of the saloon and away from the town's center, where his mother meets him and walks behind him. The camera records this scene from an ever increasing height, suggesting a god ascending or looking down.

The death scene remains ambivalent because the viewer must rely only on what is pictured without any words as a guide. Taking the doctor's advice, Books has arranged a death in keeping with his life. The gun that had been his life now has ended it. Yet when Gillom comes to his rescue and kills the bartender, Books approves when he throws the gun away. So clearly the gun is not to be a part of Gillom's world, yet the creed that provoked this gunfight remains a part of that world. What then of the gun? Is tossing it aside only a gesture? Will it still be needed? In the final scene Mrs. Rogers remains excluded from the new male world her son has just entered by killing. She cannot console him and can only walk behind him. The creed remains, and the male and female worlds are still separate.

He emptied himself out.

—Philippians 2:7

THE DEATH OF JESUS IS A CENTRAL COMPO-nent in the belief structure of the Christianity underlying the New Testament. Strange though it may seem, the death of Jesus need not be at the heart of Christianity. Both the *Gospel of Thomas*, which may well be dated to the first century, and the Synoptic Saying Source Q, a document used by both Matthew and Luke in writing their gospels, do not deal with the death of Jesus, nor do they make it critical for salvation (Kloppenborg 1988; Kloppenborg et al. 1990).

For Thomas "Whoever discovers the interpretation of these sayings will not taste death" (*Gospel of Thomas* 1). In Q Jesus' death is like that of the prophets in that it illustrates Israel's resistance to God's wisdom: "That is why the wisdom of God has said, 'I will send them prophets and apostles, and some of them they are always going to kill and persecute.' So this generation will have to answer for the blood of all the prophets that has been shed since the world was founded, from the blood of Abel to the blood of Zechariah" (Luke 11:49-51). Likewise in the Gospel of Luke, as in *Thomas* and Q, not Jesus' death but his preaching is central. Hans Conzelmann has put it well: "The most important finding in this connection for our purposes is that there is no trace of any Passion mysticism, nor is any direct soteriological significance drawn from Jesus' suffering or death. There is no suggestion of a connection with the forgiveness of sins" (Conzelmann 1960, 201). In Luke, at Jesus' death the centurion remarks on his innocence (Luke 23:47).

But in other parts of primitive Christianity, the death of Jesus figured more prominently. One of the earliest extant meditations on the death is found in the hymn embedded in Paul's letter to the Philippians. This hymn predates Paul's writing of the letter (therefore pre-50s) and was not composed by Paul, as its unique vocabulary indicates. Setting it in lines gives a good indication of the hymnic character:

1	He was in the form of God
2	yet he laid no claim to equality with God,
3	but made himself nothing,
4	assuming the form of a slave.
5	Bearing the human likeness,
6	sharing the human lot,
7	he humbled himself,
8	and was obedient, even to the point of death, [death on a cross].
9	Therefore God raised him to the heights
10	and bestowed on him the name above all names,
11	that at the name of Jesus every knee should bow
12	in heaven, on earth, and in the depths,
13	and every tongue acclaim
14	"Jesus Christ is Lord"
15	to the glory of God the Father. (REB)

While there is almost universal agreement that the note about the cross at the end of line 8 was added by Paul and breaks the hymn's original rhythm, the debate still rages about whether the hymn draws on the myth of the gnostic redeemer or some form of the Adam myth. Although the debate probably is irresolvable without new evidence, nevertheless it is important to recognize that the Christ event is here understood in a mythical pattern. The hymn has three stages: the incarnation, death, and exaltation of the divine being. The first stanza describes the status of the redeemer. His form is that of God but he takes on the form of a slave. The Hellenistic world could not imagine a more absolute and drastic contrast. He has moved from one extreme in the hierarchical structure of that world to the opposite end. Line 3 describes the exchange of form. The REB says "but made himself nothing" trying to capture the sense of the Greek word *ekenōsen*. The NRSV translates the same line as "he emptied himself." The sense of the verb is to divest oneself of one's privileges (Bauer et al. 1979, 428; similarly Louw and Nida 1989, 1:87.70). "Make himself nothing" captures the sense well, for God has all possible status in the Hellenistic world and a slave has none. The incarnation is a loss, a complete loss. The hero's identification with humanity leads to a very low mimetic presentation, the opposite of the superhero.

In the second stanza the redeemer's identification with humanity is complete even to the point of death. But the hymn emphasizes that he does not resist or fight against death, but is obedient to his fate.

Because of this humbling obedient death, God raises "him to the heights" or, as the Greek says, "superexalts him." God raises him back to the status he enjoyed at the hymn's beginning. But the function of this exaltation is not to restore the being but to give him a new name. Naming is not simple labeling; it indicates something essential about the one named. For this reason Moses asks for God's name in the burning bush. The name given Jesus is "Lord" (*kurios*). The significance of this name is manifold. First, it is the name for Yahweh in the Septuagint, the Greek translation of the Hebrew Bible. In English translations this had led to the convention of translating this Hebrew name for God as "the Lord." Thus, God is giving Jesus God's own name. Second, this title is also widely used as an imperial title for the Roman emperor. Thus, Jesus is proclaimed the Lord of all because of his becoming nothing and his humility. Implicitly, his nothingness (emptying out), humility, and obedience stand in sharp contrast to the Roman emperor. Ironically, employing mythical elements in an unexpected way in contrast to the expectations of power gives the hymn its real power.

There are remarkable correspondences between *The Shootist* and the Philippians' hymn. They both mark a shift in the ages. The eschatological shifts in *The Shootist* are clear. It contains not only the generic tonality of a shift, but the actual signs: the death of Queen Victoria, the modernization of Carson City, the sheriff's remark that Books has outlived his time, the contrast between Books's horse and the trolley and cars, and the ambivalent repudiation of the gun. Likewise the cosmological motion of the Philippians' hymn marks out an eschatological shift for the cosmos from one lord, Caesar, to another, the obedient and humble Jesus. Although we are often told that New Testament eschatology is outdated, that eschatology still survives in a movie like *The Shootist*. We still mark out the passing of ages, and there is little doubt that we are living through such a period now. Even though *The Shootist* is set in 1901, it really mourns the passing of the American century, the twentieth century.

This passing of the ages in hymn and movie involves the hero's violent death. Here the contrast is the sharpest. Both deaths are violent, though Christianity tends to mask the violence of Jesus' death, itself a mythical move. Actually, one might see in Paul's reference to "death on the cross" an unmasking and reminder of the violence of Jesus' public execution. Books brings on his own death. It is a planned death. He even has his tombstone delivered on the day of the shootout. This death is a suicide that the movie attempts to ennoble by invoking the tradition of the Western shootout. It also masks his co-opting of three men who forfeit their lives to facilitate his suicide. That they are pictured as less than innocent or deserving of death, as Books had remarked to Mrs. Rogers ("I never killed a man who didn't deserve it"), only masks and hides the violence of their deaths. In the Philippians' hymn, the death is a sign of humility and obedience signaling God's complete solidarity with the fate of humanity. The act of solidarity liberates. The implicit contrast is with the Roman emperor who liberates by conquering and lording it over his subjects. In this hymn, the son liberates by becoming a subject slave, humble and obedient. The death scene in Mark's Gospel catches this point. Jesus dies after crying out, "My God, my God, why have you forsaken me?" (Mark 15:34). This death unmasks violence and Jesus is truly nothing.

He is pictured in despair. Yet this sight provokes the centurion to make the same christological confession that the Father had made at the baptism (1:11) and the transfiguration (9:7): "Truly this man was God's Son." For the centurion, seeing Jesus in this death of despair becomes the liberating moment. In *The Shootist* Gillom is drawn into the web of death and leaves for a new age in disgust and revulsion. In the Philippians' hymn and in Mark, solidarity leads to liberation; in *The Shootist* it leads to killing.

Books had declared that death is about the most private thing that happens to a man, and yet ironically he chose to die in public, not in the privacy of his boarding-house room. This ambivalence between private and public represents a failure to come to terms with the purpose of death. Why is Books dying? For whom is he dying? Is he dying to escape the pain of cancer? To avoid being a burden to Mrs. Rogers, as he promised? To make a final statement about his life— that it ends as it has been lived? The death of Jesus is a public event because it is for the public. This word play also works well in English, because *public* comes from the Latin *publicus*, which means the people or the state. In the Philippians' hymn Jesus dies for the public, accomplishing for the people what the emperor could not accomplish for his public, creating a community of equals rather than a hierarchical society of elites and slaves. And the centurion, in the service of the emperor, acknowledges this liberation by his confession.

WORKS NOTED

BAUER, Walter, et al. 1979.
A Greek-English lexicon of the New Testament and other early Christian literature. 2nd ed. Chicago: University of Chicago Press.

BROWN, Raymond E. 1966.
The Gospel according to John (i–xii). Anchor Bible series. Vol. 1. Garden City, N. Y.: Doubleday.

CALDER, Jenni. 1975.
There must be a Lone Ranger: The American West in film and in reality. New York: Taplinger Publishing Co.

CONZELMANN, Hans. 1960.
The theology of St. Luke. Reprint 1982. Philadelphia: Fortress Press.

COOPER, James Fenimore. 1954.
The leatherstocking saga. New York: Pantheon Books.

GALLAGHER, Tag. 1986a.
John Ford: The man and his films. Berkeley: University of California Press.

———. 1986b.
Shoot-out at the genre corral: Problems in the 'evolution' of the Western. In *Film genre reader,* 202–16. Edited by Barry Keith Grant. Austin: University of Texas Press.

JEREMIAS, Joachim. 1969.
Jerusalem in the time of Jesus: An investigation into economic and social conditions during the New Testament period. Translated by F. H. and C. H. Cave. Philadelphia: Fortress Press.

KLOPPENBORG, John S. 1988.
Q parallels: Synopsis, criticial notes & concordance. Facets & foundations. Sonoma, Calif.: Polebridge Press.

KLOPPENBORG, John S., et al. 1990.
Q Thomas reader. Sonoma, Calif.: Polebridge Press.

LOUW, Johannes P., and Eugenc A. Nida. 1989.
Greek-English lexicon of the New Testament based on semantic domains. 2nd ed. 2 vols. New York: United Bible Societies.

MCDONALD, Archie P. 1987.
John Wayne, hero of the Western. In *Shooting stars, heroes and heroines of Western film,* 109–25. Edited by Archie P. McDonald. Bloomington: Indiana University Press.

PERCY, Walker. 1962.
The moviegoer. New York: Knopf.

PYE, Douglas. 1986.
The Western (genre and movies). In *Film genre reader,* 143–58. Edited by Barry Keith Grant. Austin: University of Texas Press.

SCHNACKENBURG, Rudolf. 1968.
The Gospel according to St. John. Introduction and commentary on chapters 1–4. Vol. 1 of *Herder's theological commentary on the New Testament.* Translated by Kevin Smyth. New York: Herder and Herder.

SONNICHSEN, C. L. 1978.
From Hopalong to Hud: Thoughts on Western fiction. College Station: Texas A&M University Press.

STOWELL, Peter. 1986.
John Ford. Twayne Filmmakers Series. Boston: Twayne Publishers.

TUSKA, Jon. 1976.
The filming of the West. Garden City, N.Y.: Doubleday.

Clint Eastwood as Dirty Harry. (Photo courtesy of Archive Photos/copyright © Fotos International)

5 MORALLY ALONE

> There is hardly any human action, however private it
> may be, which does not result from some very general
> conception men have of God, of His relations with the
> human race, of the nature of their soul, and of their
> duties to their fellows.
> —*Alexis de Tocqueville (1835–1840)*

CRITICS WERE UPSET WHEN RUDOLF BULT-
mann said that theology is anthropology, but it has become a truism
(Bultmann 1955, 2:191). Perhaps in a graphic age this should be printed
*theo*logy (a word about God) is *anthro*pology (a word about humanity). We cannot say something about God without disclosing
something about ourselves. Although Bultmann had Paul's theology
in mind, his saying would seem to be true anytime one deals "with
God not as he is in Himself but only with God as He is significant
for man, for man's responsibility and man's salvation."

Alexis de Tocqueville, one of the earliest and most profound thinkers about the American experience, thought that the inverse is likewise true: Anthropology is theology. To speak about *anthropos* (humanity) is to speak about *theos* (God). The usefulness of this
hypothesis is perhaps not immediately obvious. Yet even those statements about humanity that have no obvious referent to God inevitably
betray a premise about God, at least implicitly. Moreover, if the way
we depict the world and humanity implicitly conjures up an image
of God, then the way movies depict humanity in the world will mirror
assumptions about God, whether present, absent, or even dead. Thus,
movies with no obvious religious theme are important theological

data because they reflect the society's implicit experience and beliefs about God.

The frontier experience, as de Tocqueville long ago pointed out, led to an emphasis on the individual and freedom of action for the individual unknown in old Europe. This individualism has combined with our ideological commitment to capitalism to produce a new version of the hero myth based on the rugged individualist or solo savior. We have already seen in John Wayne the emergence of this distinctive American version of the traditional hero/savior myth.

The power of myth is such that unknowingly we force our other heroes to conform to the pattern of our myth. As we have noted before, the invasive power of myth allows it to operate in and shape our construction of reality without our being aware of it: "Myths operate in men's minds without their being aware of the fact" (Lévi-Strauss 1969, 12). We inevitably, almost naturally, reconstruct and constrain the way we perceive reality so as to fit it into our readily available mythical structures. And we expect others, whether modern or ancient, to behave according to the coordinates of our myths. It takes effort, consciousness, and self-criticism to stand back and examine our mythical heritage.

A classic example of reshaping an ancient hero fit our reigning mythological pattern is the standard image of the apostle Paul. Although various scholars have protested for over a generation against the individualization of Paul (Stendahl 1976), in the popular imagination he tends to be viewed as the lone individual, standing up against the Jerusalem group for the rights of the individual as symbolized in the slogan "by faith alone." Paul struggles alone in his missionary activity.

This individualized picture of Paul seriously distorts the historical record. Paul's self-understanding is corporate, and he emphasizes not the individual or even individual conversion but the community as the body of Christ or the people of God. In baptism and faith the individual is lost into the body of Christ, so "it is no longer I who live, but Christ who lives in me" (Gal. 2:20). Paul frequently refers to coworkers, and most of his letters have several addressees. Abetted by the image of him in Acts, we imagine Paul as a powerful speaker and preacher even though the Corinthians warn us otherwise: "His letters are weighty and strong, but his bodily presence is weak, and his speech of no account" (2 Cor. 10:10). Though we think of Paul as constantly involved in preaching, a recent work on Paul the tent-maker reminds us that his occupation placed him among the scorned lower classes (Hock 1980). When Paul protests that "we worked night and day, that we might not burden any of you" (1 Thess. 2:9), he is not exaggerating. His ministry was carried out not in the parish, the boardroom, the television studio, or even the *agora* (marketplace), but in the workshop.

The rugged individualist myth is not a constant. It has developed as our culture and history have shifted. We have seen a version of it in Natty Bumppo, James Fenimore Cooper's fictional hero, and a recent incarnation, in Hollywood's depiction of the cowboy.

The John Wayne persona became the epitome of the myth. John Wayne summarized his own persona in his description of Rooster Cogburn as someone who knows that you must use any means to bring outlaws to justice (Tuska 1976, 575). This hero is loyal to his family and those he loves. Though often on the perimeter of society and even engaging in semilawless activity, he is never an outlaw. To bring about justice, though, he must at times violate the letter of the law. Such behavior was justified mythically in a variety of ways. The expanding and almost limitless frontier created less-than-normal situations that required extraordinary responses. Normal was the settled East with its crowds and established law. But in the empty spaces of the West, the individual had to be self-sufficient and resourceful. As one of the characters in *Shane* notes, there was no law in the valley. So individuals had to take the law into their own hands. The myth of the West also supported a strong belief in the integrity of the individual who can rise above the circumstances to triumph over the immediate. Like almost all Westerns, John Wayne's Westerns were nostalgic. They looked back to the past as a way of providing a guide to the present. It was indeed a powerful mythos.

The connection of moral courage and lonely individualism is even tighter for that other, more modern American hero, the hard-boiled detective. . . . When the detective begins his quest, it appears to be an isolated incident. But as it develops, the case turns

out to be linked to the powerful and privileged of the
community. Society, particularly, "high society," is
corrupt to the core. It is this boring into the center of
society to find it rotten that constitutes the fundamental
drama of the American detective story.
                                    —*Robert N. Bellah et al. (1985)*

TRANSLATING THIS MYTH INTO URBAN AMERI-
ca has proved somewhat problematic and has exposed a vulnerability
in the myth that makes it a good conversation partner for Paul's letter
to the Romans. In a series of movies built around the character
Inspector Harry Callahan, Clint Eastwood has transplanted the Duke
myth to urban America. Toward the end of his career, John Wayne
was quoted as saying that Clint Eastwood was "my only logical successor" (Vnijewski 1982, 10). Both actors were the most popular male
box-office attractions of their generation, and Eastwood's first real
success was in the television series "Rawhide," which was inspired
by *Red River* (1948), Howard Hawks's classic Western that starred
John Wayne.

The very popularity of the Dirty Harry movies indicates that they
have hit on a theme of importance, a conflict point in American life
between reality and belief. The conflict that these movies attempt to
resolve is easy to spot—the perceived breakdown of civilized values
in urban American life. This conflict is frequently projected onto the
legal system, which is perceived as protecting the rights of the criminal at the expense of the rights of the victim or law-abiding citizen.
Though these movies followed in the wake of the U.S. Supreme Court's
decisions in *Miranda v. Arizona* (1966) and other cases that delin-
eated the rights of the accused, the conflict goes deeper. These movies
expose a profound ambiguity in American life—our perception of
ourselves as peace loving—the new Israel, the blessed nation—and
our history of violence in defense of that peace. As Virginia's early
motto has it, "Don't tread on me!" As we will see later, so powerful
is our need to resolve this conflict that in *Birth of a Nation*, we tried
to understand the Ku Klux Klan as the restorers of peace to the South.

Some of these themes are part of the western myth as represented
by the Duke. As we have seen, the West was frequently portrayed as
a place where law must sometimes be established by extralegal methods. Yet, in the Dirty Harry movies, the city is a place of terror where

the law is frequently interpreted in a way that turns against those who are lawful. The threat and terror are much more ominous than in traditional Westerns. The world of the traditional Western looks to the future for salvation (eschatological), whereas Dirty Harry's world is corrupt and fallen from salvation. In Westerns God is present as future promise, but in the Dirty Harry movies God is absent. There is no possible end to the evil, and only the lone individual can triumph or, perhaps more accurately, survive against the system.

The shift from the wide open spaces of the West to a western city creates conflict for the hero. An urban police officer with the Duke's values is a dinosaur, a reactionary. Other characters frequently refer to Harry Callahan as outdated and regard him a product of a bygone age. He does not belong to the modern urban period. Even critics describe the movies as reactionary and fascist (Kael 1984, 148).

A double conflict drives the mythical structure of the Dirty Harry movies. The primary conflict derives from this attempt to translate the Duke's values into the city, which sets Harry's values at odds with those of the modern world. Westerns also faced this problem because their values were nostalgic from the perspective of the contemporary viewer and filmmaker. But Westerns employed a romantic solution to this conflict by placing the action in another time and place. As such they looked forward to a new future when all would be right and we would return to the mythical equivalent of the Garden of Eden. To put it in more cinematic terms, the hero would ride off into the sunset. In contrast, the Dirty Harry movies are realistic and unromantic because the conflict between values is real, felt, and unresolved. At the movie's end there is no Garden of Eden to provide an eschatological escape.

A second conflict in the Dirty Harry movies stems from the view of the world (the city) as irredeemably evil. Theologically, this strikingly parallels the beliefs of the ancient Manichaeans. Not only do the Manichaeans and Dirty Harry share a dualist view of the world, but they both advocate a type of asceticism as a solution to the problem. Though Callahan is not a religious ascetic, he does practice an asceticism. He has neither family nor wife, cannot keep a partner, forms few human relations, and is isolated within the police department. Unlike James Bond, he is not addicted to technological marvels. He is an urban ascetic. But the question remains, why is the world irredeemably evil?

Thus, underlying the Dirty Harry films and generating their narrative tension is a conflict between the values of the Duke and those of the modern city in the midst of an evil world. Each of the five movies uses a similar structure to study a different problem in an effort to apply a moral calculus to resolve the conflict.

Each movie opens with a set sequence that establishes its tone. The hero, Inspector Callahan, never appears in these opening shots. *Dirty Harry* (1971) opens with a high shot of a woman swimming in a penthouse pool. The setting is urban with skyscrapers all around. The camera swoops in on another rooftop and sights down the barrel of a rifle. The rifle fires and the woman floats dead in the pool. In the next scene the penthouse rooftop is covered by police going about their various tasks. Callahan walks about alone and then goes by himself to the adjoining rooftop where he finds the spent cartridge.

This initial scene defines the world and the protagonist. The world is urban, ominous, dangerous, and violent without warning. The high point of view taken by the camera does not signify transcendence but evil. No god looks on from the horizon; rather evil lurks on the rooftop. Callahan is defined by silence and isolation from the other police. He is without a partner. Physically, he is tall, lean, and hardboiled, a man of few words—the archetypal cowboy in a suit. There is a strong intertextual referent because Eastwood began his career in Westerns.

Early in each of the movies Callahan faces a test that establishes his derring-do. All take place while Harry is eating, normally an act of bonding or socializing with other people. In *Dirty Harry* he is eating a hotdog at a luncheonette when he spots a car parked in front of a bank. He coolly waits for the action to begin while telling the short-order cook to phone the police. "Now if they'll just wait until the cavalry arrives." But, of course, that is not going to happen—it never does in Dirty Harry's world. The robbers run out of the bank, and Harry takes off after them, a .44 Magnum in one hand, the hotdog in the other. He shoots the robbers down one by one, creating mayhem in the street. Finally, he walks up to a wounded robber who is reaching for a sawed-off shotgun. Standing over him, sighting down the long barrel of the .44 Magnum, Callahan says, "I know what you're thinking, punk. You're thinking, 'Did he fire five shots or six?' Well, to tell the truth, in all this confusion I forgot myself. But being as this is a .44 Magnum, and the most powerful handgun in the world—it can clean blow your head off—you've got to ask yourself one question: 'Do I feel lucky?' Well, do you, punk?" As the man withdraws his hand from the shotgun, Harry turns and walks away. Then the robber calls after him, "I gotta know." Harry turns, points the gun at him, and pulls the trigger. The gun is empty.

These recurring formula scenes in each movie set the mythical landscape for the hero. It is a type of western shootout, in a crowded urban street, instead of the dirt street lined with wooden storefronts. The urbanism and crowds underscore the sense of evil attacking innocent bystanders at random. Callahan always acts alone in such a situation; his gun is his partner. In these scenes the gun sight is often the camera view, or we see Callahan carrying his huge weapon at his side. In *The Enforcer* (1976) he rescues a group taken hostage during a robbery by driving a car through the window and shooting the robber-terrorists; afterward the police captain complains that Callahan put on a wild west show. In *Magnum Force* (1973) he leaves his meal at an airport restaurant to rescue a hijacked airplane. In *Sudden Impact* (1983) he takes on a group of urban, black toughs robbing a diner where he regularly eats. Though obviously alone, he tells them to put down their guns "because we're just not going to let you walk out of here." When they ask "Who's 'we'?" he replies, "Smith and Wesson." The gun is all Callahan needs in his contest against the more numerous foe. In *The Dead Pool* (1988) the scene is a Chinese restaurant. Callahan and his partner are outside when a sudden explosion sends a man careening through the front window. Callahan sends his partner to call for backup while he goes to the rescue. Inside the restaurant several bandits are terrorizing the clients during a robbery. One robber points his gun at Callahan who has snuck into a booth. Callahan hands him a fortune cookie wrapper and says, "It says you're shit out of luck." He draws his gun and begins to blow the bandits away. One robber escapes into the street only to be met by Callahan's new partner, a Chinese American who proceeds to subdue the robber with an exhibition of oriental martial arts. Callahan is impressed.

In these scenes, all of which are unrelated to the movie's plot, the action clearly demonstrates that not only does Callahan act alone, but the cavalry is not going to come. The one exception is *The Dead Pool* where the partner does not exactly come to the rescue, but does subdue the last robber. The irony and symbolism of situating these testing scenes in the midst of eating should not be overlooked. Eating is a social act of bonding, but as we noticed in *Witness*, urbanites have problems with eating. The rugged individual does not know how to eat or bond. In Philadelphia, Detective Book ate fast food by himself; in Amish land he has to be taught how to join others in a meal. The symbolism in the Dirty Harry movies is clear. Harry does not bond; rather meals are a dangerous time.

> Well, the law is crazy and Harry gets all the shit.
> —*Harry Callahan,* Dirty Harry

THE PLOT OF *DIRTY HARRY* REVOLVES AROUND the pursuit of a vicious killer who has sent a ransom note signed Scorpio to the mayor of San Francisco threatening to kill "a priest or a nigger" next unless he is given $100,000. This is not a simple chase movie in which the object is to catch the killer before he kills again. The movie's subtext paints the breakdown of a society. Callahan and Scorpio (Anthony Robinson) are as much symbols of values as they are characters in a story.

Scorpio has kidnapped a fourteen-year-old girl and buried her alive, or so his note says. The mayor agrees to pay the ransom although Callahan believes the girl is dead and they should not pay. He is selected as the bag man and against orders takes his partner along. After leading them on a merry chase, Scorpio brutally attacks Callahan under a towering cross in a park. The killer shouts, "I've changed my mind. I'm going to let her die." Callahan's partner comes to his aid but is shot by Scorpio. With a knife he had taped to his ankle, Callahan stabs Scorpio in the leg, but Scorpio escapes, hurling himself down a steep hill and limping away, while Callahan passes out at the foot of the cross. The brutality of this scene is typical of the climactic scenes in Dirty Harry movies. The symbolism of the cross is blatant, yet this sacrificial slaughter saves no one. It's a kind of madness that ends nothing. Though bleeding and wounded, both Scorpio and Callahan escape.

Callahan traces Scorpio to his hiding place in a large stadium. After Callahan shoots him in his good leg, Scorpio begins shouting "I have a right to a lawyer." Callahan stands over him with his .44 Magnum demanding to know where the girl is while Scorpio calls for a lawyer. The scene dissolves with the implication that Callahan will get the information he wants. The next scene shows a nude girl's body being removed from a shallow grave in the early morning mist.

If this were a chase movie, it would climax with Callahan's capture of Scorpio. But its narrative object is not Scorpio's capture. Because Callahan violated Scorpio's rights, the district attorney releases him. Scorpio is the innocent victim while Callahan is the criminal. To which Callahan replies, "Well, the law is crazy." This scene stakes out a double point of view—Callahan's and the law's. Callahan represents the values of the Duke—sometimes you have to bend the law to bring about real justice—while the district attorney represents the law. From Callahan's perspective he is the hero, doing his job and bringing the slime of the earth to justice. From the district attorney's perspective Scorpio is innocent until proven guilty, and his rights clearly have been violated by Callahan. The Duke faced crooked law enforcement officers, but for Callahan the law itself is the enemy.

Scorpio responds with a vendetta against Callahan. He pays to have himself horribly beaten and then blames Callahan, claiming police brutality. Callahan simply remarks, "Anyone can see I didn't do it 'cause he looks too damn good."

At the plot's climax, Scorpio kidnaps a group of children in a school bus and demands money and a plane to take him out of the country. The mayor agrees. Callahan doesn't. "When are you guys going to quit fooling around with this man?" he says. On the way to the airport, the bus goes under a train trestle. From the bus Scorpio (and we through the camera, which takes up Scorpio's viewpoint) see the lone silhouette of Callahan on the trestle. The final chase scene concludes with Scorpio holding a gun to a child's head and demanding that Harry throw down his gun. At first he seems to comply but then rapidly raises his gun, aims, and fires. The blast knocks Scorpio down. Scorpio starts to reach for his gun, and Callahan repeats the scene with the bank robber that began the movie. "In the excitement I plum forgot how many times I fired. Do you feel lucky?" Scorpio goes for his gun and Harry shoots him. The focus shifts to Harry's badge. He throws it away. The camera moves to a high vantage point, like an omniscient narrator. But again this is a world of loss—a gravel pit, the dregs of a culture. Callahan has abandoned the law.

All five Dirty Harry movies emphasize the danger in being Callahan's partner. As he himself remarks, "They usually end up dead." Because Callahan is a loner, he never has a partner at the beginning and end of the movies, but in between, a partner provides a foil for the Dirty Harry character.

In *Dirty Harry* the partner, Gonzales (Reni Santoni), is a college graduate with a degree in sociology. Callahan remarks to Gonzales on first meeting, "Don't let your college degree get you killed." Gonzales is typical of Callahan's partners. They come from minority groups, appear to be better educated than he is, and represent urban values opposed to Harry's Duke values. Yet, like Harry, they are marginalized. In *Magnum Force* the partner is an African American, in *The Enforcer* a woman, and in *The Dead Pool* a Chinese American. Inevitably, there is a bonding between Callahan and his partners, and a grudging respect develops on both sides. In several cases the partners serve to modify Callahan's worldview.

These partners serve as bridges or mediators between Callahan and the world he believes has betrayed him. The bonding between Callahan and Gonzales reaches its height when Callahan takes him on the ransom drop against the chief's express orders. Frequently, the bonding between Callahan and his partner is symbolized by an episode in which the partner steps over the line and breaks the law. At the level of plot, Gonzales provides a backup for Callahan, but more importantly, by disobeying orders and following Callahan, he becomes lawless or dirty like Callahan. Gonzales is seriously wounded in the encounter with Scorpio in the park, and when Callahan visits him in the hospital, he confesses that he is not coming back. Gonzales's wife remarks that it is her fault, that she just cannot stand being a police officer's wife. When she innocently asks how Callahan's wife takes it, he replies that she was killed by a drunk. "Why do you stay in?" she asks. "I don't know, I really don't," he replies. Thus, Callahan ends as he began, alone, alienated from a world he is trying to save. Even more, he is a hero who does not know why he continues his quest.

The first movie provides several explanations of how Callahan got the nickname "Dirty Harry." One comes from the captain who says that Harry hates everybody. Callahan promptly demonstrates his hatred by spitting out a list of derogatory names for ethnics. Gonzales provides another explanation when he catches Harry watching a couple making love. Harry is dirty because he is a voyeur. Indeed, the movie contains a certain amount of voyeurism. During one stake-out Harry spots an attractive naked woman through his binoculars. When she turns out to be a lesbian, he is disgusted. One of the most famous posters of Dirty Harry shows him with his sunglasses. He frequently hides behind them, looking out at an alien and, to his tastes, disgusting world. Even more, the movies themselves are a type of voyeurism in that we see things that would be out of our view without the movie camera. A final explanation of Harry's nick-name comes when he is selected as the bagman for Scorpio's ransom. Another character remarks, "No wonder they call him Dirty Harry. He always gets the shit job." In the end all these explanations boil down to the same thing—Harry is an unclean scapegoat, whose violence protects and purifies a society that rejects him and his values.

> The terrorist and the policeman both come from the same basket. Revolution, legality—counter moves in the same game; forms of idleness at bottom identical.
> —*Joseph Conrad (1907)*

THE MORAL CALCULUS OF *MAGNUM FORCE* IS very different from that of *Dirty Harry*. In the latter Callahan is something of a vigilante, but in *Magnum Force* he is faced with a death squad within the San Francisco police force. Vigilante justice was a theme of many Westerns. These modern vigilantes ride motorcycles.

During the initial credits of *Magnum Force*, the camera focuses on a .44 Magnum, Callahan's gun. This is one kind of Magnum Force. In the first scene an unsavory-looking character with an Italian name leaves a murder trial after being set free on a technicality. The crowd outside the courthouse is obviously hostile to the defendant. We see him next in a limousine being driven by a couple of hoods. A motorcycle policeman trails the car and then signals for it to pull over. In an example of the voyeurism characteristic of the series, this entire scene is shot through windows and mirrors so we never see the policeman's face. He pulls his gun and shoots all four men in the car.

The juxtaposition of the .44 Magnum and the murder of the four men sets up the movie's moral calculus. What is legitimate violence?

The death squad is made up of four young rookies assigned to the motorcycle patrol led by Lieutenant Briggs (Hal Holbrook). The rookies' innocent boyish faces and Holbrook's distinguished bearing give these characters a respectability and credibility that Dirty Harry could never emulate.

After the death squad eliminates several stereotypical villains, Callahan is assigned to investigate under Lieutenant Briggs's direction. Callahan's first response is to say that the murders are all right with him. Yet when the motorcycle squad confronts him, he begins by saying sarcastically, "You heroes have killed a dozen people this week." They contend that they are the first generation that has learned to fight back. They are simply ridding society of people that the legal system would put away if it worked properly. They conclude by saying, "It's not a question of whether to use violence; there's simply no other way." Ironically, this should be Callahan's speech, since it has been his basic *modus operandi*, but he replies that they have misjudged him. It now becomes a battle to the death—one side must eliminate the other. This conflict has no logical, discursive solution. Only violent death can resolve the conflict and demonstrate the superiority of Harry's position. As the movie reaches its violent conclusion, Callahan's partner, the rookies, and Lieutenant Briggs are all killed.

The conflict in *Magnum Force* presents maximum stress to the mythical structure because in the rookies Callahan comes face to face with his own self-image. Exactly how does Callahan see himself as different? Briggs admits that they are vigilantes and insists that evil demands evil. But Callahan argues that the police can't be executioners: "I hate the system, but until someone comes along and makes some better changes, I'll stick with it." This may be less eloquent than Winston Churchill's defense of democracy, but it does indicate where Callahan draws the line. He's not an executioner; he just takes care of the dirt.

Mythically, this movie exacerbates an important conflict in the solo savior's profile. The world is evil, and since justice is perverted, there is no real way to save the world. Yet the demands of justice must be respected. The four rookies and Lieutenant Briggs have the trappings of civilization on their side. They are youthful, innocent looking, and distinguished, all the things Dirty Harry is not. Never-theless, Harry knows that respect for justice, even when it fails, divides civilization from bestiality. Like the Duke on the frontier, Dirty Harry in the jungles of San Francisco has to find that dividing line so that civilization can eventually emerge. Yet is this really a solution or a mythical sleight of hand?

> Man's discovery that his genitalia could serve as a weapon to generate fear must rank as one of the most important discoveries of prehistoric times, along with the use of fire and the first crude stone axe. From prehistoric times to the present, I believe, rape has played a critical function. It is nothing more or less than a conscious process of intimidation by which *all* men keep *all* women in a state of fear.
> —*Susan Brownmiller (1975)*

THE ENFORCER FOLLOWS THE FORMULA SET up in the first two movies, but as a movie it is not nearly as good. It lacks their crisp direction, and the formula has become too predict-able. The law is still in the hands of those who would placate criminals, and the criminals are supervillainous, here a group of revolutionaries led by a sadistic homosexual. Yet the movie has an extremely good performance by Tyne Daly as Inspector Kate Moore, Callahan's part-ner. This is appropriate because her role is pivotal in introducing a new conflict into the Dirty Harry mythology. Now the Duke mythology must not only adjust to the modern city but must cope with a liberated woman. We have already seen the Duke's own version of this mythical problem in *Rooster Cogburn* (1975) with Katharine Hepburn.

Callahan first encounters Moore after he has been reassigned from homicide to personnel. As a member of an examining board, he clashes with a woman, the mayor's representative. Her gender and her association with the mayor identify her with two systems with which Callahan is in conflict. He does not believe that female police officers should be assigned to the field. She replies that the police force should be brought into the mainstream of the twentieth century and that the Neanderthals should be winnowed out. Moore is the woman whom the board is examining. She has worked for ten years in records and now is applying for the rank of inspector (the same as Callahan). He ridicules her experience. She tries to defend herself, but Callahan is not convinced.

In this conflict Callahan and Moore play predictable mythical roles. He represents the priority of males while she represents the intelligent female trying to get ahead but without the male's experience. She is Marian from *Shane* trying to make it in the city. The real tension in the movie is the resolution of this conflict at the mythological level. Can the Duke accept a partner as an equal? Or does Marian have to return to the kitchen? What is the price she must pay to enter the male world?

When Callahan is reassigned to homicide to investigate the revolutionaries, Moore becomes his partner. She initially makes mistakes that vindicate Callahan's opinion. At a demonstration of a portable rocket launcher, she stands behind the launcher until Callahan jerks her away, saving her life. To all her antics, he responds with a deadpan "Marvelous." Yet in the first real confrontation with the criminals, Moore spots the suspect and helps him give chase.

Callahan's view of Moore begins to change after he has been fired from the police force because he refuses to participate in a sham ceremony. As he walks out, she follows him and says she will help him in any way she can, implying that she will bend the law to do so. For the first time they call each other "Harry" and "Kate." In one of the rare occasions when Dirty Harry's façade cracks, he asks her why she isn't married with a couple of kids. Standing in the shadow of Coit Tower, she makes a joke about coitus interruptus. The scene is not played as a seduction; instead, Callahan and Moore relate as two people who are learning to care for and respect each other. The mythological armor of Dirty Harry has experienced a significant dent.

In fact, she does help him, and her experience in records proves highly valuable as she discovers some important information that breaks the case open. The movie's final scene takes place at Alcatraz, where the revolutionaries have taken the mayor hostage. Harry and Kate assault the island. In the inevitable concluding shootout, she performs as an equal with Callahan, shooting one of the revolutionaries and freeing the mayor. But when Harry gets caught in the cross fire, Moore steps in and takes the bullet. Mortally wounded, she dies in Callahan's arms telling him to get her killer, and he says, "You can count on it."

What standards should we use to judge the relationship between Callahan and Moore? By feminist standards both fall short, but I would suggest that these standards are inappropriate. Moore forces a shift in the mythological world of Dirty Harry. She is a female with whom he eventually learns to relate as an equal. Nevertheless, Dirty Harry's worldview does not break down. The movie ends with Callahan returning to the body of his dead partner, but Moore has paid a heavy price to gain this acceptance. Not only is she dead, but like Harry she has become dirty. First, she violates the rules of the system; then, in a very mythically male gesture she steps into the cross fire to take the bullet; and in the end she calls down vengeance on her killer. This behavior is not the typical self-sacrifice appropriate to the female's mythological role. Moore has adopted a new role, a male role. This film demonstrates how a mythological structure can adapt to accept a new conflict. Women can gain acceptance into the myth, but only by playing a role sanctioned by the myth. Since acceptance comes at the high price of her death, this acceptance must be considered ambivalent. Nevertheless, Callahan has changed—women play prominent roles in the next two movies.

> Vengeance is mine, and recompense, for the time when their foot shall slip; for the day of their calamity is at hand, and their doom comes swiftly.
> —*Deuteronomy 32:35*

> Beloved, never avenge yourselves, but leave it to the wrath of God; for it is written, "Vengeance is mine, I will repay, says the Lord."
> —*Romans 12:19*

SUDDEN IMPACT ADVANCES ANOTHER PROBlem in the moral calculus. Jennifer Spencer (Sondra Locke) and her sister were gang-raped under the boardwalk at San Paolo (the movie was actually filmed at Santa Cruz) about ten years before the story opens. As a result, the sister is comatose, described by her doctor as "a vegetable." To compound the injustice, the local sheriff covered up the crime. Thus, we have the classic situation of a Dirty Harry movie—really bad criminals and a breakdown of justice.

The movie opens with Spencer exacting the first step in her revenge. A man and a woman are making out in the front seat of a car. She unzips his fly, draws a chrome-plated revolver, and shoots him in the genitals.

As Spencer later explains to her unresponsive sister, the first murder was opportunistic. She saw one of the men who had raped them on the street in San Francisco and watched him for days. Then she let him pick her up in a bar. "He touched me, then I killed him. I love you, Beth."

Now Spencer's revenge becomes systematic. She returns to San Paolo under the pretext of restoring a carousel and begins to eliminate the other gang members in a similar manner.

Callahan, who is "vacationing" in San Paolo, notices the pattern between the killing in San Francisco and those in San Paolo. He correctly identifies the killer as Spencer, a woman with whom he has become involved. Since Harry is generally an ascetic, this relationship with Spencer is important. When he does become attached to a woman, she is a "dirty" woman, one who has been wounded by the system.

The violent conclusion of *Sudden Impact* takes place at the same amusement park on the boardwalk where the gang rape had occurred. Mick (Paul Drake), the particularly nasty gang leader, has taken Spencer to the park to kill her. She remarks, "This time you'll have to rape my dead body" and fights back ferociously. He begins to beat her viciously. Then the camera shifts, and in the distance on the boardwalk, Dirty Harry stands backlighted, with his huge gun at his side. Once again no cavalry comes to the rescue, but Callahan is there, ready to fight to the death. He repeats the now famous epithet, "Make my day," and shoots Mick who falls through the roof of the carousel and is impaled on the horn of the unicorn, an appropriate punishment for his crime.

As the police are removing the bodies, Spencer asks him what happens now, what about justice? At this moment a young officer informs them that he found a .38 in Mick's belt. Callahan responds that if he checks its ballistics against those of the gun used in the killings he will find they are the same. Only he and Spencer know that the .38 is her gun. The police assume it is Mick's.

This resolution presents multiple ironies for Callahan. He has always made fun of psychologists and sociologists, whom he thinks cater to criminals. Yet he subscribes to a psychological explanation of Spencer's acts, believing that she acted not simply out of revenge but out of compulsion. Her comatose sister is a clue to her own psychological state. Throughout the movie Spencer has been painting a self-portrait with a haunted, ghastly visage. Even though the painting is one of Callahan's clues that she is the killer, he spends the night with her. Thus, the ending suggests that Spencer's psychological state is sufficient reason to let her go.

Unlike the rookies in *Magnum Force*, Callahan does not execute those who have done evil. Yet because he does not turn Spencer in, he does not let justice take its full course. Because the law-and-order mentality does not work in this case, the moral calculus becomes more complex. In a real sense the fate of this woman deconstructs a part of the Dirty Harry mythology.

> This brings us to a fourth and final mode of generic transformation that might be described as the affirmation of myth for its own sake. In films in this mode, a traditional genre and its myth are probed and shown to be unreal, but then the myth itself is at least partially affirmed as a reflection of authentic human aspirations and needs.
>
> —*John G. Cawelti (1986)*

THE LAST, AND ONE HOPES FINAL, EPISODE IN the Dirty Harry series is *The Dead Pool*. By now the formula has become tired, and the hero seems to have run his course. Perhaps a new version of the solo savior is emerging. Clint Eastwood seems to agree, as his more recent projects including *Bird* (1988) and *Unforgiven* (1992) and the morally ambivalent *A Perfect World* (1993) suggest.

The Dead Pool advances along two fronts already established in the Dirty Harry series. Callahan has to deal with another woman, and the moral calculus must justify itself when Callahan becomes the intended victim. The killer is yet another psychopath, named Harlan Rook (David Hunt). The plot revolves around an elaborate game that the director of a horror movie plays with several of his production assistants. They list people they think are likely to die during the filming. Callahan's name appears on the director's list. The psychopathic killer gains access to the director's list and begins to kill the people on it so that the director will appear to be the killer. Callahan is assigned to investigate his own potential murder.

The female relation is Samantha Walker (Patricia Clarkson). She is a television reporter, a profession that Callahan views with contempt. The movie depicts television reporters as vultures who descend on the scene of a crime to pick the bones dry, interfering with the police investigation in the process. They are interested only in sensationalism, not justice.

Walker is involved in the story both because the killer chooses to send her important clues and because she wants to do a story on Callahan. Thus, two people are pursuing Callahan in this movie: the killer and Samantha Walker. In many respects Walker is the more dangerous because she threatens to expose Callahan and strip away the sunglasses he hides behind.

The development of the relation between Callahan and Walker is more interesting than the solving of the murders. They first meet in a set scene typical of a Dirty Harry movie. Callahan is investigating the murder of a rock star, when the victim's girlfriend arrives in distress. The television crews swarm around her. Callahan comes to her rescue and in the process trashes a camcorder. When Walker threatens a lawsuit, Harry's superiors tell him to cooperate with her. She says she'll drop the suit if he will go to dinner with her. At dinner she proposes to do an in-depth story on him, but he refuses, saying, "All you are interested in is blood." She protests, but to no avail.

Callahan's accusation is most interesting. At the rock star's burial, Callahan confronts the director, who at that time is a suspect. When asked whether there is any relation between his movies and the dead pool murders, the director replies, "People are fascinated with death and violence." Callahan's antipathy to blood in the media seems a bit disingenuous, in that both his life as Dirty Harry and the movies themselves are built on the public's fascination with violence. The constant mayhem is one of the films' chief attractions, and obtaining an accurate body count in any one of them is virtually impossible.

The conclusion of the movie drives this point home. It takes place at night against the background of Guns and Roses playing "Welcome to the Jungle." As befits a plot in which Callahan is the one pursued, the killer manages to obtain Callahan's gun and chases him. When the killer thinks he has Callahan cornered, Callahan suddenly appears behind him, silhouetted against the light. He says "you're out of bullets," an allusion to the bullet-counting episodes in *Dirty Harry*. This time Callahan announces that the gun *is* empty and then says, "You're shit out of luck," a phrase also used in the formulaic opening confrontation in the Chinese restaurant. Harry then impales his would-be killer with a harpoon. *The Dead Pool* ends with an overhead view of Callahan walking away as the police and television reporters swarm over the killer's impaled body. Walker doesn't get her story.

The myth of Dirty Harry exposes itself as a fraud. If the gun indeed was empty, there was no need to kill the villain. Callahan has become an executioner. When chased, he attacks and hides from the light of day. But the purpose of *The Dead Pool* is not to deconstruct or demythologize the myth of the solo savior. Rather the fascination with violence and death misleads the viewer into reaffirming the myth in a new guise. The world is so evil, so irrational and nonrational, that the hero can always create a new moral line to separate himself from evil. The mutation of the Duke hero was precipitated by the shift from the wide open spaces to the urban world. But as part of the transformation, the dinosaur must recalculate the moral space, and in the Dirty Harry movies the myth keeps searching out that line. By playing out the moral calculus, Callahan has run out of formulas, but in myth do we notice that Harry has now become judge and executioner? The driving force of the myth overcomes itself. We have become fascinated with the violence needed to guarantee "life, liberty, and the pursuit of happiness." Thus, the myth continues to work as long as we don't ask any embarrassing questions.

> Don't you know what Bronco Billy and the Wild West Show are all about? You can be anything you want. All you have to do is go out and do it.
> —*Lorraine Running Water*, Bronco Billy

IT IS UNFAIR TO CLINT EASTWOOD TO PRESENT him only as the maker of violent movies. The Eastwood persona, developed not just in the Dirty Harry cycle but also in spaghetti Westerns such as *A Fistful of Dollars* (1964) and *The Good, the Bad and the Ugly* (1966) and other films, is like the John Wayne persona— it's larger than the real person. But the persona also obscures another side of Eastwood. Beginning with *Play Misty for Me* (1971) and including *Bird* (1988) and *Unforgiven* (1992), he has made a number of fine films, some of which are at variance with his mythological projection. *Bronco Billy* (1980), made in the middle of the Dirty Harry cycle, shows the positive side of the western myth while rejecting the stereotype of Dirty Harry.

John G. Cawelti has developed a fourfold typology for the transformation of genre in film: (1) burlesque (*Blazing Saddles*); (2) nostalgia (*True Grit* or *Raiders of the Lost Ark*); (3) demythologization (*Chinatown* or *Bonnie and Clyde*); and (4) the affirmation of myth for its own sake (*The Wild Bunch* of 1969) (Cawelti 1986). While the Dirty Harry cycle clearly belongs to this latter typology, *Bronco Billy* combines the characteristics of burlesque and demythologization and thus is a powerful lens on the myth itself.

The scale of this movie is different from that of the Dirty Harry series. It is a small, quiet movie, whose atmosphere is reassuring rather than threatening. It never even explains its title. Only the *cognoscenti* would know that Bronco Billy was one of the first cowboy film stars. The movie's vision of the world is also at variance with Dirty Harry's. Although the characters are threatened, the movie conveys a sense of hope, no matter how bad or desperate things might seem. Identifying the reason for this different worldview illuminates much about the other side of the solo savior.

The plot, which derives from the zany comedies of the 1930s, is almost irrelevant to the movie's mythical development. Antoinette Lily (Sondra Locke), an extremely rich and spoiled woman, has married a man simply to inherit her father's estate. He promptly abandons her in the middle of Montana. She falls in with the Bronco Billy Wild West Show, a small ragtag group that travels the outback playing mostly to audiences of small children. Since Lily has been left with literally nothing, she wears a threadbare cotton jumper throughout much of the movie. Her disdain for the Wild West Show is evident throughout. She joins initially as a way of returning to civilization, although Billy (Clint Eastwood) and his group believe they are taking pity on a poor bereft waif. Just when she is ready to leave the group, she sees a newspaper headline announcing her death and the conviction of her husband for the murder. He has agreed with the family lawyer to plead insanity in exchange for a short prison term and a payoff of $500,000. She decides to play along. All goes well until the show stops at an asylum for the criminally insane where the incarcerated husband spots his wife and blows the whistle. This leads to the denouement.

In this movie the whole is greater than the parts; the group is more than the individuals that make it up. The show itself is only a small-time outfit that is perpetually broke. Most of its members are ex-cons who met Bronco Billy when he too was serving time. Billy does do a rather nice trick-riding and shooting act, but it must be exactly the same every night—he gets upset whenever his female partner deviates from the script by even one word. Chief Big Eagle (Dan Vadis), who is writing the great American Indian novel at night, does a snake dance where he insists on using real rattlesnakes, which are always biting him. Bronco Billy buys him some gopher snakes to use instead, but Big Eagle refuses. Billy remarks that Big Eagle is a proud man and then adds the scurrilous comment, "The only good Indian is a dead Indian." As individuals they fail, but as a group they heal.

An initial scene sets the tone for this oscillation between group and individual. The show's caravan of trucks is on the move with Bronco Billy in the lead truck. Doc Lynch (Scatman Carothers), the group's spokesman and Billy's sidekick in the tradition of Gabby Hayes, asks Billy when the performers are going to be paid—they've not been paid in six months. In great disgust Billy stops the truck in the pouring rain and accuses the group of being disloyal. He listens to their excuses: Lefty (Bill McKinney) needs a new hand to replace his hook, Leonard (Sam Bottoms) needs some new lassos for his roping act, and Big Eagle and his wife Lorraine Running Water (Sierra Pecheur) need a new bed. Billy squelches each complaint just as he had put down Big Eagle with the dead Indian line. Although Billy puts on his best tough man act and plays the lone hero, the viewer is struck by the irony of the scene. All the members of the motley crew begin to regret that they have provoked the boss, and he concludes by invoking the group's recurring mantra: "Someday we'll get enough money to buy a ranch so city kids can see what cowboys

were really like." Throughout the movie this dream of a ranch functions as a type of eschatology, underlining what the Wild West Show
is all about.

Miss Lily is the ironic observer of this crazy menagerie although
the irony is compounded because they believe they are helping her
in her time of destitution. She notices how happy they are as a group
even though they have failed as individuals. They are constantly giving
free shows for orphanages, insane asylums, and other collections of
humanity like themselves.

Several scenes play on the ironic distance between Miss Lily and
the group. Although she constantly puts them down, the members of
the troupe think she is depressed at being abandoned and try to be
nice to her. When they gather at a bar to celebrate the impending
birth of a baby to Big Eagle and Running Water, Billy asks the snooty
Miss Lily, "Did you ever think what it would be like to be nice to
people?" She replies, "People only want to take." When she leaves
the bar alone, some men attempt to rape her, and Billy and the group
come to her rescue. For the first time she begins to see the importance
of group solidarity.

Now Miss Lily gradually begins to understand the Wild West Show.
At one point Billy confesses to her that he served seven years in
prison for attempting to murder his wife after catching her in bed
with his best friend. Miss Lily is incredulous—"You tried to kill your
wife?"—but he responds that the man was his best friend. At this
point in a Dirty Harry movie, Harry would establish his solitary nature,
his disregard for women, and his male bonding, but Bronco Billy is
not Dirty Harry. Miss Lily has seen the love within the troupe and
has begun to appreciate Billy as a gentle if daffy soul. He also tells
her that he met Big Eagle, Doc, and Lefty in prison and that he was
formerly a shoe salesman in New Jersey. When she asks him if he's
for real, he replies, "I'm who I want to be."

As the inevitable romance between Miss Lily and Billy begins to
develop, she resists it as completely improbable, which, of course, it
is from her ironical point of view. But the turning point comes when
Running Water tells Miss Lily, "Don't you know what Bronco Billy
and the Wild West Show are all about? You can be anything you want.
All you have to do is go out and do it."

But the real world keeps intruding into the Wild West Show. When
their tent burns down, they attempt a train robbery in imitation of

the old West. Miss Lily points out that there aren't any cowboys and Indians any more; this is the real world, and people could get killed. But her protests are in vain. They charge off after the train, but it speeds on, ignoring them. In another scene Leonard, the young roper, is arrested and beaten by the deputies when they discover that he is a Vietnam deserter. Even Bronco Billy denounces him as unfit to be in the Wild West Show, calling him a poor example for "our little partners," the kids who come to their show. Yet Billy takes all the money the group has been able to squirrel away for a ranch and offers the sheriff a bribe to let Leonard go. The sheriff accepts the bribe but in a scene patterned after an old-fashioned shootout humiliates Billy by making him admit that the sheriff is the faster draw. The sheriff sneers, "Bronco Billy, you're nothing but a yellow belly egg sucker." But both these scenes conclude the same way—the group stays together. Billy disapproves of Leonard's past behavior, especially keeping it secret, but he spends the troupe's money to reunite Leonard to the group. Even though the train robbery is a fiasco, their effort ironically brings joy to its only witness, a little boy looking out the window who sees cowboys and Indians chasing the train. The group goes to the insane asylum where they have performed over the years, and the inmates make them a new tent, pieced together from the American flags the inmates produce.

Miss Lily's conversion comes at the movie's conclusion. She has returned to her penthouse in New York, while the Wild West Show goes on its way. But the performers, especially Billy, miss her. She is in bed swallowing a bottle of sleeping tablets, when Running Water calls to say that Billy needs her. Miss Lily promptly spits out the pills. Her suicide attempt, like so much else with Miss Lily, was a front.

Though both *Bronco Billy* and the Dirty Harry cycle are dependent upon the lone savior myth, they reference it in quite different ways. The Dirty Harry movies reinforce the myth by playing to the public's fascination with violence. Bronco Billy subverts the myth by burlesquing and demythologizing it.

None of these movies appeals to a divine figure. Yet the way they construct a fictional world implies a great deal about God or God's absence.

The Dirty Harry movies have often been condemned as apologetics for right-wing, antiliberal ideologies. But that misses the point. These movies play on a common fear in urban America, namely, that the system does not work and is out of control. That is why the villain is frequently psychopathic. People feel at risk; they are afraid to go out or travel alone. This sense of fear leads them to regard the outside world as evil and hostile. In the Dirty Harry cycle this vision becomes extreme because the world is treated as irredeemable. Callahan stands alone against the evil; even the criminal justice system and the police force are at times aligned against him and with the criminals. As the lone savior, Callahan himself is forced over the bounds into lawlessness, although he is constantly trying to redefine the line that defines what is really justice.

One of the primary functions of savior myths is to provide a sense of redemption from chaos. Abstractly, redemption is the resolution of a fundamental conflict that creates separation from the desired object. The function of the savior is to bridge that gap. Frequently, discussions of redemption overlook that what one is redeemed from and redeemed for determines the savior's role. In the Dirty Harry cycle the conflict is created by the world, which is a place of evil. This is not a classic dualism because there is no clear antipole, no completely good principle to counter the evil world. Nor is there even a heaven to escape from "this vale of tears," as the medieval hymn has it. Callahan as a savior partakes of the very structures he finds so repulsive. Consequently, the solution to the problem of evil is overwhelming violence that temporarily holds the evil at bay and produces a catharsis, the illusion of a period of redemption.

Bronco Billy dramatizes what Dirty Harry lacks, a sense of community and eschatology, a beneficent present and a possible future. Since the world is evil, Callahan is essentially alone. His partners have quit or been killed off, and his wife is dead. At best he can form temporary alliances, which are doomed to fall apart. By contrast, evil and betrayal are part of the world of *Bronco Billy*, but it is presided over by a comedic sense. The whole story has the character of a tall tale where everything is exaggerated. But more importantly, the world of *Bronco Billy* is redeemable because it has a future. Each character in the movie clearly is flawed and remains flawed, yet within the group they have a chance to be whatever they want, to be redeemed. They do not want just anything. The Wild West Show is not a utopia or even a fantasy, as Miss Lilly mistakenly believes. It is a place where flawed people become more than themselves, where they reach out to serve others, the "little partners."

Bronco Billy paints a sharp contrast with the world of Dirty Harry. Three issues seem to be primary: community (world), eschatology, and freedom. In the world of Dirty Harry there is no community, and, in fact, society (world) is evil or corrupted. Dirty Harry is a potential savior, but he cannot save the world—does not even pretend to save it—because it is too evil to be saved. In the Dirty Harry movies the world and the individual are set at odds. In contrast, the community of *Bronco Billy* is a group of flawed individuals who have all experienced the warmth of forgiveness. That forgiveness does not eliminate their flaws, but it does provide them the freedom to be. In that freedom they have a *telos* (goal)—the ranch—that has a purpose for others, so that the "little partners" can see what real cowboys and Indians were like.

> We face a profound impasse. Modern individualism seems to be producing a way of life that is neither individually nor socially viable, yet a return to traditional forms would be to return to intolerable discrimination and oppression.
> —*Robert N. Bellah et al. (1985)*

THE CINEMA'S REALISM POSES A PROBLEM OF images for those of us who espouse the Christian virtues of community, freedom, and eschatology. When these theological categories are translated from abstractions to concrete images, we may see something other than what we expected. As a way of probing this issue, I wish to compare the apostle Paul's vision of these issues with the visions of Dirty Harry and Bronco Billy.

At certain points the anthropologies of Paul and Dirty Harry are not far apart, although there are important and telling differences. Harry views the world, its systems, and those in it as evil, and Paul agrees that humans are weak, ungodly, and sinners (Rom. 8:6, 7). But for Harry the human situation appears to be irredeemable. Although he can stave off the inevitable disaster momentarily, none of the Dirty Harry movies offers any hope for the world's eventual redemption. These movies call for vigilance, not unlike most apocalyptic texts (e.g., Mark 13), yet this vigilance has no ultimate redemption or solution. Vengeance is the only reprieve for humans caught in a web of systemic evil.

Paul takes a somewhat different tack: "While we were still weak, at the right time Christ died for the ungodly" (Rom. 5:6). For our purposes this verse can summarize Paul's position. "Still" describes humanity before faith as godless, a position essentially in agreement with Dirty Harry. The Greek word for "still" is repeated twice in the verse, an indication of its importance. Although many manuscripts omitted the second "still" because it is grammatically redundant, it means precisely the "right time," the appropriate time, for Christ to die for weak sinners. This same thought is repeated in the parallel formulation of verse 8: "But God proves his love for us that while we were still sinners Christ died for us." Thus, Paul sets up a paradox in which the love of God is the contrary of "ungodly" and "still" is the bridge between the two. That this is a paradox is shown by the question it provokes in the imaginary dialogue: "Should we continue in sin in order that grace may abound?" (Rom. 6:1). This question goes to the heart of the essential difference between Dirty Harry and Paul. For Dirty Harry the world's ungodliness leads to its irredeemability; there is nothing in it to love. Paradoxically, for Paul God loves the ungodly. Paul does not resort to the cliché of hating the sin and loving the sinner. That misses the power of what he is proposing. "While still ungodly" is the state of those whom God loves. Paul even underlines the paradox by arguing that one would hardly die for a righteous person, although one might dare to die for a good person (Rom. 6:7). The solution to the problem of evil in both Dirty Harry and Paul is violence, but in Dirty Harry the violence is a continuing spasm of revenge, whereas in Paul Jesus' death is an act of love "on our behalf."

The domination of human beings is an important theme in both Dirty Harry and Paul. In the Dirty Harry cycle people are possessed by evil, driven by evil, because the system itself is corrupt. Evil cannot be explained by psychology or sociology. In most Dirty Harry movies such explanations are considered a way of coddling criminals. Paul similarly notes that he does not understand his actions: "For I do not do what I want, but I do the very thing I hate. . . . But in fact it is no longer I that do it, but sin that dwells within me" (Rom. 7:15, 17). Paul and Dirty Harry exhibit both a basic similarity and a basic difference at this point. Paul speaks in the first person (a first person that represents both himself and all humans), whereas Dirty Harry looks out on the world from behind his sunglasses and exempts himself from this judgment. In *Tightrope* (1984) Eastwood's Dirty-Harry-like detective approaches Paul's point of view. He turns out to have proclivities similar to those of the criminal and should by all rights be one of the suspects. A second difference is that Paul finds the solution to this problem in the death of Jesus, in that while humans are still ungodly and acting under the dominance of sin, God demonstrates love for them. Just as Paul finds it a principle that when he seeks to do good, evil is close at hand (Rom. 7:21), so likewise after faith: "I have been crucified with Christ; and it is no longer I who live, but Christ who lives in me" (Gal. 2:20). For Paul, human existence must recognize its subordinate character and acknowledge a lordship. When one seeks to do good, evil lies close at hand because to do good is to risk idolatry. To seek to do good is to risk setting oneself up as God. Harry falls into the trap set for those who would do good. In each of the movies, he becomes responsible for determining the moral line, the calculus as I have called it. He keeps trying to distinguish what he does from the actions of those he condemns, until in the end he does become the executioner, something he has always been in reality. Harry is the perfect example of what it means to be "under the law." "I discover this principle, then: that when I want to do right, only wrong is within my reach" (Rom. 7:21, REB).

Paul recognizes that the desire to do good is how the law seduces human behavior (Rom. 7:11). Unlike the rabbinic notion of evil inclination, Paul sees what might be called the good inclination as the seduction to do evil. So, like Dirty Harry, he sees humanity as surrounded by sin and evil. Even one's efforts to do good allow sin in. Paul experiences himself as torn between a "delight in the law of God" (7:22) and his body as "captive to the law of sin" (7:23). He calls himself a wretch (7:24) and concludes, "So then, with my mind I am a slave to the law of God, but with my flesh I am a slave to the law of sin" (7:25). But immediately after expressing this extremely negative view of human existence, Paul concludes: "There is therefore now no condemnation for those who are in Christ Jesus" (8:1). "Now" indicates the time of those wretches who are in Christ, justified by faith; and "no condemnation" describes their situation. If Paul experiences the *now* as a battle between his desire for good and the law of evil that rules his members, how can he say that now there is no condemnation? What happens to the struggle, the battle, that forms the plot of the Dirty Harry movies? Paul is open here to an antinomian interpretation that he believes there is no law. The Corinthians apparently drew such a conclusion when they employed the slogan "All things are lawful for me" (e.g., 1 Cor. 6:12). But Paul's point is not antinomian. Rather, for him God "passes over former sins" (Rom. 3:25), or in the language applied to Abraham, sin "is not reckoned" (4:8).

Thus, the death of Jesus creates for those in faith a field of action in which there is great freedom because one need not risk condemnation. That the whole is greater than the parts is evident in Paul's image of the body of Christ. Since it is no longer the "I" but Christ who acts, the body is made of many members, not one member. *Bronco Billy* exhibits this idea that "the whole is greater than its parts" and, in fact, is an interesting exemplar of Paul's understanding of community. Like the Pauline communities, the members of the Wild West Show are far from perfect. They are flawed human beings, at war with their members. Within the group acceptance gives them the freedom to be whatever they want to be, as Running Water explains to Miss Lily. Thus, acceptance within the group permits freedom. Paul expresses a similar notion when he notes that "all things work together for good for those who love God" (8:28). This provokes him to ask, "If God is for us, who is against us?" (8:31). These optimistic pictures of human freedom in both Paul and Bronco Billy are situated in the context of flawed human communities and are purchased at a price. In the very next sentence after asking who can be against us if God is for us, Paul says, "He who did not spare his own Son, but gave him up for us all; how can he fail to lavish every other gift upon us?" (8:32, NEB). Likewise Billy purchases the freedom of Leonard, the Vietnam deserter, after being humiliated by the sheriff. Although Billy suffers violence to redeem Leonard, it is not Dirty Harry's violence of vengeance.

One of the most depressing aspects of Dirty Harry's vision of reality is that it is without a future—there is no end to the garbage with which he has to deal. Dan O. Via notes that clinical psychologists have drawn connections between depression and the absence of a future (Via 1985, 63–64). Bronco Billy's Wild West Show has a future represented by the ranch where the troupe will show their "little partners" what real cowboys and Indians were like. This dream, however trite and childish it may seem to the film's adult viewers, is what infuses the group with hope and purpose. Paul too speaks often of a future, a future derived from an apocalyptic model. Yet what Paul does not say is as important as what he does say. Paul offers little speculation about the future life; he provides no final judgment scenes or promises of the apocalyptic destruction of the world or evildoers. The closest he gets to the final war mythology of apocalyptic is 1 Thess. 4:13-18. More often he speaks of transformation, as in 1 Corinthians 15. He also identifies creation with the believer. Creation has been subjected to futility, is groaning in labor awaiting the revelation of the children of God (Rom. 8:19-22). Thus, creation has an eschatological aspect. It awaits the same hope as the believer, so it is not to be separated from the believer, but is the arena "for the setting of human history" (Käsemann 1980, 232). Furthermore, creation groans together with the believer, awaiting the final adoption when the body will be redeemed (8:23).

Paul in this regard is much closer to Bronco Billy than to Dirty Harry. After each setback for the Wild West Show, Billy announces their eschatological purpose. So too does Paul: "I consider that the sufferings of this present time are not worth comparing with the glory that is to be revealed to us" (Rom. 8:18). Both Paul and Billy have a future because they have hope—a dream. Eschatology is a type of dream, as witness the dreamlike language of much of apocalyptic. Dreams are powerful phenomena and should not simply be dismissed as wishful thinking. In his famous speech in 1963, Martin Luther King, Jr., intoned, "I have a dream," and in many ways that dream changed a nation. The power of a dream is its ability to create a new present in anticipation of a future.

Not just any dream will do, however; you could have a bad dream, as the visions of Charlie Manson and David Koresh testify. As Paul testifies, what makes a dream salvific is that it builds up the group (1 Cor. 8:1). Dirty Harry represents a version of life in urban America to which many subscribe. It is an alienated life in which people feel threatened by random violence that strikes without warning. This constant prospect of violence creates terrified individuals in search of someone who will strike out at those who appear threatening to them. Dirty Harry feeds on that urban experience. The gritty realism of violence in the Dirty Harry movies and their even more violent successors, such as *Robocop* (1987) and *Lethal Weapon* (1987), warns us of the price society will have to pay if we adopt their position in reality. Even recent political life has appealed to these mythologies while seeking to make them more palatable. Ronald Reagan's "America Standing Tall" campaign, his actual quoting of Dirty Harry's famous "Make my day!" and George Bush's efforts to show that he was not a wimp, and Bill Clinton's "Three strikes and you're out" get-tough-with-criminals campaign demonstrate how much this mythology underwrites public life. This myth allows us the fantasy of revenge on our enemies without admitting any price. Lévi-Strauss's remark that myth thinks for us without our knowing it can serve as an antidote.

Are Paul's dream of a restored creation, Bronco Billy's dream of a ranch, and Martin Luther King's dream of an America where blacks and whites dwell in harmony utopian fantasies? Yes, if they are taken as a narcotic that banishes our present trials and sufferings, but not if they infuse the present with meaning and purpose. Not just any meaning or purpose will do, however; the dream must provide a purpose of service to others, where the whole is greater than the parts. We may think Bronco Billy's dream is childish, but to such belong the kingdom. Billy reminds us in vivid images that the body of Christ, if it abandons its perfectionist claims, may well look childish, as Jesus says, or foolish, as Paul says. "For Jews demand signs and Greeks seek wisdom" (1 Cor. 1:22), and Americans seek vengeance—"Don't tread on me."

How do we conceive of God? Bronco Billy and Paul present an alternative to the image of God as a religious, cleaned-up Dirty Harry who will right all wrongs and defend and underwrite our use of power (violence). Their God is a slightly daffy presider over a community of flawed folks acting in the service of others, the little partners in Billy's dream or the poor in Jesus'!

WORKS NOTED

BELLAH, Robert N., et al. 1985.
   Habits of the heart: Individualism and commitment in American life.
   Berkeley: University of California Press.

BROWNMILLER, Susan. 1975.
   Against our will: Men, women and rape. New York: Simon & Schuster.

BULTMANN, Rudolf. 1951, 1955.
Theology of the New Testament. Translated by Kendrick Grobel. 2 vols.
New York: New Charles Scribner's Sons.

CAWELTI, John G. 1986.
Chinatown and generic transformation in recent American films. In *Film
genre reader*, 183–201. Edited by Barry Keith Grant. Austin: University of
Texas Press.

CONRAD, Joseph. 1983.
The secret agent. The World's Classics. Oxford: Oxford University Press.

HOCK, Ronald F. 1980.
The social context of Paul's ministry: Tentmaking and apostleship. Philadelphia: Fortress Press.

KAEL, Pauline. 1984.
5001 nights at the movies. New York: Holt, Rinehart & Winston.

KÄSEMANN, Ernst. 1980.
Commentary on Romans. Grand Rapids: Eerdmans.

LÉVI-STRAUSS, Claude. 1969.
The raw and the cooked: Introduction to a science of mythology. Trans-
lated by John Weightman and Doreen Weightman. New York:
Harper & Row.

STENDAHL, Krister. 1976.
The apostle Paul and the introspective conscience of the West. In *Paul
among Jews and Gentiles*, 78–96. Philadelphia: Fortress Press.

TOCQUEVILLE, Alexis de. 1969.
Democracy in America. Translated by George Lawrence. New York: Doubleday, Anchor Books.

TUSKA, Jon. 1976.
The filming of the West. Garden City: Doubleday.

VIA, Dan O. 1985.
The ethics of Mark's Gospel—In the middle of time. Philadelphia:
Fortress Press.

VNIJEWSKI, Boris. 1982.
The films of Clint Eastwood. Secaucus, N.J.: Citadel.

Orson Welles stands tall as the newspaper magnate Charles Foster Kane in his 1941 classic *Citizen Kane*. (Photo courtesy of Archive Photos)

6

THE POOR YOU HAVE ALWAYS WITH YOU

Only fools laugh at Horatio Alger, and his poor boys who make good. The wiser man who thinks twice about that sterling author will realize that Alger is to America what Homer was to the Greeks.
— *Nathanael West and Boris Ingster (1940)*

MYTH WORKS ITS MAGIC THROUGH ENDLESS repetition. It tells the same story over and over; the story is renewed and updated with new characters and new situations, so it appears different, but it is actually the same story solving an ever recurring conflict. The Western provides one important mythical source for expressing the American belief system. The tales for young boys written by Horatio Alger in the late nineteenth century are another source. He created a formulaic pattern that functions like a mantra, an aphorism of the American way, to give us a set of easily recognizable heroes: "impoverished boys who through hard work and virtue achieve great wealth and respect" (*American Heritage Dictionary* 1992, 45).

The appeal of Alger's stories stems from a fundamental conflict in the American experience. Our founding document, the Declaration of Independence, confesses as a self-evident truth that all men are created equal. Even though the U.S. Constitution never mentions equality, its prominence in the Declaration has implanted a commitment to equality in our national psyche. By moving this notion to the center in his Gettysburg Address, Abraham Lincoln reinvented the nation: "Fourscore and seven years ago our fathers brought forth on this continent a new nation, conceived in liberty, and dedicated to the proposition that all men are created equal." As Lincoln also noted, this great work is "unfinished." The Civil War itself was a testimony to the strife implied in that proposition, or as Aldous Huxley has said, "That all men are equal is a proposition to which, at ordinary times, no sane human being has ever given his assent" (Huxley 1927, 1). Our failure to live up to this noble proposition is as assured as death.

Thus, this noble notion was doomed to failure because everyday life reminds us that we are not equal. Yet at another level the American experience has vindicated this proposition. As a land of great wealth and possibilities, with an ever expanding frontier providing a seemingly endless series of new chances, America seemed to offer boundless opportunities for success. If we forget the true natives (as our myths have), America as a nation of immigrants is a land of opportunity compared to the old country. With its large middle class it gives the appearance of a classless society. The Horatio Alger hero appeals to this side of the American experience, while masking and discounting the protests of is darker underside.

Alger wrote over one hundred juvenile novels and many short stories. He considered himself a moral and religious teacher and offered his readers heroes like his classic Ragged Dick, who "would not steal, or cheat, or impose upon younger boys, but was frank and straight forward, manly and self-reliant" (Alger, as quoted in Scharnhorst 1980, 67).

Ironically, the Alger hero has changed over time, and our notion of that hero is not exactly what Horatio Alger himself conceived. Alger receives credit for developing the myth, whereas a myth has arisen from his own creation. Gary Scharnhorst has carefully traced this development (Scharnhorst 1980; Scharnhorst and Bales 1985). He summarizes the invariable Alger formula:

> A teen-aged boy whose experience of the sinister adult world is slight, yet whose virtue entitles him to the reader's respect, is cast unexpectedly into that sinister world and forced to struggle for a livelihood. At some point in this picaresque novel, the hero enters the City, both a fabled land of opportunity and a potentially corrupting environment, where he meets an array of allies and confidence men. His exemplary struggle to maintain his social respectability, to clear his or another's name of false accusations, to gain a measure of economic independence from those stepmothers or squires who wish to oppress him—this is the substance of the standard Alger plot. Alger always offered a foil

to his virtuous hero, usually a parochial snob who neither travels nor struggles, whose behavior is supremely selfish, who aspires to wealth, and who invariably ends the novel clinging to a rung lower on the social ladder than the one attained by the hero. At length, the hero earns the admiration of an adult patron who rewards him with elevated social station, usually a job or reunion with his patrician family, and the trappings of respectability, a watch and a new suit, which he flaunts before the deflated snob. (Scharnhorst 1980, 68)

Alger's morality plays actually reflected his abhorrence of the greed of the Gilded Age. His values, like those of the Western, were rooted in preindustrial America (Scharnhorst and Bales 1985, 150.) The pure moral insight his heroes possess descends from James Fenimore Cooper and from an even earlier model, *The Autobiography of Benjamin Franklin*. As Scharnhorst observes, it is ironic that Alger has become the icon for an American myth, for he was not a gifted writer and sales of his books were moderate during his lifetime.

Sales increased after his death, however, and reached their peak between 1900 and 1920 when over a million copies were sold annually. This was the age of Progressive reform, and the Alger hero came to be viewed as less of a moral character who is rewarded with success than as a prophet for Progressivism. The repetitive pattern of success became a protest demanding that similar opportunities be made available to all. As Scharnhorst argues, "Whereas in his own time Alger was credited with inventing a moral hero who becomes modestly successful, during the early years of this century he seemed to have invented a successful hero who is modestly moral" (Scharnhorst and Bales 1985, 151).

By far the most radical transformation of the Alger hero occurred between the 1920s and World War II. Although his books were no longer selling, the myth came into full bloom, now that it no longer was anchored to the actual stories. The phrase "Horatio Alger hero" was coined in the 1920s, and the myth was boiled down to a rags to riches story. During the Great Depression, "Alger was at last transformed into a patriotic defender of the social and political status quo and erstwhile advocate of laissez-faire capitalism" (Scharnhorst and Bales 1985,152). Now the myth took its definitive form as a celebration of the common man, rugged individualism, and economic success in the land of opportunity.

Like most myths, the Horatio Alger myth is ever changeable and flexible and frequently combines itself with other myths. *Pretty Woman* (1990), for example, draws on the fairy tale of the princess in the tower, although its more explicit mythical contact is Cinderella. Her rise to riches invokes aspects of the Alger hero, although this is not the primary myth employed in the film. Yet the elements are clear. The film's heroine is not a fallen woman but a working woman. Although she is a hooker, her virtue is protected in many ways; she doesn't take drugs, practices safe sex, and has had a hard life. Her opponents are grasping upper-class types, and most importantly, she instills in her hero/savior a moral point of view. Thus, in the end she is rewarded for her virtue and hard work with the hero as shining knight.

On the other hand, point of view sometimes determines which myth dominates. In *An Officer and a Gentleman* (1982) the primary myth is the Horatio Alger story but with a number of contemporary updates. The hero is Zack Mayo (Richard Gere), the wop as he refers to himself. As more Americans climb the social scale, the myth has had to accommodate non-WASP heroes. And in a further adaptation to our psychological concerns, Mayo is his own opponent in that he has to overcome himself. Because of his upbringing by a mother who committed suicide and then an alcoholic and neglectful father, he has become a loner who is always trying to beat the system. His patron is a black drill instructor named Emil Foley (Louis Gossett, Jr.), a tough unrelenting Marine who views his job as washing out those who are unfit to be pilots and unable to be team players. Mayo's encounter with this regimen leads to self-discovery. In the end he is rewarded with the title "an officer and a gentleman."

Yet from a female point of view the underlying myth is quite different. A subplot of the movie involves a relationship between Mayo and a local woman, Paula Pokrifki (Debra Winger), who works in the paper mill and dreams of a knight/sailor who will take her away. From her point of view the myth is Cinderella, which is clearly invoked at the movie's ending. After graduation Mayo sweeps into the mill on a motorcycle to carry her away, while a chorus of working women cheer them on. From a female perspective, the plot is nearly identical to *Pretty Woman.*

But women do not have to follow Cinderella. As they have moved out of the home into previously male jobs, reality has come up against belief. "All men are created equal" has become "All are created equal," and the Horatio Alger story has mutated to accept a female hero.

Working Girl (1988) is a slick, clever comedy that follows the Horatio Alger hero model. All the pieces are in place. The new hero is a Staten Island secretary with a Brooklyn accent and long, wild hair. Tess McGill (Melanie Griffith) is not satisfied with her background but is upward bound in the great American tradition. She is taking a speech class even though her friend asks why. "You talk fine," says the friend in her Brooklyn accent. Tess is continuing her education even though she is thirty years old and took five years to get her night degree with honors. Although she is brighter than her stockbroker bosses, she is hitting the glass ceiling. Clients don't want to talk to a secretary, even when she knows the answers. When her boss tells her she has been turned down again for an executive training program, she asks why. "Why? You've got to remember you're up against Harvard and Groton graduates. All you got is some night school and secretary on your time sheet," he explains. Then he tells her about a quick path in another division and sets up a luncheon interview. But this turns out to be a sexual setup. "I'm hungry but not that hungry," she says. Thus, we see her virtue as well as her talent and frustration.

In the true tradition of the Alger hero, Tess's big break comes when she finds a patron, Katharine Parker (Sigourney Weaver), who has the calm, cool upper-class look of a Harvard graduate. Katharine imparts to Tess a code for success. Even though Tess is Katharine's secretary, she is to address her boss as "Katharine" and they will form a team. Katharine wants Tess's input: "It's a two-way street." She also instructs Tess about dress: "We have a uniform, simple, elegant, impeccable. Dress shabbily, they notice the dress. Dress impeccably, they notice the woman. Coco Chanel."

Katharine also reveals a philosophy of success and serves as Tess's coach: "You don't get anywhere in this world by waiting for what you want to come to you. You make it happen." When Tess is despondent, Katharine drills her: "Tess, who makes it happen?" "I do," she says, "I make it happen." To which Katharine replies, "Only then do we get what we deserve."

Despite Katharine's posturing as a mentor/patron, she turns out to be no different than the men for whom Tess has worked. While Katharine is in the hospital with a broken leg following a skiing accident, Tess arranges her notes and discovers that Katharine has stolen Tess's idea for a merger prospect for Trask Industries. Cynical and disappointed, she says, "A two-way street. You make it happen."

Following Katharine's advice, Tess decides to make it happen by following up on her own idea for a potential merger for Trask Industries. She also begins to make herself over, lowering the pitch of her voice and adopting an upper-class Ivy League accent. She changes both her hair ("Want to be taken seriously, you need serious hair") and her clothes. She literally borrows Katharine's expensive clothes. As in *Pretty Woman*, clothes do make the woman. Finally, she seeks a new series of patrons, beginning with Jack Trainer (Harrison Ford), a deal maker from another firm. He does the numbers; she does the concept. When Trainer first meets this new Tess McGill, he remarks that she doesn't look like all the other women trying to look like men. She retorts, "I have a head for business and a bod for sin. Anything wrong with that?" The second patron she seeks is Oren Trask, head of Trask Industries. She even crashes his daughter's wedding to get the crucial meeting to pitch her deal. Like the typical Alger hero, she demonstrates resourcefulness in rising above her situation.

This shift in career and social class does not go unchallenged. She quickly loses her Brooklyn boyfriend. But the strongest challenge comes from her woman friend Cyn (Joan Cusack). Aware of Tess's involvement with Jack Trainer, she confronts her: "First, tell me even in your wildest dreams you're not thinking that Mr.-Briefcase-Let's-Have-Lunch is going to take you away from all this?" Tess tries to deflect the question, but Cyn persists: "If you're so smart, act smart. You're not going to have this job or any job. You're out of man and home already." Cyn argues for an unchanging status quo symbolized by man, house, and job. In the mode of the Horatio Alger myth, Tess protests that she is trying to make her life better: "I'm not going to spend the rest of my life working my ass off and getting nowhere just because I have to play by rules I had nothing to do with setting up." She echoes the Alger hero's protest. America is an egalitarian society, and rules that hold one down violate that commitment. But in this exchange Cyn gets the last word, an aphoristic word that warns against change: "Sometimes I dance around my house in my underwear. It doesn't make me Madonna and it never will."

At first, it appears that Cyn's prediction will come true. At the climactic meeting when the deal is going down, Katharine rushes in, exposes Tess as her secretary, and claims that Tess stole the idea from her. Yet in the end, Tess's two male patrons come to her aid. After initially doubting her, Jack refuses to proceed with the deal without Tess, and Oren Trask asks what prompted the idea for the merger? The answer is faithful to Tess's social origins. She got the idea from reading the *New York Daily News,* a tabloid quite different from Katharine's *New York Times.* In the end, Trask not only removes Katharine from the deal but vows to destroy her career. True to the Horatio Alger tradition, the heroine succeeds at the expense of the upper-class snob who had stood in the way.

A major backdrop in this movie is the pink ghetto, those countless, nameless secretaries who make a modern corporation work. Tess is trying to escape from this ghetto. Her accent, hair, and dress identify her as a member of the caste. Her friend Cyn is a permanent member of this group with no hope or apparent desire to escape. In the film the pink ghetto functions almost like a Greek chorus. When Tess is fired after the confrontation with Katharine, the secretaries gather around while she collects her things at her desk. They give her some money they have collected and admonish her to spend it on herself, not on the ConEd bill. When Trask confronts Katharine in Tess's defense, they are in the background. And after Katharine's defeat, when Tess kisses Jack, the pink ghetto oohs and aahs and claps in celebration. Finally, when Tess reports to work at Trask Industries, she sees another woman sitting in the office and takes up her place outside as secretary, the job she thought Trask had offered her. But it turns out that the other woman is Tess's secretary and Tess belongs in the office. Looking out the window at the Manhattan skyline, she dials Cyn and announces the news, at which Cyn lifts her arms in a gesture of victory and shouts out to the pink ghetto.

The upward mobility so celebrated by the Horatio Alger myth has its own eschatology. The goal is success, and that success is not simply, or even mostly, a matter of financial rewards. Despite the assumption that the Horatio Alger myth is a rags to riches story, success really means escape from the lower classes and is achieved in most cases at the expense of an antagonist, who is a member of the upper class. Thus, the myth celebrates the middle class over the two extremes, the lower class and the cultural elite. The middle class mediates between the lower and upper classes because it affirms the primary belief that all are created equal. Hence those who work hard and play by the rules should be rewarded. The Carly Simon song, "Let the River Run" invoking the "New Jerusalem," which plays in the background at important moments in *Working Girl*, and the high view of the Statue of Liberty that opens and closes the film reinforce its eschatology. The new Jerusalem image and the Statue of Liberty join the Horatio Alger hero in a triad that indicates that Tess has fulfilled the American dream. Her story is the new American story.

> We have talked long enough in this country about equal rights. We have talked for a hundred years or more. It is time now to write the next chapter, and to write it in the books of law.
> —*Lyndon B. Johnson (1963)*

IF A PRIMARY MYTHICAL FUNCTION OF THE Horatio Alger hero story is to undergird American upward mobility as a way of affirming our foundational belief that all are created equal, then the application of this myth to African Americans is very problematic because the boundary between black and white is one of the strongest taboos in American society. *Driving Miss Daisy* (1989) exposes some divisions imposed by this taboo and at the same time tries to show how genuine human engagement can bridge the boundary. Unlike Lyndon Johnson who wanted the taboos legislated away, *Driving Miss Daisy* calls on individual action in the spirit of the 1980s.

Sounder (1972) received critical acclaim, including Academy Award nominations for best picture, best actor (Paul Winfield), and best actress (Cicely Tyson), and praise as an uplifting family movie. Inasmuch as it implements the Horatio Alger story line, it is uplifting, but the points where it must deviate from that line are telling. The story is set in Louisiana during the Great Depression, so times are hard, a classic situation for a Horatio Alger tale. The Morgans are a hard-working family, struggling to take care of themselves, and thus they meet the moral requirement for an Alger tale. The hero is David Lee (Keven Hooks), the oldest of the Morgans' three children. Although his age is never given, he appears to be preadolescent. Quiet, intent, and a hard worker, he is often shown at the side of his father, Nathan Lee (Paul Winfield).

The movie opens with an unsuccessful possum hunt. Though the dog Sounder trees a possum, Nathan's aim is off. With food and survival on the line, he steals some meat for his family. When he is arrested, the sharp line between black and white is evident. The law is white and makes no exceptions for blacks. Nathan is sentenced to a year at hard labor in a parish work camp. When David Lee visits his father in the county jail, the sheriff subjects them both to repeated humiliations, both large and small. Rebecca (Cicely Tyson) bakes a cake for her husband, but a deputy says he must search it and destroys it in the process. Nathan's despair is palpable, as he tells David Lee, "Don't ever get yourself caught in a place like this."

Various people attempt to come to the family's aid. Mrs. Boatwright (Carmen Mathews), a white woman, previously had befriended David Lee and encouraged his reading by providing him with books. He pleads with her to find out where they have sent his father. When she approaches the sheriff, he refuses to divulge the information and throws up the taboo: "Just because you're in love with a little colored boy." His remark insinuates that she not only has crossed the line, but has broken a deep taboo because a white woman should not be "in love" with a little colored boy. Nevertheless, she persists and rifles through the sheriff's files until she finds the information. When the sheriff discovers her, he threatens to expose her so that she will be shunned by the community. When Mrs. Boatwright tells her where they have sent her husband, Rebecca remarks, "You're sure a crazy acting woman." She is as amazed as the sheriff that Mrs. Boatwright has violated the taboo. But the sheriff's threat is effective—Mrs. Boatwright makes it clear that she can no longer risk crossing the line.

Unable to make contact with her husband and unsure of his safety in prison, Rebecca sends David Lee on a journey to find him. Though a young boy, he already is being forced into adult roles. Dressed in his finest clothes, he sets off with his dog Sounder to find the work camp. He never makes contact with his father, but he does come across a black school run by Miss Camille Johnson. Like most mythic travelers, David Lee finds a new world, in this case one where blacks are not subordinate to whites. The black school stands in stark contrast to his own school, where he must sit in the back, pretend that he is not there, and endure insults about his inability to learn. In Miss Johnson's school, all the students are black, and she and her school represent black pride. When Miss Johnson takes him into her house,

David Lee remarks on how pretty it is and how many books she has. Hers is only a modest middle-class home, but it contrasts sharply with his sharecropper's shack. Once again, the middle class represents the eschatological goal.

Upon his return home, David Lee proposes to his mother that he attend Miss Johnson's school, but Rebecca thinks that is impossible. Nathan's return from the work camp with an injured leg makes the school appear even more unlikely because now David Lee is needed at home. Yet, when Miss Johnson writes to David Lee, his father understands that David Lee needs school like air: "I'm going to beat this leg; you beat this life they've laid out for you."

The father's commission to David Lee underlines the hurdle to adapting the Horatio Alger hero story to the African American experience. For the white hero, society lays out a clear-cut path: all are created equal; therefore you need only follow your destiny and all will work out. So strong is this mythological imprint on the American psyche, that we tend to attribute the failure of those who do not succeed to some fault of their own. One reason we have had a great deal of societal conflict about welfare is our conviction that those on welfare are undeserving. That so many found President Reagan's welfare queen story convincing, even though he never produced the queen, demonstrates my point. As Nathan remarks, David Lee has to beat the life they (the whites) have laid out for him. Yet the path David Lee will follow is not integration, but Miss Johnson's black school. Education is the classic American path to upward mobility, but it operates in a different way for African Americans because all are not created equal.

In *Sounder* the upper-class opponents are white society itself. In the typical Alger story, they get what is coming to them in the end, as happened to Katharine Parker in *Working Girl*. Such is not the case in *Sounder*. The only comeuppance for the whites is the ironic view of the movie, which casts them in the role of villain.

In the movie's final scene as father and son are riding off in the wagon to Miss Johnson's school, David Lee looks back and says, "I'm going to miss this old ragged place, but I sure ain't going to worry about it." David Lee has the skills to leave home, and his father hopes this will happen. But will the rest of the family make it too? This story is about David Lee's success, not his family's success. In the Horatio Alger myth, the rugged individual makes it, not the group.

One might think that the progress made in recent years would significantly modify the application of the Horatio Alger myth to blacks. After all, for several years during the Reagan era, "The Bill Cosby Show" was one of the top rated shows on television, and a number of blacks, for example, Michael Jackson and Eddie Murphy, have become major figures in the entertainment industry. Yet each of these in his way is problematic. The idyllic life of Bill Cosby's family replicates in the 1980s the "Leave It to Beaver" model of the 1950s; Michael Jackson's remake of his body might be interpreted not as black pride but shame, and his recent legal difficulties leave his future in doubt; and Eddie Murphy, while laughing all the way to the bank, manages to live up to every white stereotype of African Americans. One might suggest that these individuals have had a major impact on American entertainment because they hide mythically the real lines that separate American society.

Our myths mask this line of separation because of our fundamental conviction that all are created equal. *Mississippi Masala* (1992) reveals that line while exposing the bogus character of the Horatio Alger myth as applied to African Americans. The movie is complex and deals with a variety of interracial issues. It follows the fortunes of an Indian family who are expelled from Uganda and settle in Mississippi to operate a motel, a business many Indians are pursuing around the country. The frequency of "American Owned" signs in front of small town motels attests to the prejudice this trend has aroused. A major aspect of the movie's plot concerns an interracial relationship between Mina (Sarita Choudhury), the only daughter of the Indian family, and a young African American, Demetrius (Denzel Washington). The movie raises the question of what race means in America. As Demetrius points out, in America if you're not white, you're black. Ironically, the Indian family was expelled from Uganda, despite living there for three generations, because the new Africa was for black Africans.

Demetrius's story follows the Horatio Alger path. Unlike his brother who spends his time on the street corner trying to be hip, Demetrius dresses in a neat blue uniform and has opened his own rug cleaning business. Through the good graces of his father's white employer, he has a loan from the bank and is on his way up the ladder. All the ingredients of the Alger story are present: the hard-working youth, the patron, and the contrast, in this case Demetrius's younger brother.

But the story comes crashing down when Demetrius and Mina cross the racial boundary and fall in love. He loses his customers and the bank recalls the loan. The Horatio Alger dream can only come true if one remains on the path laid out by the dominant white culture. It referees who is deserving and who is not.

> With the consciousness of standing in the fullness of God's grace and being visibly blessed by Him, the bourgeois business man, as long as he remained within the bounds of formal correctness, as long as his moral conduct was spotless and the use to which he put his wealth was not objectionable, could follow his pecuniary interests as he would and feel that he was fulfilling a duty in doing so. The power of religious asceticism provided him in addition with sober, conscientious, and unusually industrious workmen, who clung to their work as to a life purpose willed by God.
> —*Max Weber (1930)*

> The goal of Jesus' proclamation was to reestablish Israel as the people of God. An alternative structure of social and economic relations was part of salvation.
> —*Halvor Moxnes (1988)*

MAX WEBER'S POSITION MAY BE EXTREME, but we Americans have suffered from a tendency to see material wealth as God's blessing. This belief is due in part to our Calvinist heritage, but other elements have also contributed. The frontier expansion gave the country not only a forward-looking spirit but also a constant sense of renewal. If life did not work out, one could always try again in the new lands on the next frontier. Likewise the frontier produced a leveling of society. The sense of our land as the new Israel, one nation under God, has given us a sense of being blessed and destined. Nativistic rhetoric about being the greatest nation in the world brings with it the sense of being special, or perhaps the sense of being God's chosen has led to a sense of being the greatest.

The Horatio Alger myth reflects this vision of America. The story's very form draws on the frontier's renewing energy. Unlike in Europe, one's place in American society was neither fixed nor a matter of inheritance. Here one could always start over and work one's way up the ladder. Success in America is marked by financial rewards and upward mobility, not inherited titles. The Horatio Alger myth undergirds and bridges our religious identity as Americans. By reinforcing our already strong Calvinist inheritance, middle-class wealth denotes God's reward. "To get religion" in our society almost inevitably means the adoption of middle-class values. One repents, reforms, quits drinking and carousing, gets a job, dresses better, and over time begins to improve one's lot. Thus, the Horatio Alger story repeats itself. The strong association of prohibition movements, women, and religion is part of this dynamic. If the men are dragged out of the saloons, they will return to work and support their families.

Scripture does not contain an exact parallel to the Horatio Alger story. Perhaps the story is too closely linked to the peculiarities of the American experience. The ancient world lacked the vast middle class so characteristic of American society. A diagram of ancient society would form an inverted funnel with a long, thin neck and a wide base, with a powerful elite at the top and the vast poor at the bottom. The reason for the absence of a Horatio Alger story in the Bible goes even deeper. The God of Israel and the early Christians fundamentally identifies with the poor. The most sustained meditation on these themes occurs in the Gospel of Luke. According to Luke Timothy Johnson, "in Luke, we have a compendium of the Gospel teaching on possessions, and so no end of attention has been paid to this 'evangelist of the poor' by scholars" (Johnson 1981, 13).

We must begin by recognizing that economics plays a different role in our society than it did in the ancient world. Economics drives our society like an engine, and we often have economic motives for our actions. In the ancient world, economics was embedded in or subordinated to other activities: family, kinship, and religion. The rich "based their power on politics and status rather than on economy" (Moxnes 1988, 31). A simple but potent example will clarify this. Our free enterprise system is driven by acquisition. Consumers must consume, capitalists must accumulate capital, and labor must sell its labor. These activities are virtues in our society. But the ancient world would castigate these modern virtues as greed. The poet in Habakkuk describes the problems of the wealthy: "They open their throats wide as Sheol; like Death they never have enough. They gather all nations for themselves, and collect all peoples as their own" (Hab. 2:5). These are powerful images of acquisitiveness. The rich are insatiable like death itself; they want the whole world. Why does our culture regard acquisitiveness as a virtue, whereas the ancient world lists it as a sin? In the ancient world, all goods were viewed as limited. Peasants, who were the vast majority of the population, worked for subsistence, not to produce a surplus. Our society believes that wealth is infinite and thinks in terms of surplus. Our inability to realize that oil is a finite resource is a perfect example. We use it as though it were infinite.

Because goods were limited, ancient societies were organized around reciprocity and exchange. You scratch my back, I'll scratch yours. Within kinship groups and villages the reciprocity tended to be balanced or equalized because mutual support was in everyone's interest. But empires distributed power very unequally. The elites used their power to ensure that they got something for nothing, as the Habakkuk text makes clear. Thus, the elites organized themselves along the lines of a patron-client model. To negotiate through the inequalities of an empire, one needed a patron to protect and advance one's interests. Without such a benefactor, one would be lost.

Although it has long been recognized that the poor hold a prominent place in Luke's Gospel, exactly how they are to relate to the rich requires careful consideration. Statements pulled out of context can misrepresent Luke's position. We must keep the social context in mind because Luke's Gospel keeps the empire in the reader's mind. The elaborate date in 3:1-2 situates Jesus' advent on the stage in Galilee in the midst of the empire's affairs. Likewise, Luke's Greek and rhetorical style, among the best in the New Testament, indicate that both the author and his intended audience have an elite social standing. It is the only New Testament document that is dedicated to a patron, the most excellent Theophilus.

The gospel's opening scenes graphically initiate the theme of rich and poor. The priest Zechariah is silenced at the announcement of his son's birth, while the lowly maid Mary breaks out in a triumphant song. The first two lines of the song address God as Lord and Savior (1:47), both titles from the imperial cult. God is set up in direct contrast to the claims of the Roman emperor. His strength is directly invoked under the additional title of the "mighty one" (1:49). "He has shown strength with his arm" (1:51) probably alludes to Ps. 89:10:

> O Lord God of Hosts,
>   who is as mighty as you,
>   O Lord?
> Your faithfulness surrounds you.
> You rule the raging of the sea:
>   when its waves rise, you still them.
> You crushed Rahab like a carcass;
>   you scattered your enemies
>   with your mighty arm. (Ps. 89:8-10)

As this quotation from Psalm 89 indicates, the Magnificat's threat of God's arm is not an idle threat but celebrates "God's revolutionary overthrow of the established governing authorities" (Horsley 1989, 112). Mary, the young maid, shouts in a "battle-like tone" (Fitzmyer 1981, 1:361) that God

> has scattered the proud in the fantasy of their hearts
> he brought down the rulers from their thrones
> and he lifted up the lowly
> the hungry he has fed good things
> and the rich he has sent away empty. (my own translation)

This song sets the gospel's tone, announcing God's overthrow of the rich and the exaltation of the humble and poor.

Jesus' own inaugural sermon in Nazareth begins with a reading from Isaiah announcing the same themes: "The Spirit of the Lord is upon me, because he has anointed me to bring good news (to gospelize) to the poor. He has sent me to proclaim release to the captives and recovery of sight to the blind, to let the oppressed go free, to proclaim the year of the Lord's favor" (4:18-19). When John the Baptist sends his disciples to inquire about whether Jesus is the one to come, Jesus' answer echoes this quotation from Isaiah: "Go and tell John what you have seen and heard: The blind receive their sight, the lame walk, the lepers are cleansed, the deaf hear, the dead are raised, the poor have the good news brought to them" (7:22). Likewise, the beatitudes in Luke repeat these same themes: "Blessed are you who are poor, for yours is the kingdom of God" (6:20). Unlike Matthew who abstracts or, perhaps one should say, deconcretizes this beatitude, Luke understands the poor in a physical sense, as those whom the empire has suppressed. The Scholars Translation nicely captures the irony and paradox of this saying: "Congratulations, you poor! God's domain belongs to you." In contrast to Caesar's empire, God's empire belongs to the poor. Furthermore, in Luke the beatitude is balanced by a woe: "But woe to you who are rich, for you have received your consolation" (6:24). In Luke, God and God's kingdom are identified with the poor, but even more importantly, in the kingdom the poor remain poor; they do not become the rich. The reversal theme does not turn the poor into the newly rich. This theme becomes even more evident when we consider how Luke deals with the rich.

A group of stories about rich people can serve as exemplars of Luke's view of the rich. Luke situates the parable of the Rich Fool in the midst of a discussion about a disputed inheritance, a problem of the rich, not of the poor. Jesus refuses to mediate between the two quarreling brothers as a judge or to serve as their patron. Instead, he warns about greed: "Be on your guard against all kinds of greed; for one's life does not consist in the abundance of possessions" (12:15). While a warning about greed in a discussion of inheritance might strike us as strange, it actually fits well within the limited goods perspective of the ancient world. Since goods are severely limited and there is not enough to go around, greed—the desire to possess all the inheritance—threatens to destroy the peace between the brothers. The parable drives the point home. The rich farmer's bountiful harvest is meant not to enrich him but to be set aside like Joseph's great bounty in Egypt for the people to use in the lean years (Scott 1989, 134). But the rich man steals the harvest for his own enjoyment, at which point God intervenes: "You fool! This very night your life is being demanded of you." God intervenes on the side of the poor because in his kingdom the harvest is for the good of all people, not for one individual's enjoyment.

The parable of the Rich Man and Lazarus (Luke 16:19-31) likewise occurs in the context of a discussion about wealth and community. In the parable of the Unjust Steward, Jesus draws the conclusion, "You cannot serve God and wealth" (16:13), and describes the Pharisees as "lovers of money" (16:14) who ridicule Jesus' teaching about God and wealth. Wealth threatens community, while God is for the poor. Divorce also appears in this context because it breaks the social bond. In the parable of the Rich Man and Lazarus, the rich man and Abraham are the two main characters. Lazarus remains passive, lying by the gate of the rich man and then in Abraham's bosom. Many commentators have noted the oddness of describing life after death as in the bosom of Abraham because it is unattested elsewhere in

Jewish literature. But the significance lies in Abraham. Abraham is famous for two things in Jewish folklore: he was rich, and he provided hospitality for the three strangers at the oaks of Mamre (Gen. 18:1-5). Abraham's hospitality contrasts with that of the rich man. Lazarus lies beside the gate every day, but the rich man does not offer him hospitality, whereas as soon as the three strangers approached Abraham, he provided for them. The issue then is not wealth itself, but rather its redistribution to the poor. In the discourse between Abraham and the rich man, he pleads with Abraham to send Lazarus to warn his brothers. But Abraham rejects his plea on the grounds that they already have Moses and the prophets to warn them. From Luke's perspective God has always been on the side of the poor, and Moses and the prophets are witness to this fact.

Only Luke introduces the story of the would-be follower who must choose between his riches and following Jesus (Luke 18:18-25) by identifying him as a ruler. Mark and Matthew use only a generic, masculine identifier, literally "a one." The identifier "ruler" places the man socially among the elite, and translating it "one of the elite" would be appropriate. After the ruler acknowledges that he has kept all the commandments, Jesus remarks that he is missing only one thing: "Sell all that you own and distribute the money to the poor and you will have treasure in heaven" (18:22). Those who remember the parallel passages in Mark (10:21) and Matthew (19:21) will notice that in Luke Jesus tells the ruler to "distribute" the proceeds to the poor, not simply to give. Though the outcome would be the same, the point is telling, for Luke envisions the redistribution of wealth within the kingdom (Moxnes 1988, 155). Thus, unlike the Horatio Alger story, Luke does not envision the poor moving up the social ladder to join the rich, but rather a new kingdom where all wealth is redistributed to the poor. The poor will make up the kingdom. We have also seen this notion of storing up treasure in the parable of the Rich Fool where Jesus warns, "That is how it is with the man who piles up treasure for himself and remains a pauper in the sight of God" (12:21 NEB). Just as the fool's life was taken because he did not redistribute his wealth, so it is with the Rich Man in the Lazarus parable. Real treasure is not wealth but found in heaven. Jesus' comment to the disciples immediately after the parable of the Rich Fool makes this point clear: "Do not be afraid, little flock, for it is your Father's good pleasure to give you the kingdom. Sell your possessions, give alms. Make purses for yourselves that do not wear out, and unfailing treasure in heaven, where no thief comes near and no moth destroys. For where your treasure is there your heart will be also" (12:32-34). The flock has the kingdom, and they respond to that kingdom by selling all they have, giving alms, redistributing their wealth, and becoming poor. Then they will have treasure in heaven.

In the story of Jesus' meeting with Zacchaeus, all these issues come to a head. Luke notes that Zacchaeus is both the chief tax collector (not an ordinary, low-level tax collector) and a rich man, although describing him as rich is redundant if he is the chief tax collector. Luke often employs these redundancies, as when he also describes as rich the man dressed in fine purple linen (16:19). In the ancient world, the two go together. When Jesus dines with Zacchaeus, *all* (19:7) object because he is eating with a sinner. In Judaism tax collecting was a forbidden occupation because it involved collaboration with the enemy, the occupying forces of the Roman Empire. In response, Zacchaeus promises half of his possessions to the poor and fourfold restitution to anyone he has defrauded. The text does not indicate whether his promise would impoverish him, but it would mean a considerable redistribution of wealth to the poor. Significantly, Zacchaeus does not promise to give up his occupation. He will remain the chief tax collector and therefore a sinner. Just as in the parable of the Pharisee and the Tax Collector, the tax collector asks, "God, be merciful to me, a sinner!" (18:13). He gives no hint of giving up his sinful occupation, yet Jesus says he went home justified, and in the case of Zacchaeus, he says, "Today salvation has come to this house" (19:9).

Jesus in Luke's Gospel proclaims a kingdom in which wealth is redistributed to the poor, not so that the poor become rich, but so that the hierarchical patron-client structure of society will be destroyed. Eschatology is not climbing the social ladder to become rich. When all the rich people refuse to attend the banquet, the man joins the outcast, the poor who dwell by the wayside (14:16-24).

> Let me tell you about the very rich. They are different
> from you and me.
>
> —*F. Scott Fitzgerald (1926)*

> Yes, they have more money.
>
> —*Ernest Hemingway (1936)*

CITIZEN KANE (1941) IS A TRULY GREAT FILM and is regarded by many critics as the finest American film ever made. Though Orson Welles is identified with the film, it was actually a collaborative venture by the Mercury radio group. Yet Welles deserves his reputation for he was the film's guiding genius. A film as rich as this one cannot be reduced to a single myth, but the Horatio Alger story furnishes a part of Kane's temper, and the film profoundly critiques that myth.

Kane's early life fits the Horatio Alger story perfectly. Born in relative poverty and raised in his mother's boarding house, he inherits enormous wealth at an early age and goes to live with a guardian, Walter Parks Thatcher, who is patterned after John D. Rockefeller.

The film ostensibly takes place after Kane's death, as the journalist Thompson (William Alland) attempts to make sense of his life by digging beneath the surface of the newsreel that opens the film. One of the first important pieces of information in the puzzle is a diary kept by Thatcher. The diary is preserved in the Thatcher Library, an imposing building with a huge statue of Thatcher dominating its entrance. This is an extrafilmic reference to the Morgan Library in New York, a memorial to John Pierpoint Morgan. Thompson is ushered into an elongated inner room that resembles a mausoleum. From a tiny vault in the wall, a guard produces the diary, as a priest might bring forth the Eucharist from a tabernacle. As he walks forward, a beam of light, like the Holy Spirit overshadowing a sacred object, pierces the darkness and shines on the little book. As James Naremore has argued, "this aura of sacredness is mixed with elements of hokum and profanity, so that we are aware of banal material goods being mystified into a spiritual nether world" (Naremore 1979, 78). This analysis goes to the film's heart. The film's strategy is to turn money into a sacred myth and then to demythologize it by showing that it cannot sustain what it promises.

The diary, narrated by Thatcher, describes Kane's early life. Thatcher, so to speak, was there at the beginning. The first episode explains how Kane got his money. In a scene that draws on the imagery of a Victorian Christmas, a young boy is playing in the snow in front of a house identified by a sign as "Mrs. Kane's Boardinghouse." Inside are Mr. and Mrs. Kane and Thatcher. The viewer is drawn into the house and gradually pieces together what is happening. While Kane's father protests to little apparent effect, his mother and Thatcher are the principal players. A previous boarder, unable to pay his bill, had signed over some seemingly worthless stock to Mrs. Kane. Now the stock has turned out to be from the lucrative Colorado Lode, and Mrs. Kane has asked Thatcher's bank to manage it and to serve as guardian of her son. The dialogue implies that Mrs. Kane is sending her son off to protect him from his father and to make sure that he is raised in a manner appropriate to his great wealth. This scene plays both with and against the Horatio Alger story. On the one hand, the scene is pure Horatio Alger—the Victorian Christmas, the poor but honest mother operating her boarding house, and Kane's resistance to being separated from his mother. These are essential ingredients in the myth. Yet there are counter signs—the mother coldly turning over her son to a bank and Thatcher's obvious dislike and disapproval of Kane. Thatcher's attitude is evident not only from his opening narration, when he remarks that Kane will surely be soon forgotten, but also from the way he handles the boy. But most tellingly, in an Alger story, money comes as a reward *after* the hero has demonstrated his worthiness, whereas in Kane's story wealth is not a reward for virtue but has become an end in itself. Capital controls the boy's life.

The last episode recorded in Thatcher's diary takes place in Kane's office at the *Inquirer*, his crusading newspaper. Thatcher is concerned about the newspaper's attacks on the Metropolitan Transfer Company in which Kane is a major shareholder. Kane confesses that he is two people:

> As Charles Foster Kane, who has eighty-two thousand, six hundred and thirty-one shares of Metropolitan Transfer—you see, I do have a rough idea of my holdings—I sympathize with you. Charles Foster Kane is a dangerous scoundrel, his paper should be run out of town and a committee should be formed to boycott him. You may, if you can form such a committee, put me down for a contribution of one thousand dollars.

But there is also another Kane:

> I am the publisher of the *Inquirer*. As such it is my duty—I'll let you in on a little secret, it is also my pleasure—to see to it that the decent, hardworking people of this city are not robbed blind by a group of money-mad pirates because, God help them, they have no one to look after their interests! (Mankiewicz and Welles 1971, 151)

This dichotomy will determine Kane's own fate. Will he use his wealth to defend the people and live up to the Horatio Alger tale in which wealth is the reward of virtue, or will he allow the demands of wealth to triumph? The film's opening has already told the tale. He will die rich and alone in his Xanadu.

> Finding is the first act
> The second, loss
> > —*Emily Dickinson (c. 1864)*

> The kingdom of heaven is like treasure hidden in a field, which someone found and hid; then in his joy he goes and sells all that he has and buys that field.
> > —*Matthew 13:44*

AS WE HAVE SEEN, THE BIBLICAL TRADITION does not contain an exact parallel to the Horatio Alger story. Nevertheless, the parable of the Treasure presents an interesting parallel to *Citizen Kane*, although the relation is not immediately obvious.

John Dominic Crossan has shown that in Judaism, as in most cultures, treasure is a reward for good deeds, so that treasure comes at the story's end (Crossan 1979). A story that occurs in several rabbinic texts perfectly exemplifies the type. A certain Judah was very generous in his support of the rabbis. When he lost all his money, he was not concerned about himself but with how he could continue to support the rabbis. According to the story, which also emphasizes the virtue of Judah's wife, "His wife, who was even more righteous than he, said to him, 'You have a single field left. Go and sell half of it and give the proceeds to them.'" Judah does as his wife suggests, and the rabbis pray for him, "May the Holy One, blessed be He, make up all the things you lack." Now the plot is set for treasure to come as a reward: "Now while he was ploughing in the half-field that remained to him, his cow fell and broke his leg. He went down to bring her up, and the Holy One, blessed be He, opened his eyes, and he found a jewel. He said, 'It was for my own good that my cow broke its leg.' " What appeared at first to be more bad luck turns out to be God's blessing, and Judah immediately gives thanks to God. When the rabbis come, they ask how Judah is doing and the people answer, "Who can [even] gaze upon the face of Abba Judah—Abba Judah of the oxen! Abba Judah of the camels! Abba Judah of the asses!" At the story's end, the rabbis gather around Judah and the scripture verse is fulfilled: "A man's gift makes room for him and brings him before great men" (Prov. 18:16; the rabbinic story is discussed and quoted in Scott 1989, 396–97).

The story furnishes a striking parallel to the parable of the Treasure in Matthew, and one probably can assume that such stories were widespread and are necessary to understand Jesus' parable. Both parables are set in a religious context although in Jesus' parable the context is the kingdom of God whereas in the rabbinic parable the context illustrates the verse from Prov. 18:16. The subject of Jesus' parable is the treasure whereas Judah is the subject of the rabbinic parable. That Judah is named while the man remains anonymous in Jesus' parable reflects this difference. It is emphasized by the multiple characters in the rabbinic parable who serve as a chorus acknowledging Judah's virtue while the anonymous man is the lone character in Jesus' parable. In the rabbinic parable the treasure is explicitly an act of God, whereas Jesus' parable is silent on this point.

The rabbinic parable makes obvious what must be inferred from Jesus' parable. Since Judah finds the jewel on his own property, there can be no question about its ownership. In another treasure parable in the Jesus tradition from the *Gospel of Thomas*, the parable goes out of its way to stress that the man owns the field by providing a list of ownership: "The Kingdom of Heaven is like a man who had a [hidden] treasure in his field without knowing it. And [after] he died, he left it to his son. This son did not know (about the treasure). He inherited the field and sold [it]. And the one who bought it went plowing and found the treasure" (*Gospel of Thomas*, 109 SV). As in the rabbinic parable no one can doubt that the treasure finder owns the field and thus has a right to claim the treasure for his own. The situation in Jesus' parable is different, although the hearer must infer this from the man's actions. That he buys the field at the parable's conclusion indicates that he does not own the field and so has no claim on the treasure.

The piety and righteousness of Judah and his wife are evident throughout the story whereas in Jesus' parable the hearer must draw a conclusion from the man's behavior. After finding the treasure, he covers it up and goes and buys the field. Thus, he is clearly unrighteous since he has no right to the treasure. This situation should not be confused with the story of the Widow's Mite (Mark 12:41). She gives all she has for charity. Her virtue exceeds even Judah's. The anonymous man, on the other hand, sells all to buy a field to claim a treasure that is not rightly his. In the rabbinic parable finding the treasure is the middle act, the reward for virtue, and in the final act, that treasure is used to do more righteous deeds. The motion in the rabbinic parable is from rich man to poor man, and back to rich man. In Jesus' parable, there is no motion. The state of the man is unknown at the parable's beginning, but he certainly is not rich since he is working for another. In his joy he impoverishes himself to buy the field. But the treasure is of little use to him because he obtained it by deceit. So he is still a poor man.

The parallel to *Citizen Kane* is very strong. If treasure is the first act, loss is the second, but this is a loss of virtue or self, not a loss of treasure. In *Citizen Kane* Kane must struggle with his two selves, one dedicated to preserving his wealth and the other a crusading publisher devoted to defending the interests of the masses. As the movie makes clear, the former Kane wins out, and that loss is symbolized by the mystery of Rosebud, that reference to the joy of his youth before the wealth. Jesus' parable ends with a similar loss. Seduced by his joy at finding the treasure, the man does not give thanks, but sells everything and impoverishes himself. In the end he is alone with his treasure and the field, unable to announce his find to the village. Unlike Judah, whose village celebrated his blessing, the anonymous man's village would ask embarrassing questions: "Where did your newfound wealth come from? You found treasure? Where? And how long have you owned the land?" The only answers he could give would show his impiety and risk the forfeiture of his treasure.

The Horatio Alger story has provided a powerful mythical engine propelling upward mobility in our national consciousness. But ironically and inevitably, it subverts the very conflict it seeks to overcome, which is based on the foundational belief that all are created equal. As Luke argues, wealth creates a dangerous hierarchy of elites lording it over the rest. In Luke's version of the last supper, Jesus provides what can almost be called a summary statement on this issue as he resolves a fight over which is the greatest:

> Among the foreigners, it's the kings who lord it over everyone, and those in power are addressed as "benefactors." But not so with you; rather the greatest among you must behave as a beginner, and the leader as one who serves. Who is the greater, after all: the one reclining at a banquet or the one doing the serving? Isn't it the one who reclines? Among you I am the one doing the serving. (Luke 22:25-27 SV)

He emphatically rejects the way the Roman Empire has structured reality. That form of hierarchy leads only to tyranny. His position runs counter to common sense, as his answer to his own question indicates. So Luke rejects upward mobility and calls instead for a redistribution of wealth. As both *Citizen Kane* and the parable of the Treasure so forcibly warn, wealth can seduce, and unless one is careful, Emily Dickinson's poem becomes a prophecy:

> Finding is the first act
> The second, loss
> Third, Expedition for
> The "Golden Fleece"
> Fourth, no Discovery—
> Fifth, no Crew—
> Finally, no Golden Fleece—
> Jason—sham—too
> (Dickinson c. 1864, 870)

WORKS NOTED

THE AMERICAN HERITAGE *dictionary of the English language.* 1992.
3rd ed. New York: Houghton Mifflin.

CROSSAN, John Dominic. 1979.
Finding is the first act. Semeia Supplements. Philadelphia: Fortress Press.

DICKINSON, Emily. 1955.
The complete poems of Emily Dickinson. Boston: Little, Brown.

FITZMYER, Joseph. 1981.
The Gospel according to Luke. Anchor Bible Series. Vol. 1. Garden City, N.Y.: Doubleday.

HORSLEY, Richard A. 1989.
The liberation of Christmas: The infancy narratives in social context.
New York: Crossroad.

HUXLEY, Aldous. 1927.
The idea of equality. In *Proper studies*, 1–30. London: Chatto & Windus.

JOHNSON, Luke Timothy. 1981.
Sharing possessions: Mandate and symbol of faith. Overtures to Biblical
Theology. Philadelphia: Fortress Press.

MANKIEWICZ, Herman J., and Orson Welles. 1971.
The shooting script. In *The Citizen Kane book*, 87–300. Boston:
Little, Brown.

MOXNES, Halvor. 1988.
*The economy of the kingdom: Social conflict and economic relations
in Luke's Gospel.* Overtures to Biblical Theology. Philadelphia:
Fortress Press.

NAREMORE, James. 1979.
The magic world of Orson Welles. New York: Oxford Univ. Press.

SCHARNHORST, Gary. 1980.
Horatio Alger, Jr. Twayne's United States Authors Series. Boston: Twayne
Publishers.

SCHARNHORST, Gary, and Jack Bales. 1985.
The lost life of Horatio Alger, Jr. Bloomington: Indiana University Press.

SCOTT, Bernard Brandon. 1989.
Hear then the parable: A commentary on the parables of Jesus. Minneapolis: Fortress Press.

WEBER, Max. 1930.
The Protestant ethic and the spirit of capitalism. Translated by Talcott
Parsons. New York: Charles Scribner's Sons.

WEST, Nathaniel, and Boris Ingster. 1940.
"A cool million." Unpublished and unproduced screenplay, quoted in
Scharnhorst and Bales, *The last life of Horatio Alger, Jr.*

Captain Willard (Martin Sheen) conveys the horror of the Vietnam War in Francis Ford Coppola's *Apocalypse Now* (1979). (Photo courtesy of Archive Photos)

7 LOSS OF INNOCENCE

> An angry man—there is my story: The bitter rancor of
> Achilles, prince of the house of Peleus, which brought
> a thousand troubles upon the Achaean host. Many a
> strong soul it sent down to Hades, and left the heroes
> themselves a prey to dog and carrion birds, while the
> will of God [Zeus] moved on to fulfillment.
> —*Homer, The* Iliad

IF, AS LÉVI-STRAUSS MAINTAINS, MYTH AT-
tempts to resolve conflict, then war presents a fertile ground for the
flowering of mythical resolutions. Homer's *Iliad* weaves a story about
the Achaean war with Troy that explores the hubris at the base of
human conflict. For him the resolution is fidelity to the will of the
gods. Although Paris's abduction of Helen provoked the war, Homer
sings about Achilles' anger and pride, which led to the quarrel with
Agamemnon, the near defeat of the Greeks, and the death of his good
friend Patroclus.

America's wars have also supplied mythical inspiration for the
nation. The Revolutionary War has served as a genesis myth, and the
Civil War, our most traumatic conflict, created the myth of a unified
nation. But our sense of the United States as a peace-loving nation
comes into conflict with the violence and frequency of our wars.
Thus, we have difficulty seeing ourselves as the aggressors and must
vilify the enemy.

In this century the movies have contributed to the war effort by
providing a public definition of the war. During World War II Hollywood was recruited for the war effort. Not only did it make many
films for the War Department, but Walt Disney Studios, even contributed artists to emblazon insignia on bombers. In 1942 the Selective

Service ruled that the movies were an essential industry, giving many Hollywood stars the opportunity to serve their country at the studio, as Ronald Reagan did. The films they made were not just propaganda. As members of the armed forces, major directors including Frank Capra, John Huston, John Ford, and William Wyler made significant documentaries about the war (Cook 1981, 394–95). These documentaries introduced a level of realism that made Hollywood's earlier war films laughable by comparison and led to many serious films about the dark days of the war. Tay Garnett's *Bataan* (1943) exemplifies the victory in defeat motif. In its final scene Robert Taylor, the only survivor in his unit, fights to the end to stop the onrush of Japanese invaders.

> The achievement of David Wark Griffith (1875–1948) is unprecedented in the history of Western Art, much less Western film. In the brief span of six years, between directing his first one-reeler in 1908 and *The Birth of a Nation* in 1914, Griffith established the narrative language of the cinema as we know it today and turned an aesthetically inconsequential medium of entertainment into a fully articulated art form.
> —*David A. Cook (1981)*

THE CIVIL WAR HAS BEEN A RICH LODE FOR movie myth making. In his *Birth of a Nation* D. W. Griffith produced an epic that helped refine and consolidate the American view of that war and helped create the filmic view of war itself. The monumental film, which premiered on February 8, 1915, established the artistic standard that defines the narrative movie to this day. It also set a number of firsts:

1. It was the most expensive movie to date, costing $110,000 (the usual film ran around $10,000).
2. At twelve reels it was the longest movie yet made. Normal distribution channels refused to handle it, forcing Griffith to set up his own distribution network.

3. It had had the longest shooting schedule. In an age when most movies were shot in a week, Griffith took six weeks to rehearse and nine weeks to shoot.

But perhaps the financial return tells the true tale. *The Birth of a Nation* was the first movie to charge the same two-dollar admission price as the legitimate theater. After the first five years of distribution, it had grossed over $15 million, an astounding record for its time (Williams 1980, 62–65).

Though the public response was overwhelming, the movie did meet with opposition. The National Association for the Advancement of Colored People (NAACP) protested strongly, and the film became an important galvanizing force in the modern civil rights movement. It also played a role in the modern revival of the Ku Klux Klan. Reportedly, President Woodrow Wilson initially said, "It is like writing history with lightning," and he did write Griffith on March 5, "I congratulate you on a splendid production" (D. W. Griffith 1993). Later, however, pressure forced Wilson to attack the film. But as Cook has shown, "If Griffith distorted history, then so did Woodrow Wilson in his five-volume *History of the American People* (1902), written while he was president of Princeton University, which tells pretty much the same story as *The Birth of a Nation*" (Cook 1981, 79).

Griffith built his tale around two families, the Camerons from the South and the Stonemans from the North. The interlocking destinies of these two families provide not only the movie's narrative vehicle but also its mythical resolution.

The movie is divided into three parts. The first depicts the pristine unity of the country before the Civil War. This is symbolized by the happy slaves working for their masters and also by the visit of the Stoneman brothers to the Cameron plantation in Piedmont, South Carolina. But a snake lurks in paradise. As the first screen reads, "The bringing of the African to America planted the first seeds of dis-Union." These seeds of disunity were sown not by the South but by the New England slave traders and their successors, the abolitionists.

The second part is devoted to the war itself. Griffith staged monumental war scenes and employed his camera with great skill to draw the viewer into the battles. His depiction of Sherman's March to the Sea is a classic example. It begins with an iris shot of a mother and her children cowering on a hillside and gradually opens up to a long shot revealing the cause of her fear, Sherman's troops marching through the valley. Though he does not neglect the glory of war, Griffith's efforts to depict realistically the senseless savagery in which brother slaughtered brother began an enduring tradition in American movies.

In the war's final battle at Petersburg, Ben Cameron, known as "the little colonel," leads a desperate charge against the Union troops under the command of Phil Stoneman, who had been visiting him in Piedmont at the war's outbreak. As the Confederates charge the Union line, the troops engage in hand-to-hand combat. When the little colonel stops to aid a fallen Union soldier before the final charge, he is cheered on by Phil Stoneman and his men. The message is clear. Despite the bloody war, South and North are still united by a common brotherhood. In the battle's last stage, with the Confederates stopped, only the little colonel remains standing, and he finishes the charge and rams the Confederate flag down the barrel of a Union cannon as Phil Stoneman calls off his own troops and looks on approvingly. The war ends with the little colonel collapsing into Phil Stoneman's arms.

Though one might think that the Civil War would be the movie's climax, Reconstruction provides not only the film's dramatic focus but also its great controversy. Here myth charges to the fore in the birth of a new nation, a radical reinterpretation of Lincoln's Gettysburg phrase. In this third phase of the movie, Austin Stoneman, the father of the Stoneman clan and a leader in the House of Representatives, is a central character. Modeled on Thaddeus Stevens, he leads the protest against Lincoln's policy of clemency. After Lincoln's death he is described as the most powerful man in the country, and the screen announces, "And now began an era of cruel chicanery and political upheaval as a result of the Carpetbaggers' studied degradation of the conquered South." By degradation, Griffith seems to mean that Stoneman insists on equality between blacks and whites. One screen reads, "The new-found freedom turns to rude insolence" and shows a number of scenes in which blacks no longer kowtow to whites as in antebellum days. Another screen proclaims, "Reaping the whirlwind. Stoneman's insistence on full racial equality brings grim tragedy." The prime example of the grim tragedy is the death of Flora Cameron, the youngest child of the family. Gus (Walter Long in blackface), who is described as a "renegade negro," proposes marriage to Flora in a nonromantic and brutish manner, "I'se a Captain now, an' I want to git married." When she refuses and runs away, he runs after her. The chase ends when she throws herself off a cliff rather than submit and dies in the little colonel's arms. When white men seek out Gus to give him a fair trial, he kills one of them. The Klansmen then try, convict, and execute him, dumping his body with a KKK warning affixed on the steps of the home of the lieutenant governor Silas Lynch, a mulatto in league with Austin Stoneman. This lynching is depicted as a reasoned execution of justice, whereas legitimate trials with blacks as jurors are portrayed as gross miscarriages of justice.

The movie now rapidly proceeds to its climax. Lynch calls out the militia, a band of black soldiers with white leaders, to arrest the Klansmen. When old Dr. Cameron is arrested, his black house servants, the "faithful souls," rescue him. Afterward the Camerons along with Phil Stoneman find refuge in a cabin with former Union soldiers. The screen proclaims, "The former enemies of North and South unite to resist the mad results of the Carpetbaggers' political folly." The "former enemies," of course, are the whites, now united against the carpetbaggers and their allies, the black militia.

Meanwhile, Elsie Stoneman goes to Silas Lynch to plead for the Camerons. Instead, Lynch proposes marriage to her and kidnaps her when she refuses. Black troops are rioting in the streets of Piedmont, and another contingent of black troops is attacking the Camerons in their rural hideout. Interspersed among the riot scenes are others showing the "Summoning of the Clans." Two Night Hawks ride throughout the Piedmont calling out the Klan. They come together on horseback like streams to form a veritable river of white knights in ordered columns. For background music, Griffith selected Wagner's "Ride of the Valkyries." Now comes a pitched battle scene in Piedmont reminiscent of the Civil War battles. The tension builds to the climax. As the Klansmen come to the aid of those trapped in the cabin, the men are ready to kill the women rather than let them fall into the hands of the black troops. In the end the Klansmen defeat the blacks and restore legitimacy to the South. As one of the final screen titles reports, the "Black Empire" has collapsed in the face of the "Invisible Empire," and "the establishment of the South in its rightful place is the birth of a new nation."

According to *The Birth of a Nation*, the Civil War disrupted the unity of a once happy land, and the South restored this unity. In myth the war's meaning has been transformed. In a logic that almost defies comprehension, slavery and the abolitionists start the war, and the Klansmen rebel and reestablish the unity of the nation. Thus, a war that had been lost from a southern perspective has now been won. The South did not secede but restored the nation. Even though Griffith clearly sympathized with the South and the movie met with considerable protest, its version became the national point of view. How did this myth succeed?

The nation born from this myth was a white nation, and race is a central element in the maintenance of this myth (Cook 1981, 79). The movie itself was based on an openly racist novel and play entitled the *Clansman* by Thomas Dixon. In fact, *The Birth of a Nation* was originally released under that name, although Griffith adopted its present title almost immediately.

In the movie blacks are depicted either as happy slaves or as surly, undisciplined troopers, who yearn to marry (in this movie a euphemism for rape) white women. Of course, any white woman would rather die than submit to such a fate. Incapable of independent action, the blacks are always under the command of carpetbaggers and mulattoes. Gus and Silas Lynch who both pursue white women are mulattoes. Thus, blacks and mulattoes are the true villains of the piece. But as Martin Williams has remarked, "Griffith, like many American whites, still had not faced the meaning of the existence of mulattoes. Who fathered them? And who mothered them? And under what circumstances? Better to make them not just scapegoats, but villains" (Williams 1980, 75).

The whites form the Klan to counteract this black villainy and, appropriately enough, find their inspiration in the blacks' naïveté and superstition. The little colonel gets the idea for the Klan and its distinctive costume while watching some black children run away in fright from a playmate dressed like a ghost in a white sheet.

Yet the myth derives its credibility from more than just depicting blacks as villainous. Griffith ties this image into history and thus, as Wilson reportedly remarked, "wrote history with lightning." He interjects a series of what he calls "historical facsimiles" based on famous images, frequently Matthew Brady photographs. These historical facsimiles not only add verisimilitude to the film, but also blur the line between fiction (the story of Camerons and Stonemans) and its underlying myth. In the first, Lincoln calls out the first 75,000 volunteers for the war. For a film with a southern viewpoint, Lincoln is pictured very sympathetically. He calls up the volunteers reluctantly with a tear in his eye. Later in the movie when Ben Cameron, a prisoner in a Union hospital, is to be tried on unspecified but false charges, Elsie Stoneman arranges an interview for Mrs. Cameron with Lincoln who is referred to as the Great Father.

The second historical facsimile is Lee's surrender at Appomattox. This is actually a tableau and remains undeveloped because it conflicts with the movie's mythical theme that the South really won the war by giving birth to the nation.

The most elaborate historical facsimile is Lincoln's assassination at Ford's Theater. This facsimile is interwoven with the movie's plot because Phil and Elsie Stoneman attend the play. Griffith went to great expense to recreate the theater and even had his actors present a performance of the play playing that night. Upon hearing the news of Lincoln's death, the Cameron family gathers and asks what is to become of them now that Lincoln is dead, surely ironical in that he had only recently been prosecuting a war in which two of their sons were killed.

One final historical facsimile completes the mythical web. Griffith recreates a session of the all black South Carolina House of Representatives. Representatives dressed in ridiculous clothes are swilling whiskey, and the speaker rules that all members must wear shoes. The chamber is so painstakingly re-created that an unwary viewer would think that this facsimile—and by association the others— depicts actual history. As the sequence in the legislature concludes with the passing of a law allowing intermarriage, "an iris begins to slowly close upon a group of Negroes on the assembly floor who are leering at something above them; then the iris moves like the lens of a telescope to reveal the object of this lustful attention: a group of frightened white women and children in the gallery" (Cook 1981, 87).

The final linchpin in Griffith's mythological construction is the incorporation of the stories of the Camerons and Stonemans into the history of the country, "so that our history becomes, in effect, the collective record of private American families" (Wood 1983, 23). The stories of the two families are symmetrical and are interwoven with each other as well as with history. Both families are led by fathers. Dr. Cameron is an aristocratic Southern planter while Austin Stoneman is a radical reconstructionist. Dr. Cameron mourns the death of Lincoln, but Austin sets out to implement his radical program of racial equality, symbolized by intermarriage. The matriarchal figure of the Cameron family follows the normal female role of nurture and submissiveness. She pleads with Lincoln, our Great Father, for her son's life.

There is no mother on the Stoneman side, although the movie implies that Austin keeps a mulatto mistress, Lydia Brown, who is in league with Silas Lynch. The significance of these mulattoes in Griffith's schema is not hard to fathom. They are played by white actors in blackface, so that they can be readily identified as mulattoes; otherwise their status would not be obvious on the screen. For Griffith these mulattoes symbolize what happens when whites and blacks mix. The blacks corrupt the whites. Such mixing of the races brings out the worst instincts of the blacks, again symbolized by a desire for white women. Griffith never seems to realize that most mulattoes resulted from white men's desire for black women. Mythically, even though mulattoes are both black and white, they do not serve as mediators between the races because they point out that the only possible relation is separation and subordination of blacks to whites.

The children of the two families establish a series of relations. Eldest sons lead both families. Ben Cameron (Henry B. Walthall) is one of the movie's stars. His counterpoint Phil Stoneman plays a much smaller part in the film. The Camerons have two daughters, Margaret and young Flora, sometimes called "pet." Elsie Stoneman (Lillian Gish) is the film's star on the Stoneman side. Both families lose sons during the war. In the movie's early scenes when the Stoneman boys are visiting the Cameron plantation, Phil falls in love with Margaret and Ben with Elsie. Ben carries Elsie's picture through-out the war, symbolizing the power of pictures to unify North and South even in wartime. When he is wounded and captured at the battle of Petersburg, he ends up in a hospital where Elsie is a nurse, and when he is falsely accused, Elsie arranges for his mother to intercede with Lincoln. When Ben founds the Klan, Elsie withdraws out of loyalty to her father, but Silas Lynch's outrageous wooing soon sends her back to Ben. Phil is with the Camerons in the cabin when the black militia attacks, and he prepares to kill Margaret rather than let her fall into their hands. In the film's final triumphant scene when the Klansmen march through Piedmont with the nation reborn, Margaret and Elsie Stoneman head the column, thereby symbolizing the nation's unity. Just as the mulattoes represent the disunity introduced into the country with the Africans, so the white women, the object of black lust, represent the nation's unity. In the end, Griffith reduces the unity of the nation to the personal story of these two families. Good families make a good nation.

The phenomenal popularity of *Gone with the Wind* (1939), both as a book and as a film indicates the continuing viability of the Civil War as a mythical vehicle for our self-understanding as a nation. Even though the producer David Selznick was determined to avoid the racial problems of *The Birth of a Nation*, and Hattie McDaniel won an Academy Award for her performance as Mammy, the film persisted in maintaining the same mythical viewpoints as *The Birth of a Nation*. It employs a nostalgia for the past, blames the carpetbaggers for upsetting race relations, and in the end reduces national values to family values (O'Brien 1983). Both films point to an event that tore the national fabric apart and cast the blame outside themselves by vilifying the other and treating the traditional family values as the core of what is authentically American.

> My solution to the problem would be to tell them [the North Vietnamese] frankly that they've got to draw in their horns and stop their aggression, or we're going to bomb them back into the Stone Age.
> —*General Curtis LeMay (1965)*

THOUGH WORLD WAR I PLAYED HAVOC WITH EUrope, it barely dented the American mythical consciousness. In many ways it marked our entrance on the world stage, a role that came to fruition in World War II. The films of World War II supported the war effort with tales of heroism, bravery, and nobility. Perhaps *Bridge on the River Kwai* (1957) and *Catch-22* (1970) define the two poles of the World War II experience. The issue is war itself, not the national self-understanding. The Vietnam conflict, on the other hand, has much more in common with the Civil War because it divided the nation, almost producing an internal civil war. Furthermore, we lost the Vietnam War. Since myth does not like to lose, it attempts to hide the loss. Our films on Vietnam have attempted to find some way to win that war. Griffith and Margaret Mitchell set about reinforcing the southern myth of the Civil War's outcome, and now we are searching to overcome the Vietnam syndrome.

John Wayne starred in and directed one of the earliest Vietnam War movies, *The Green Berets* (1968). Though not one of his better efforts, the film did well at the box office. In 1968 the war was extremely controversial, and the nation was confused about the path it should take. The campuses had not yet exploded, but they were seething and the "incursion" into Cambodia in 1970 would set them afire, beginning at Kent State University. Hollywood stayed out of this debate, however. Aside from *The Green Berets*, movies did not deal directly with Vietnam until the late 1970s, although the conflict did form part of the background in such movies as *Easy Rider* (1969), *American Graffiti* (1973), and *One Flew over the Cuckoo's Nest* (1975).

The Green Berets is explicitly pro-war and evokes earlier American war films to develop a myth about this war. John Wayne plays Green Beret Colonel "Big" Mike Kirby, and David Janssen is a liberal newspaper reporter (Beckworth) whom Kirby invites to his command post in Vietnam to see what the war is really about. The journalist's conversion to the war effort is a major driving mythical force in the movie. The logic of the film is that Beckworth's conversion will demonstrate the bias of American newspapers and simultaneously draw a skeptical viewer to the movie's position. Thus, his conversion becomes the vehicle for convincing the viewer that the war is justified. The final exchange between Kirby and Beckworth sums up this aspect of the film. Kirby asks, "Whatya gonna say in that newspaper of yours?" To which Beckworth responds, "If I say what I feel, I may be out of a job." With dialogue like this the movie attempts to establish its credibility against the presumed liberal bias of the newspapers.

The soldiers under Kirby's command appear to incorporate every movie cliché from World War II. First, Kirby himself embodies the John Wayne myth. We have already dealt extensively with this. Kirby's outpost in Vietnam sports a ranch-style wooden signpost reading "Dodge City," an explicit reference to Western stories. Peterson (Jim

Hutton) is the goofy kid who scrounges for supplies; Muldoon (Aldo Ray) is the dependable sergeant straight out of all of John Wayne's old cavalry movies; Sergeant Provo (Luke Askew) is the all-American farm boy who is a great fighter; and Hamchunk (Craig Jue) is the war orphan adopted by the company. There is even a beautiful spy (Irene Tsu) who charms a Vietcong general so Kirby can lead a kidnapping raid. When her people reject her for consorting with the Vietcong, Kirby persuades her cousin, a South Vietnamese officer, to welcome her back. All the stereotypes of male military behavior are brought out in an effort to assure us that this war is just like the war in Europe. Americans are coming to the rescue of a fledgling democracy.

But *The Green Berets* is not interested in the Vietnamese. Its target is the home front. The Vietcong are almost literally demonized. They don't fight; they commit atrocities. Their bamboo traps bedevil the American soldiers causing slow and painful death. Numerous stories of Vietcong atrocities form the backdrop for Beckworth's continuing conversion. The turning point is a story about the little daughter of a Montagnard village headman. She was raped by five men while his wife was raped by forty. This Manichaean view of the war drives the viewer to Kirby's side. His position is the only possible one, and the conflict about the war at home is misguided, if not traitorous.

In the end *The Green Berets* views the Vietnam conflict as a mythical extension of World War II. The Vietcong and their Communist patrons are the new Nazis, and their demonic attack on the poor South Vietnamese demands our response. On an even deeper level, it reduces the war to a conflict between the cowboys (Dodge City) and Indians (the savage natives), another Manichaean view of the world.

A feeling is widely and strongly held . . . that "the Establishment" is out of its mind . . . that we are trying to impose some U.S. image on distant peoples we cannot understand, and that we are carrying the thing to absurd lengths. . . . [What loomed was] the worst split in our people in more than a century.
—*John McNaughton, aide to Robert McNamara (1966, quoted in Karnow, 506)*

A DECADE AFTER *THE GREEN BERETS*, MI-
chael Cimino's ambitious *The Deer Hunter* (1978) swept the Academy
Awards, winning best picture, director, and supporting actor (Chris-
topher Walken), with nominations for best actor (Robert De Niro),
best supporting actress (Meryl Streep), and best screen play (written
for the screen). The following year the long-awaited *Apocalypse Now*
(1979) garnered many nominations, but no awards.

The Deer Hunter revolves around the Vietnam War, but its subject
is not the war itself but rather the effects of the war on the main
characters' lives. Though many critics have complained that the movie
gives too few clues to how its various parts and symbols are inter-
related (Halliwell 1988, 46), on one level its structure is quite simple.
The movie traces the stories of three blue-collar buddies from a
Pennsylvania mill town through a simple chronology: before the war,
the war, and after the war. On another level, however, the film is
built around a series of interlocking scenes that cross-reference
each other:

> Wedding/Celebration
> Hunting/Killing
> Russian Roulette
> Hunting/No Killing
> Funeral/Breakfast

This general structure accommodates even more detailed cross-
referencing. For example, the hero Michael (De Niro) works at a
flaming foundry in a steel mill and wields a flamethrower in Vietnam.
Furthermore, the interlocking arrangement of the film is not at odds
with the chronological order but correlates with it, making it easier
for the viewer to follow the mythical structure.

As this outline suggests, the themes of the movie are survival,
violence, renewal, and reconciliation. Perhaps, at the risk of reduc-
tionism, its basic theme can be summarized as how to survive Vietnam, and its answer fits the American myth: the strong, independent,
loyal, rugged individual holds on to the basic American values.

The movie follows a group of men through their Vietnam experience. Though only three go to Vietnam, Michael, Nick (Walken), and
Steven (John Savage), the war affects all the men in the group. In a

sense the men represent us, just as their small mill town is a micro-cosm of the nation. The movie opens with Steven's wedding and the reception is both a celebration of the wedding and a farewell party for the three buddies who are about to enter the army. During the party they come across a Green Beret drinking silently at the bar. The trio tries to engage him in conversation and camaraderie about the war, but the Green Beret responds, "Fuck it," as a toast. This interchange ominously portends the war itself.

The Vietnam section of the movie deals only indirectly with the war. The image of a fan blade revolving in a bar is slowly transformed into the whop-whop-whop of a helicopter blade. The hell of war is evident immediately. Unlike *The Green Berets*, this movie does not glorify the Vietnam experience. But as in the tradition of *Birth of a Nation* and *The Green Berets*, the enemy is dehumanized. In the opening war scene, a Vietcong guerrilla tosses a hand grenade into a shelter filled with women and children.

Almost immediately and by coincidence, the three comrades end up in the same prison camp where they are kept in rat-infested bamboo cages partially submerged in a river. The guards only release the prisoners from the cages to play Russian roulette, while they bet on the outcome. In a brutal movie, this is one of the most brutal sequences. The viewer is thrust into the scene without any prepa-ration. The guards jabber incomprehensibly in Vietnamese and slap and beat the prisoners to force them to play. The metallic click of the gun when the chamber is empty and the explosion when it is not create a chilling effect. Nick's hysteria tops off a stunning perfor-mance. Michael, however, maintains his control and actually con-vinces the guards to add more bullets to the gun. When the first two chambers come up empty, he turns the gun on his captors, kills them, and then escapes with his two friends. When they finally are rescued from the river by a helicopter under fire, Steven falls back into the river. Michael, ever the hero, jumps back into the river, brings him to shore, and carries him through the jungle to safety.

But all three have been wounded by this passage through hell. Steven's legs were broken when he fell into the river and must be amputated. He returns home to a veteran's hospital where he avoids his wife and imprisons himself in bitter resentment at his fate. Nick's experience in the prison camp leads him to pathological withdrawal. He goes AWOL from a Saigon hospital and discovers a gambling den

where they bet on Russian roulette. He becomes one of the professional players, not a wagerer, but the one who plays roulette. Russian
roulette is a major metaphor in the movie. One shot ends it all, and
there is no way to know whether the chamber is empty. Roulette is
like the war itself—one can be in the wrong place at the right time.

A deer hunting scene occurs both before the Vietnam sequence
and after Michael's return home. Michael puts great emphasis on
killing the deer with one clean shot. The similarity to Russian roulette
is obvious. The serenity and purity of the mountain contrast starkly
with the bleakness of the mill town and the horror of Vietnam. As
the men ascend the snow-capped mountain, they climb out of the
mist into the clear, pure air. The music shifts appropriately—not quite
heavenly strings, but close. The sense of pure space is palpable. On
the mountain the men can commune with nature, and return to the
natural life of the hunter. Through the contest with the massive buck,
they revive the American frontier spirit. Michael, the deer hunter, is
another Natty Bumppo in James Fenimore Cooper's *The Deerslayer*.
Like Natty, he has pure moral insight, always sees what to do, and
does it.

In the first hunting sequence before Vietnam, Michael gets his deer,
but the second hunt, after Vietnam, is less successful. He has trouble
just getting the deer in his sights. No longer pure and whole after
Vietnam, he is unworthy to kill the deer. When he finally sights a
buck, in frustration and anxiety he shouts, "Okay! Okay!" and does
not pull the trigger.

Instead of killing, he sets out to make his wounded buddies whole.
In part, Michael's decision seems to be due to his recovery of his
pure moral insight, the symbol for which the film borrows from his
ethnic heritage. Like most of the people in the town, he is of Russian
descent and follows the Russian Orthodox religion. The archangel
Michael is the patron of Russia, and Michael fulfills the guardian
angel role for his friends. He goes back to Vietnam to find Nick who
is still playing Russian roulette and sending his winnings home to
Steven. Though Michael confronts him and even joins in the game,
he cannot get through to Nick who seems catatonic, without feeling
or emotion. Michael tries to persuade Nick to stop the game. When
Michael says, "I love you," a brief flicker of recognition flashes across
Nick's face as he pulls the trigger. Unfortunately, his luck had just
run out.

Michael brings Nick's body home for burial. He convinces the bitter Steven to leave the hospital for the funeral and be reconciled with his wife. In the final scene, the remaining members of the original group, all wounded in some way by the war, all healed in some way by Michael, gather for breakfast after the funeral and quietly sing "God Bless America." Thus, the movie affirms that after the chaos and contamination of Vietnam, the nation can restore itself by returning to the simple American virtues of family, patriotism, and individualism, the same virtues that Natty Bumppo embodied and the hunters discovered on the mountain. Like a boat floundering on the sea, the myth will right itself.

The similarity between the mythical solutions in *The Birth of a Nation* and *The Deer Hunter* are striking and the contrast with *The Green Berets* illuminating. John Wayne, usually so sure in his mythical grasp, missed in *The Green Berets* because he seized on the wrong myth. He thought Vietnam was World War II. In that war, the nation was unified and myth had only to glorify and ennoble the war. In Vietnam, like the Civil War, the nation was divided and myth must find a way to heal that breach. Even more, the entire nation, not just the South, lost the war. Like *Birth of a Nation*, *The Deer Hunter* constructs a fictional view of history. The war is telescoped into the capture of the three friends and the metaphor of Russian roulette. The artist's prerogative includes fictionalizing history, but when fiction distorts by appealing to racial prejudice, it becomes very problematic. It also provides a perfect hiding place from which myth can sally forth to resolve the conflict. Griffith appealed to the prejudice against African Americans just as Cimino appeals to our prejudice against Asians. In Griffith's case the appeal to prejudice unifies the North and the South (crusading whites against blacks), and in Cimino's film it unifies those wounded by the war (whites against Asians). Both directors also find the same unifying factors: the basic American virtues of family, patriotism, and individualism. Even though most people consider the Ku Klux Klan unpatriotic, Griffith portrays them as patriots restoring the nation. Both films are based on a myth of reconciliation, restoration, and rebirth. Both announce the trajectory along which myth works out a way to resolve a conflict that we lost: the strong individual with pure moral insight who is in touch with his roots can triumph.

You Can't Go Home Again.
—Thomas Wolfe (1940)

IN 1978 VIETNAM WAR MOVIES DOMINATED THE
nominations for Academy Awards. Hal Ashby's *Coming Home* won
awards for best actor (Jon Voight), best actress (Jane Fonda), and
best screenplay. The latter is somewhat baffling in that the script by
all accounts leaves much to be desired (Simon 1982, 351). The film
is set in the carefree atmosphere of balmy southern California, but
it addresses serious issues raised by the war in Vietnam. The time is
shortly after the Tet offensive (1968). There are no war scenes, because the film deals exclusively with the war's aftereffects. It follows
the lives of three people, Marine Captain Bob Hyde (Bruce Dern),
his wife Sally (Jane Fonda), and a paraplegic veteran, Luke Martin
(Jon Voight). Each character undergoes a transformation because of
the war, and Sally Hyde bridges the two male characters.

Bob is a career Marine, dedicated to the service. He refers to
Vietnam as Combat City and has been looking forward to serving
there. Not only will a tour in Vietnam give him a chance to make
major, but, as he says, it's like representing the United States in the
Olympic Games. His attitude is simple: "There's where I belong. I am
a Marine."

When he's sent to Hong Kong for rest and recreation, Sally flies
to be with him. But the reunion fails. Bob is upset that Sally has gone
to work in a veterans' hospital. He objects both to her working there
and to her working at all: "It's the pits. I just don't want you to work."
What really disturbs him, though, is the way the war has changed
the Marine Corps. When Sally asks what the war is like, he replies,
"I don't know what it's like. I only know what it is. TV shows what
it's like. They sure as hell do not know what it is." The captain's
disillusionment is total. "It used to mean something to be a Marine."
He complains that his men are chopping off the heads of Vietcong
and putting them on posts "because it scares the hell out of the VC."
His disgust and impotence are evident.

At the same time that Bob and Sally are moving in different directions, her life and Luke's are beginning to intertwine. Sally appears
at first to be a proper military wife, even a 1950s woman. When her
high school yearbook asked what she would take on a desert island,
her answer was "a husband."

After Bob ships out to Vietnam, Sally volunteers to work in the local base hospital where she meets Luke. The hospital itself is near bedlam, and the patients are treated almost inhumanely. On her first day Sally collides with Luke as he maneuvers about on an orderly's cart. To her humiliation, she upsets his urine bag. When he becomes enraged, the nurses sedate him to control him. The scene defines their characters: she is an uptight wife with carefully set hair, he is an embittered paraplegic. Both need liberation.

And gradually both find it. Sally goes to work, gets her own apartment and car, and lets her hair go natural. When Luke leaves the hospital, he gets a specially equipped car, an apartment, and most important a wheelchair. The wheelchair symbolizes his liberation just as Sally's naturally frizzy hair symbolizes hers. "You got a chair!" she exclaims. "You changed your hair!" he retorts. Inevitably, as the story progresses, they become emotionally and sexually involved.

Luke's liberation evolves into a protest against the war, sparked not so much by his own fate as by the suicide of a friend in the hospital. Wearing his old uniform, Luke chains himself to the front gate of a Marine Corps recruiting center. Gradually, he becomes increasingly involved in the anti-war movement.

All the interlocking threads begin to unwind when Bob comes home. Though wounded in the leg, his deeper and more serious wound is psychological, not physical like Luke's. Bob was wounded on the way to the latrine, when his gun went off accidentally, shooting him in the leg. To add insult to injury, in a gesture that symbolizes the bureaucracy and deceit of the war, the Marines propose to give him a medal as a hero. He protests but to no avail. To compound his problems, the FBI tells him about Luke and Sally's affair. In a tense confrontation, Luke begs Bob to give Sally a chance: "If you give her a chance, she can help you. She wants to listen to you and she wants to understand you." He goes further and blames all their fates on the war: "I'm not the enemy. Maybe the enemy is the fucking war. But you don't want to kill anybody here. You have enough ghosts to carry around." At one point the argument is disingenuous, but this speech is the film's vehicle for resolving its deeper conflicts. The war is to blame for what has gone wrong in their lives. To overcome the war, Bob must liberate himself, as Sally and Luke have. Bob replies, "I just wanna be a hero, that's all. I want to go out a hero. That way I did something that's mine." Bob's speech hints at a deeper issue, but the movie fails to pursue this mythical trail for that would lead to deeper questions about the American ideology that led to our involvement in the war. The male view of heroism is submerged deep in the mythical mist.

In the movie's closing sequence, the three characters go their separate ways. The unifying thread comes from a talk Luke is giving to a high school convocation. After a Marine recruiting officer speaks, Luke talks about the war: "You want to be a part of it and patriotic; get your licks in for the US of A. When you get over there, it's a totally different situation. You grow up really quick because all you're seeing is a lot of death." The camera cuts away to the captain walking to the beach in full dress blues, while Sally speeds along the highway to the shopping center. "I know some of you are going to look at that uniform and think of the glory of other wars and think of some vague patriotic feeling and go off and fight this turkey too." The captain begins to undress. "And I'm telling you, it ain't like in the movies. I wanted to be a hero and wanted to go out and kill for my country." Now the captain is running naked into the sea. "I have killed for my country or whatever and I don't feel good about it. For there's not enough reason, man. To feel a person die in your hands or see your buddy get blown away, I'm here to tell you, it's a lousy thing, man. There's no reason for it. And there's a lot of shit I did over there that I find fucking hard to live with. And I don't want to see people like you, man, coming back and having to face shit like that. It's as simple as that. I'm just telling you there's a choice to be made here." When Luke finishes, there's not a dry eye in the room—even the recruiter has been moved. In the final shot Sally enters a grocery store through the "OUT" door to buy steaks for her now-dead husband.

Coming Home is a much more ambivalent movie than *The Deer Hunter*. Both depict the war as evil and disturbing to the American moral compass. But *Coming Home* goes deeper and challenges aspects of the American hero myth. In *The Deer Hunter* contact with the enemy contaminates the nation, but in *Coming Home* our very involvement in the war and the need to be a hero have corrupted the very nobility of the Marines. Somewhat like the grandfather in *Witness*, Luke begins to see that there is a choice. But the movie does not present a thoroughgoing critique of the system, or even a countersystem as *Witness* did with the Amish. The rugged individual, though wounded, is still intact. The captain fails because he cannot be a hero; Luke succeeds because he discovers within himself the strength to stand against the war. Although one hopes it is not the movie's intention, the final shot of Sally entering through the OUT door at the grocery suggests that our involvement in Vietnam was likewise an absentminded mistake.

> My film is not about Vietnam. It's Vietnam; it's crazy.
> —*Francis Ford Coppola (1979)*

BY GENRE, *APOCALYPSE NOW* (1979) IS A WAR movie, but unlike the other films we have explored, it takes place completely in Vietnam and was one of the first films to launch an explicit attack on America's participation in the war. It eschews the war movie tradition of World War II, however. *The Green Berets* tried to follow that heroic genre and failed. The noble and heroic model, which has been applied to war at least since Homer celebrated the battle for Troy, does not work in Vietnam. Captain Hyde's walk into the sea ends that dream. The heroic genre falsifies the nation's experience in that war.

Instead, *Apocalypse Now* adopts the quest genre, which also implies a journey of self-discovery. The movie follows its protagonist Captain Willard (Martin Sheen) up a river in search of Colonel Kurtz (Marlon Brando) whom Willard has been assigned to assassinate. Throughout the journey Willard reads an extensive dossier on Kurtz and speculates about the meaning of his life. In many ways that life mirrors what has gone wrong with America in Vietnam.

Initially, Willard thinks he has the wrong dossier because Kurtz is the all-American soldier. A third-generation officer, he graduated at the top of his class at West Point. He was being groomed for one of the top spots in the "corporation," as Willard calls the army, maybe even Chief of Staff. In 1964 Kurtz did a tour in Vietnam, in the advisory command, but his report to the Joint Chiefs of Staff and President Lyndon Johnson caused such consternation it was restricted. Then, at the age of the thirty-eight, he entered airborne training and after that the Special Forces. As Willard notes, things had begun to slip.

Now Kurtz has formed his own army of Montagnard villagers and is fighting out of Cambodia.

Willard receives his assignment in a scene that echoes the archetype of the knight sent out on an quest, although with a chillingly modern and bureaucratic cast. The participants sit around a round table, sharing nicely prepared cold cuts, while the other soldiers in Vietnam are eating K-rations. The general's aide reviews Kurtz's current status, culminating with the crime with which the army is charging him. He murdered several men he determined were Vietcong informers.

A nameless general offers his explanation of what went wrong with Kurtz. Since he refers to Kurtz as "Walt," he obviously knows him well. "Well, you see, Willard, in this war things get confused. Out there . . . there with these natives, it must be a temptation to be god because there is a conflict in every human heart between the rational and irrational, between good and evil, and good does not always triumph." Unlike many other movies, as a rule, this film does not demonize the opponent. But the general's speech harkens back to a strong mythical element in the American story. The natives are inferior to us, so naturally the strong American, being natively so superior, might be tempted to play God. The general continues, "Sometimes the dark side overcomes what Lincoln called the better angels of our nature. Every man has a breaking point. You and I hav'em. Walt Kurtz has reached his and very obviously he has gone insane." The solution to this insanity, an insanity produced by the extremes of "out there," is not treatment but extermination. When aide tells Willard he must terminate Kurtz, a third man, who has been silent to this point, adds "with extreme prejudice." He is dressed in civilian clothes and is obviously CIA. He then offers Willard a cigarette in a gesture of sharing that reminds one of Judas at the last supper. The bureaucratic language that drains the blood out of war demonstrates the corporation-like character of this war. At the meal's end, the general reminds Willard that "the mission does not exist nor will it ever exist." Even the army now operates outside the boundaries, and there is to be no official memory of the war's insanity.

Kurtz's counterpart in the film is Lieutenant Colonel Kilgore, played by Robert Duvall in a stunning characterization. His dossier probably resembles Kurtz's, but he has stayed within the bounds of practical military necessity, as the general termed it. Kilgore strides, even struts, through the battle scene, never flinching or ducking during the shelling. With a pistol on his hip, a yellow scarf around his neck like the cavalry officers of old, and a black twenty gallon hat, he goes under the code name Big Duke. The references to John Wayne are clear and persistent.

Kilgore is a throwback to World War II and officers in the mode of Patton. He loves his men and after a raid holds a barbecue with them on the beach. He tries to make Vietnam like home, although as Willard ironically notes, the more he tries, the more they miss it. As he strides through the enemy dead, he leaves playing cards inscribed with the unit's insignia to let the Vietcong know who did this. Another time, when he comes upon a South Vietnamese soldier torturing a Vietcong who is holding his guts in with a pot, Kilgore drives him off and offers the prisoner a drink saying, "Any man with the courage to fight me can drink from my canteen." In the middle of this act of compassion, however, Kilgore learns that Willard's navy escort includes a famous California surfer. He drops the canteen in midsentence and begins talking about surfing, his real passion. The unavoidable conclusion is that this Duke/Patton officer is crazy.

One of the famous and technically most stunning scenes in the movie is Kilgore's assault on a Vietcong village. The helicopters take off at dawn while a bugle sounds the charge again, as in cavalry forces of old. They stream across the sky like giant grasshoppers, with powerful speakers blaring out Wagner's "Ride of the Valkyries." Kilgore explains, "The music scares the hell out of the slopes." Wagner's music with its overtones of Hitler paints Kilgore as a fascist. This piece also figured prominently in the rally of the Klan in *Birth of a Nation*.

The camera pans the Vietcong village, a quiet, peaceful place, populated by well-dressed, orderly schoolchildren. At the sound of the music and helicopters, they run for the trenches, and the fire fight begins. During the evacuation of a wounded GI, a girl lobs a hand grenade into the helicopter and blows it up. Kilgore attacks her from the air, calling her a savage. In the middle of the fight, while the Vietcong are still shelling, Kilgore sends surfers out to ride the waves.

The battle ends with Kilgore calling in a napalm strike that produces an almost apocalyptic explosion along the tree line. Kilgore remarks to a dazed Willard, "I love the smell of napalm in the morning. It smells like [long pause as he searches for the right word] victory.

Some day this war is going to end," he concludes with evident disappointment.

As Willard continues up river in search of Kurtz, he sums up his impression of Kilgore: "If that's the way Kilgore fought the war, I began to wonder what they really had against Kurtz. It wasn't just insanity and murder. There was enough of that to go around for every one." As Willard says at another point, "Charging a man with murder in this place is like handing out speeding tickets at the Indy 500."

Colonel Kurtz is the object of Willard's quest, the prize at the end of the river. But is Kurtz a hero or villain? Is he the only rational American in Vietnam or is he crazy like everyone else? And what will Willard do—join Kurtz or kill him? Another officer sent up the river earlier to terminate Kurtz joined forces with him instead. Certainly, as Willard works through Kurtz's dossier, his admiration for him grows. As Willard says, "He really set his hooks in me."

When we finally meet Kurtz, the ambiguity persists. When Willard arrives at Kurtz's camp, he is met by a photojournalist (Dennis Hopper), festooned with cameras and speaking the argot of a leftover hippie. He insists that Kurtz is a warrior-poet and a genius. Indeed, Kurtz quotes from T. S. Eliot's "The Hollow Men" and keeps Jessie L. Weston's *From Ritual to Romance* and Sir James Frazer's *The Golden Bough* by his bed. Chiaroscuro lighting and a shaved head give him the look of a giant mystic Buddha. A typewriter and stack of papers suggest that he is working on a manuscript. The journalist explains that the Montagnards regard Kurtz as a god, and he calls them his children.

Yet bodies hang from the trees on the outskirts of Kurtz's hideout. The compound itself is littered with bodies and decapitated heads. Upon seeing all this death, Willard remarks that Kurtz surely is crazy. After a short time at the camp, a member of Willard's crew attempts to send a coded radio message. In the very next scene, a camouflaged Kurtz tosses his head onto Willard's lap.

When Kurtz asks Willard if his methods are unsound, Willard responds, "I don't see any method at all, sir." Kurtz then tries to justify himself by telling his story, which begins with an incident in which the Vietcong hacked off the arms of children whom his Special Forces troops had inoculated against polio. In a movie that resists the tendency to demonize the enemy except at key moments, it is significant that Kurtz uses this story to justify what he has done. Furthermore, just as there is no evidence of the Vietcong playing Russian roulette with their prisoners as in *The Deer Hunter*, there is no evidence that such an atrocity ever occurred (Adair 1981, 165).

"I cried, I wept like some grandmother. Then I realized like I was shot with a diamond bullet right through my forehead. Then I thought, my God, the genius, the will to do that. The perfect genius complete, crystal, pure." This insight washes away moral ambiguity for Kurtz. How far Natty Bumppo has come! In American mythology the frontier, the wild place, has always been susceptible to a double meaning, one positive, the other negative. On the one hand, the wild place is dangerous and full of savages; on the other hand, it is the place of pure moral insight. Now this wild place has corrupted the pure moral insight, or more insidiously, corruption is masquerading as pure moral insight. "Then I realized that they were stronger than we because these were not monsters but trained cadres. These men fought with their hearts, they had families and children, and fought with love. They had the strength to do that." Though this sounds like a tribute to the enemy, Kurtz is actually arguing subtly and implicitly that this war, these people, have corrupted our pure moral insight. "If I had ten divisions like them, then our troubles would be over quickly. You have to have men who are moral, and at the same time who are able to utilize their primordial instincts to kill without feeling, without passion, without judgment. Without judgment, because it's judgment that defeats us." This almost Nietzschean superman, this Promethean stand against conventional morality, is truly mad, and Kurtz apparently senses that because he ends his speech with a reference to his son: "I worry that my son might not understand. If I was to be killed, Willard, I would want someone to go to my son and tell him. If you understand me, Willard, you will do this for me." This final sentence implies that Kurtz knows he's beyond the pale and that Willard will kill him.

The film never makes clear whether Kurtz is the antagonist or Coppola's vehicle for his own viewpoint. Both this ambiguity and what many considered to be a very poor performance by Brando as Kurtz received much criticism. But both of these complaints may be unfair. For over two hours we await Kurtz's appearance. The suspense is perhaps too much for either actor or screenwriter to sustain and so is a fault in the film's design. Yet Brando's performance wears well. Since for Coppola the war ultimately *is* mad, the very ambiguity of

Kurtz's characterization leaves the viewer without a resolution, with no way out, no way to mythically win the war except to blame "them," whoever "they" may be.

The actual killing—the termination—is almost anticlimactic. Dressed like a native, Willard hacks Kurtz to death with a machete as the natives sacrifice a bull by hacking it to death. By putting Willard in native dress and intercutting the sacrifice of the bull with Kurtz's murder, the movie suggests that the real fault lies in Vietnam and our involvement there, not in ourselves. As he dies, Kurtz slowly intones, "The horror, the horror," the movie's last words.

The title of *Apocalypse Now* conjures up the final cataclysmic battle between the forces of good and evil that brings about the end of the world, the ultimate, final conflict, or, as Sadam Hussein might say, the mother of all battles. *Apocalypse Now* offers plenty of evidence that this meaning is intended. Its scale and length are grandiose—no miniatures or models were used, no process screens for the air battles, and no tank work for the river scenes. No expense was spared. The film took so long to shoot that it became known as Apocalypse Later. But more than the production style signals this apocalyptic gesture. The movie begins with Jim Morrison singing "This Is the End." Painted on the dock of the temple at the river's end are the words, "apocalypse now." Yet the movie does not conclude with an apocalyptic destruction. Rather, faithful to Colonel Kurtz's quotation from Eliot's "The Hollow Men" ("This is the Way the World Ends, Not with a Bang but a Whimper"), Willard, the narrator, slips quietly downriver in the night.

The real apocalypse in this film is not the final battle between good and evil but the insanity of the war. The metaphor of insanity pervades the film. Kurtz must be eliminated because he has gone mad, and Willard's eyes constantly reveal his disbelief and amazement, even though he is a trained assassin who has killed men whose last breath he could feel on his face. He makes a poor knight because he himself is not innocent. The movie's opening scenes, which introduce Willard, cast him in the mode of a hardboiled Raymond Chandler detective and suggest that he too may be mad. When two soldiers come to escort him to his meeting with the general, he asks, almost like Kafka's character K in *The Trial*, what are the charges. The film's combination of the real and the surreal reinforces this sense of madness. For example, many regard Kilgore's helicopter attack on the

Vietcong village as one of the most realistic battle scenes ever filmed, yet the sound track during the initial formation of the helicopters gives the scene the appearance of something out of science fiction. This interweaving of real and surreal is so constant throughout the movie that the disbelief in Willard's eyes becomes the film's presiding image. Adding to the surreal effect are several references to the Disneyland-like quality of Vietnam.

Because no character mediates between Kilgore and Kurtz, and Willard himself is implicated in the war's madness and horror, no pure moral insight emerges from the film, and myth fails to work its amnesic magic. And yet there is still "them," the natives, to blame.

> By God, we have kicked the Vietnam syndrome once and for all.
>
> —*George Bush (1991)*

BECAUSE THE VIETNAM CONFLICT SO DEEPLY seared the American soul, myth has sought in George Bush's words to kick "the Vietnam syndrome once and for all." This battle has been fought on both the right and the left, and since *Coming Home* and *The Deer Hunter* inaugurated the solution, we need not tarry long, but only observe the elaborations and developments.

In a series of movies that parallel his highly successful Rocky series, Sylvester Stallone has followed the character John Rambo, a Special Forces Vietnam vet. In the first movie, *First Blood* (1982), Rambo is a loner and drifter, a veteran destroyed by the war. When he arrives in a no-name western town, the sheriff tries to run him off as a hippie. This provokes a kind of Vietnam conflict in the town. The sheriff and his deputies are the U.S. forces in Vietnam, and Rambo is the Vietcong who wages a guerrilla war on them. Now the war has come home. *First Blood* feeds upon the unresolved rage left over from our involvement in Vietnam. It plays upon the plight and at times rejection of the veterans, our rage at having lost, and the dis-solution of American society that resulted from the war. Much like Kurtz in *Apocalypse Now*, Rambo goes native and the army takes responsibility. As the colonel who trained him says, "God didn't make

Rambo, I did." Like *Rocky*, this movie has a confusing but truthful ending. Rambo is defeated and sent to prison, although not before wreaking vengeance on the town. As the series progressed, the ambiguity disappeared and myth won out. In *Rambo First Blood, Part Two* (1985) Rambo leads a successful raid to rescue prisoners of war in Vietnam. Again the government is to blame, but the rugged individual triumphs. In the final movie of the series, *Rambo III* (1988), he leads an attack on the Soviets in Afghanistan and, as in the final Rocky movie, gets to defeat the real enemy, the Soviets. As silly as these movies may appear in comparison with a serious film like *Apocalypse Now*, they did and do meet the real anger that many Americans feel about the war and they provide a way of dealing with and resolving, at least in film and myth, the agony of that conflict.

Oliver Stone has made two powerful and acclaimed films that address the Vietnam conflict from what might be called the liberal position. In *Born on the Fourth of July* (1989), he follows the true story of Ron Kovic (played by Tom Cruise), a true believer, who is wounded in Vietnam. Like Luke Martin in *Coming Home*, he has to endure the inhumanity and neglect of the veterans' hospital. Eventually, he becomes an anti-war activist in a wheelchair. Though the war is evil and the nation has changed because of it, the individual triumphs by persistence and integrity.

In *Platoon* (1986) two sergeants contend for the soul of Private Chris Taylor (Charlie Sheen). Taylor is not exactly a true believer in the war, but he has dropped out of college where he wasn't learning anything and volunteered for Vietnam because he thought others besides the poor should fight. Stone's movie celebrates the grunts. As Chris writes to his grandmother, "They come from small towns you never hear of . . . two years of high school is about it; maybe if they're lucky a job waits for them back in a factory. But most of them got nothing. The bottom of the barrel and yet they're fighting for their country. Maybe that's why they call themselves grunts, because grunts can take it." Unlike most Vietnam movies, this one is not about the officers, who are barely in evidence and do not come off well. Blacks and whites populate these battle scenes, and racial tension at times bubbles to the surface. Since Vietnam was disproportionately a black experience, it is good to see a movie that acknowledges their presence in more than a perfunctory way.

But the real conflict pits Sergeant Barnes (Tom Berenger) against Sergeant Elias (Willem Dafoe). The two sergeants are allegorical stand-ins for evil (Barnes) and good (Elias). Elias's biblical reference to the prophetic forerunner only accents these allegorical overtones. Taylor's allegiance alternates between these two figures. Both are excellent soldiers, and Barnes has a reputation for protecting his men and getting his people out. Elias is, in Barnes's terms "a water walker," or do-gooder.

As we have so often seen, the plot turns on an atrocity by the Vietcong. A black American is captured, garroted, and left on the trail for the squad to find. Barnes then leads a Mai Lai-type raid on a village, and Elias threatens to expose him. During a fire fight in the jungle, Barnes shoots Elias and leaves him for dead. As the helicopters are lifting off and the Vietcong are charging, the wounded Elias comes running out of the jungle. He is finally shot down in front of a church with his hands extended in a Christ-like gesture. Chris gives Barnes a knowing look since Barnes had told him that Elias was dead. Now Chris becomes concerned that Barnes will kill him. In the film's final climactic nighttime fire fight, Barnes almost kills him but is hit by an American bomb. In the morning Chris finds Barnes wounded, calling for a medic. Barnes challenges Chris to kill him and Chris shoots him.

As a helicopter evacuates Chris, who has been wounded and is now on his way home, he looks down on the scorched landscape and reminisces. Although the soliloquy occurs during Chris's evacuation, its point of view is much later: "I think now looking back we did not fight the enemy but fought ourselves and the enemy was in us." The enemy becomes irrelevant. The war becomes almost gnostic and Manichaean, a contest between the forces of light and darkness within ourselves. "The war is over for me now, but will always be there for the rest of my days as I'm sure Elias will be fighting with Barnes for possession of my soul. . . . There are times since then when I feel like a child born of those two fathers." Barnes and Elias, like yin and yang, eternally vie for the American soul absolving Chris or us of any responsibility for what happened. Underscoring this is Chris's total lack of reflection on his own action or possible guilt for killing Barnes. That act only represents Chris's resolution of the conflict over who will possess his soul. "But be that as it may, those of us who did make it, have an obligation to build again, to teach to

others what we know, and to try with what's left of our lives to find
a goodness and meaning to this life." What Chris has learned is not
at all evident, except that we were fighting ourselves. But in the end,
it doesn't matter, because the American eschatology has triumphed.
On the frontier, in the jungle, one sometimes has to take morality
into one's own hands. In the jungle Chris has seen the pure moral
insight and has gained control of his own soul. He is now the rugged
individualist reborn, getting on with the present and future, rebuilding
America.

> You know, you know what my philosophy of life is?
> That it's important to have some laughs, no question
> about it, but you got to suffer a little, too. Because
> otherwise, you miss the whole point of life. And that's
> how I feel. . . . My Uncle Sidney, a man, you know,
> hmm, lovely uncle—dead, completely—used to say
> three things. Used to say, "Acceptance, forgiveness,
> and love. . . . And that is a philosophy of life."
> —*Woody Allen,* Broadway Danny Rose

IN A CHAPTER ON WAR, PERHAPS THE MOST
appropriate biblical companion for a conversation would be the holy
war theme or perhaps Jesus' view of war. Was he, for example, a
pacifist? But I propose to examine Matthew's understanding of the
kingdom of God because it exposes what I think is the fundamental,
underlying issue in the American mythology of war, the preservation
of our sense of innocence. The parallel with our Vietnam experience
allows us to see Matthew in an unaccustomed context. Even though
the Vietnam War has corrupted us, as the movies have made clear,
we are still in search of a way to get back to that pristine innocence
of the frontier.

When we hear the phrase "kingdom of heaven" (or God), we
conjure up an image of a spiritual reality, a kingdom not of this world,
as the Johannine Jesus tells Pilate (John 18:36). Martin Luther's notion
of the two kingdoms reinforces this spiritualist understanding of the
kingdom of God and leads to a dualism in our political and spiritual
existence. Nevertheless, we maintain a militarist understanding of

the kingdom, as evidenced in hymns like "A Mighty Fortress Is Our God" and "Onward Christian Soldiers."

When the Gospel of Matthew was composed, such a fine distinction was not available. The Greek word *basileia* (kingdom) was widely used for the Roman Empire. To speak of the kingdom (*basileia*) of God implicitly challenged the empire (*basileia*) of Caesar. This is precisely why Pilate became involved in Jesus' death. Speaking of it as the kingdom of heaven instead of God makes no difference since "heaven" is only a circumlocution for "God." "Empire" or "imperial rule" is a better translation of *basileia* than kingdom, which for us has been disembodied and lost its political and earthly aspect. The Matthean version of the Lord's Prayer makes the interconnection between heaven (sky) and earth evident:

> Our Father in the heavens,
> your name be revered.
> Impose your imperial rule,
> enact your will on earth as you have in heaven.
> Provide us with the bread we need for the day.
> Forgive us our debts
> to the extent that we have forgiven those in debt to us.
> And please don't subject us to test after test,
> but rescue us from the evil one. (SV)

We have often overlooked the prayer's first-century, Mediterranean overtones. "Impose your imperial rule" may sound strange to ears long accustomed to "thy kingdom come," but it nicely catches the apocalyptic overtone and threat inherent in that phrase. One begins to see why Pilate might be concerned. The very next phrase concerning the enactment of God's will on earth as in heaven indicates that the sphere of God's imperial rule includes earth as well as heaven. Finally, the concern with debts reminds us that in the first-century world where patronage dominated social and political organization, patrons burdened clients with personal indebtedness for all sorts of things, not just or even mostly money (Crossan 1991, chap. 3; Moxnes 1991). One was always having to exchange favors. As in the year of Jubilee when all debts are canceled, the prayer calls on the ultimate patron, God, to set up a cycle of forgiveness that will make the earth a place of Jubilee.

In chapter 13 of Matthew's Gospel, Jesus uses a series of parables to instruct both the disciples and by implication the reader in the "secrets of Heaven's imperial rule" (Matt. 13:11 SV). Jesus provides interpretations for some parables but leaves others uninterpreted. Thus, the reader/interpreter must extrapolate from the interpreted parables to the uninterpreted ones in order to meet the challenge issued at this sermon's conclusion when Jesus asks whether the disciples have understood everything. They reply yes, and he responds with the aphorism, "Therefore every scribe who has been trained for the kingdom of heaven is like the master of a household who brings out of his treasure what is new and what is old" (13:58). The old things are the interpretations by Jesus, and the new things are the interpretations supplied by the disciple/reader.

The first parable of the Sower indicates that "When anyone hears the word that tells of the Kingdom" they will be judged by how they bear fruit (13:23). The pivotal parable of the whole sermon is the Wheat and Tares with its interpretation. An enemy sows darnel, a type of weed that looks like wheat, in a man's field. When his field hands ask whether they should root out the darnel, the master warns them to wait until harvest. This response is astounding because, as Douglas Oakman has shown, the weeding process began "at the earliest possible time in the growing season" (Oakman 1986, 117), and once harvested together, wheat and darnel are almost indistinguishable. Even more, in Judaism and unlike modern America, the mixing of wheat and darnel not only implies poor farming practices, but violates established purity codes. It makes the field impure and unclean.

In the interpretation of the parable, which Matthew presents in Jesus' voice, Jesus explains that the field equals the world. As one could intuit from the interpretation of the first parable, the Sower, the good seeds are the children of the heavenly empire, and the weeds are the children of the evil one. The sphere of operation for the children of the kingdom is the world. The parable does not describe the community or church, as is sometimes maintained. The children of the kingdom and the children of the evil one live together in the world and, in fact, are difficult to distinguish. Only at the end will the angels "gather out of his kingdom" (13:41 REB) all evildoers. The logic of the explanation and the mythological pattern explicitly invoke certain images and hide or avoid others. The world as the sphere of activity is a place of the unclean and impure. The angels gather the evildoers *out of* the kingdom; therefore the world is *now* the kingdom!

Matthew does not employ the myth of the righteous ascending to heaven. The wicked are removed from the field/world/kingdom: "Then the righteous will shine like the sun in the kingdom of their Father" (13:43). "What has been hidden from the foundation of the world" (13:35) the parables proclaim, namely, the secret that the world is God's empire or, in the terms of the Genesis story, that creation is good. There is no need for a dualist escape to heaven.

The four uninterpreted parables of the sermon are all descriptions of activity in the field/world/kingdom. The first, the Mustard Plant (13:31-32), again describes the kingdom as a mixed place, for mustard like darnel is a weed that mixes with other plants in a field. Or, as Oakman has remarked, "It is hard to escape the conclusion that Jesus deliberately likens the rule of God to a weed" (Oakman 1986, 127). One should add that Matthew emphasizes that point both in his interpretation of the Wheat and Tares and in his arrangement of the parables so that those of the Mustard Plant and Leaven come before the interpretation of the weeds and those of the Treasure and Merchant come immediately afterward. These parables make a point similar to that of the Mustard Plant. Leaven (13:33) is a sign of moral corruption in the ancient world (Scott 1989, 324-25), as Jesus' warning against the Pharisees (Mark 8:15; Matt. 16:12) and Paul's use of the aphorism about the corrupting power of a little bit of leaven remind us (Gal. 5:9; 1 Cor. 5:7). In a religious environment where unleavened bread functions as a sign of the holy, overtones of moral corruption jump out. The treasure (13:44), as Crossan has shown, corrupts the man who finds it (Crossan 1979). He is not rewarded for virtue, but forfeits his virtue by reburying the treasure (see chap. 6 above). And unlike our capitalist society, which values the merchant's entrepreneurial activities in seeking out the pearl (13:45-46), the ancient world always suspected such activity because it reeks of greed.

Though each of these four parables has its dark or unclean side, each also has a valuable side. Mustard was a valuable spice, and leavened bread was indeed the staff of life, the primary vehicle for protein in the ancient world. The value of the treasure and pearl are obvious. These parables present, as images of the kingdom, an intermingling of clean and unclean, pure and impure, valuable and corrupting. Like the wheat and the darnel, in the kingdom one cannot always so easily distinguish the two.

Using the other interpreted parables as a key, the scribe trained for the kingdom can see that in Matthew "The parables do not confine pollution in the world and value in the kingdom. Rather, they envision the kingdom as both polluted and valuable" (Dean 1993, 70). Matthew does not depict the kingdom as a place of innocence to which the righteous can retire. Rather the empire of heaven is both valuable and polluted, simultaneously clean and unclean. While apparently presenting an empire of moral chaos, Matthew's Jesus described it as a kingdom of higher righteousness (5:20). Such mixedness and confusion force one to the limits, to the very borders of imposed order. In loving one's enemy, one is challenged to go to the very limits, the ends (*teleios*, frequently translated *perfect*), just as the heavenly father goes to the limit (5:48). While threatening chaos, it also lays the groundwork for creativeness and generativity. It allows one to move on. The antitheses of the Sermon on the Mount, by mocking the fine order of case law, throw the hearer into creative responsibility (Tannehill 1975, 67–77). Case law defines, for example, the when and wherefore of adultery, showing one precisely where the moral boundaries are. The "but I tell you" overturns these boundaries and makes moral responsibility more precarious, as Jimmy Carter found out in the famous *Playboy* interview where he said he had lusted in his heart.

The final sermon where Jesus describes the last judgment drives home the kingdom's mixed nature. The inevitability of a final judgment is evident in both the interpretation of the parable of the Wheat and Tares and in the parable of the Net (13:47-50). A final reckoning is a major theme in Matthew, and his gospel is the only one to narrate such an event. The judge separates the nations as a shepherd separates sheep and goats. If one has followed Matthew's argument, this analogy is somewhat strange in that the difference between sheep and goats is obvious. Besides they make a poor image of good and bad because both are valuable to the shepherd. To those on his right, he says, "Come, you who have the blessing of my Father, inherit the domain prepared for you from the foundation of the world" (25:34 SV). The reference to the "foundation of the world" echoes back to the parables of chapter 13. The kingdom has remained hidden since the beginning. "You may remember, I was hungry and you gave me something to eat; I was thirsty and you gave me something to drink; I was a foreigner and you showed me hospitality; I was naked and you clothed me; I was ill and you visited me; I was in prison and you came to see me" (25:35-36 SV). The righteous protest, when did they see Jesus? "I swear to you, whatever you did for the most inconspicuous members of my family, you did for me as well" (25:40 SV). Jesus here identifies himself and his kingdom with the marginalized and inconspicuous, who are also usually the unclean and impure. The kingdom demands not innocence but solidarity with the least; it demands the risk of pollution, not protection from or containment of pollution.

In Vietnam our nation lost its innocence. We ran out of frontier into which to expand or, one might say, the westward expansion got lost in the east. In the mythical West we have sought with Natty Bumppo our pure moral insight—we were on the side of right. Mythically, the movies about Vietnam have been trying to put that syndrome behind us. Some have done so by harking back to the celebration of war as an ennobling event. Yet that does not fit our national experience in Vietnam. Others have tried to find some way to win the war, as in the Rambo series, while still others have sought the noble individual who triumphs through insight into the situation. That pattern has been by far the most prominent. Matthew's understanding of the kingdom dispenses with the dualistic myth of innocence and evil. The field has both wheat and weeds in it, and they are not easy to distinguish. The kingdom is not Barnes and Elias fighting for possession of our souls; it is Barnes and Elias and Chris. Kurtz found what he thought was the pure moral insight, the diamond bullet, and like the man who found a treasure and sold all to buy that field, he was seduced by the treasure. Like those on the right of the shepherd, we will not know the answer until the end. Until then we are to labor in the field, the world, taking care of the least and knowing that from the foundation of the world, God's empire has been mixed—like our experience in Vietnam.

WORKS NOTED

ADAIR, Gilbert. 1981.
Vietnam on film: From The Green Berets to Apocalypse Now. New York: Proteus.

CLOUD, Stanley W. 1991.
Exorcising an old demon. Time. Vol. 137, no. 10:52.

COOK, David A. 1981.
A history of narrative film. New York: W. W. Norton.

CROSSAN, John Dominic. 1979.
Finding is the first act. Semeia Supplements. Philadelphia: Fortress Press.

———. 1991.
The historical Jesus: The life of a Mediterranean Jewish peasant. San Francisco: HarperSanFrancisco.

DEAN, Margaret. 1993.
Reading Matthew's treasure map: Territoriality in Matthew's five sermons. M.Div. Thesis, Phillips Graduate Seminary.

GRIFFITH, D. W. 1993.
The father of film. Public Broadcasting System.

HALLIWELL, Leslie. 1988.
Halliwell's film guide. 6th ed. London: Paladin Grafton Books.

HOMER. 1938.
Iliad. Translated by W. H. D. Rouse. New York: Mentor Books.

KARNOW, Stanley. 1983.
Vietnam: A history. New York: Viking Press.

LeMAY, Curtis E., with MacKinlay Kantor. 1965.
Mission with LeMay: My story. Garden City, N.Y.: Doubleday.

MOXNES, Halvor. 1991.
Patron-client relations and the new community in Luke-Acts. In The Social World of Luke-Acts: Models for interpretation, 241–68. Edited by Jerome H. Neyrey. Peabody, Mass.: Hendrickson.

O'BRIEN, Kenneth. 1983.
Race, romance, and the southern literary tradition. In Recasting: Gone with the Wind in American culture, 153–66. Edited by Darden Asbury Pyron. Miami: University Presses of Florida.

OAKMAN, Douglas E. 1986.
Jesus and the economic questions of his day. Studies in the Bible and Early Christianity 8. Lewiston, N.Y.: Edwin Mellen.

SCOTT, Bernard Brandon. 1989.
Hear then the parable: A commentary on the parables of Jesus. Minneapolis: Fortress Press.

SIMON, John. 1982.
   Reverse angle. New York: Clarkson N. Potter.

TANNEHILL, Robert C. 1975.
   The sword of his mouth. Semeia Supplements. Philadelphia: Fortress
   Press; Missoula: Scholars Press.

WILLIAMS, Martin. 1980.
   Griffith: First artist of the movies. New York: Oxford University Press.

WOLFE, Thomas. 1940.
   You can't go home again. New York; London: Harper & Brothers.

WOOD, Gerald. 1983.
   From *The Clansman* and *Birth of a Nation* to *Gone with the Wind:* The
   loss of American innocence. In *Recasting:* Gone with the Wind *in American culture*, 123–26. Edited by Darden Asbury Pyron. Miami: University
   Presses of Florida.

Robotlike laborers at work in Fritz Lang's *Metropolis* (1926). (Photo courtesy of Archive Photos)

8

FROM THE DESTRUCTION OF THE TEMPLE TO *MAD MAX*

What we call the beginning is often the end. And to make an end is to make a beginning. The end is where we start from.

—*T. S. Eliot, "Little Gidding" (1943)*

PERHAPS FROM THE BEGINNING THE END HAS fascinated humankind. Any idea with such a long pedigree should not be too easily dismissed. Furthermore, a conversation between the New Testament and movies can hardly avoid the topic because apocalyptic speculation had currency in early Christianity and, despite its problems, still has currency today. When we think of ancient apocalyptic, we imagine Jesus' prophecy of nation rising up against nation and the sun being darkened, the Lord wreaking vengeance, and the myriad and odd speculations of the Book of Revelation. The modern has its own strong images: the fire and brimstone preacher shouting "the end is near," nuclear holocaust, and the publishing success of Hal Lindsey's *The Late Great Planet Earth*. Some of us tend to distrust apocalypticism because we associate it with the fantastic and the absurd. Certainly, the easiest reason to dismiss apocalyptic speculation is its abysmal track record. All predictions of the end of the world have so far proven wrong!

Yet the failures of apocalyptic speculation have not dampened the enthusiasm of its supporters. The flurry of speculation during the Gulf War with Iraq testifies to its endurance. According to *Newsweek*, over one million copies of John Walwood's *Armageddon, Oil and the*

Middle East Crisis were sold during January and February 1991 (Woodward 1992). An idea that has so fascinated humanity should not be underestimated.

Thus, apocalyptic makes a fine basis for a conversation, but before we begin, we need some notion of what we are dealing with, and defining apocalypticism is notoriously difficult. Justice Potter Stewart's remark about pornography fits well here, too: "I may not be able to define it, but I know it when I see it." The English word *apocalypse* or *apocalyptic* derives from a Greek word meaning to uncover or to reveal, and this sense fundamentally orients us. Part of the problem, however, is distinguishing between the genre *apocalypse* and the phenomenon *apocalypticism*. They are intertwined because the phenomenon is most often expressed in the genre, and so we associate the two.

The Seminar on Apocalyptic of the Society of Biblical Literature published a definition of the genre apocalypse that can help us determine how the ancient text and modern movies are related (Collins 1979). We will also borrow three of Klaus Koch's eight groups of motifs from what he calls the apocalyptic "attitude of mind" to help round out our discussion (Koch 1972, 28, 33). This involves, of course, some mixing of apples and oranges, but at this point a fruit salad is better than nothing at all.

The seminar defined an apocalypse as "A genre of revelatory literature with a narrative framework in which a revelation is mediated by an otherworldly being to a recipient, disclosing a transcendent reality which is both temporal, insofar as it envisages eschatological salvation, and spatial, insofar as it involves another, supernatural world" (Collins 1979, 9). The definition can be broken down into four aspects: (1) Apocalypse involves a narrative framework; (2) it discloses a transcendent reality that is both (a) eschatological and (b) supernatural; (3) it is revelatory; and (4) it is mediated by an otherworldly being.

All this is the language of mythology, and the origin of the various themes can be easily traced in the contemporary mythology of Jewish Apocalyptic and in

the redemption myths of Gnosticism. To this extent *the kerygma is incredible to modern man, for he is convinced that the mythical view of the world is obsolete.* (Bultmann's emphasis)
—*Rudolf Bultmann (1961)*

IN WHAT SENSE DO MODERN APOCALYPTIC MOV-ies belong to the genre apocalypse? The first requirement of the definition is easy enough to meet, because movies are narratives or stories. The second poses a problem, however, because no modern apocalyptic movie envisions the revelation of a transcendent reality. Yet this only exposes a shift between ancient and modern (and now postmodern) worldviews. With the Enlightenment and science's abandonment of the two- (or three-) storied universe as a realistic explanation of reality, such a model of transcendence is no longer available in realistic narratives. We can no longer envision heaven as literally up there. Thus, the conversation reaches a critical and essential moment at its very beginning.

Rudolf Bultmann built his famous or infamous program of demythologization partly on this insight of a disjunction between the modern worldview and the ancient myth of a two-storied universe (of earth and heaven) or a three-storied one (of hell and earth and heaven). Many people in their religious and everyday lives still believe in and base aspects of their lives on transcendence as understood in this way. According to a recent survey, 90 percent of Americans say they believe in God; 82 percent believe in an afterlife with a heaven and hell; and 55 percent believe in Satan. Further, 46 percent of Americans expect to spend eternity in heaven while only 4 percent expect to go to hell (Patterson and Kim 1991, 199–204). Yet these surviving beliefs operate in a fundamentally different way from prior eras. For example, a medieval artist who wanted to represent transcendence could simply draw a conventional vision of heaven. The magnificence of the Sistine chapel is a witness to the reality of this vision. For the people in the Middle Ages, such a picture of the universe was literal and, more importantly, part of the public discourse. Such is not the case today. One might blame the Enlightenment and Thomas Jefferson's wall between church and state. The First Amendment begins, "Congress shall make no law respecting an establishment of religion." The disestablishment of the churches, a process already well developed in colonial America, protected the state from the church and moved religion into the private sphere. But not only was religion disestablished, Congress may not make any law "prohibiting the free exercise thereof." Jefferson's famous message to the Danbury Baptist Association begins with a notice of the private character of religion:

> Believing with you that religion is a matter which lies solely between man and his God, . . . I contemplate with sovereign reverence that act of the whole American people which declared that their legislature should make no law respecting an establishment of religion, or prohibiting the free exercise thereof, thus building a wall of separation between Church and State. (Jefferson 1984, 510)

Such a wall has made belief private and the three-storied universe a matter of private discourse, for the separation of church and state denies the claims of any one religion to enforce its version of ultimate reality on the society as a whole. The wall creates the conditions and necessity for pluralism. Reinhold Niebuhr made this point very precisely: "Religion is so frequently a source of confusion in political life, and so frequently dangerous to democracy, precisely because it introduces absolutes into the realm of relative values."

Thus, a moviemaker faces a real dilemma in depicting the transcendent. Movies, even those that are fantasies, are realistic. They derive their authority from their visual credibility. If they do not correspond to the reality and conventions of public discourse, they will be rejected. The gradual demise of the movie musical underlines the increasingly realistic character of our films. The efforts of some recent movies to envision a literal transcendence illustrate the problem. Albert Brooks's *Defending Your Life* (1991) envisioned life after death as a trial at a Disneyland-like park, complete with shuttle buses and fantasy hotels. In Steve Martin's *L.A. Story* (1991), an electronic billboard speaks to him in mysterious, enigmatic sayings. Likewise, the chief character in *Field of Dreams* (1989) hears a voice telling him, "If you build it, he will come," and baseball becomes a transcendent reality. Woody Allen in *Alice* (1990) restores Chinese magic to modern-day New York. Finally, *Ghost* (1990) has all the earmarks of a medieval morality play with ghosts coming back to avenge wrongs and protect their loved ones, but the ghosts seem to live in the subway, awaiting their eventual fate. Thus, we see moviemakers striving for some way to depict the transcendent realistically, yet almost inevitably they end up picturing it in an earthly fashion. One need only remember the Sistine chapel to recognize that the Middle Ages also pictured the transcendent in images of this world.

Apocalyptic movies intensify this problem because they have no realistic way to depict the intervention of the transcendent into this world's reality. Yet these movies retain fragments of the older transcendent image, and these fragments are important building blocks in our conversation. The genre of apocalyptic movies began with Fritz Lang's masterpiece *Metropolis* (1926). In the mythical map of *Metropolis*, the laborers live underground, while the managers inhabit skyscrapers. The division of the world between an underground and skyscrapers reaching to heaven replicates the older model of heaven and earth with one essential difference. There is no God in the skyscraper, only an evil business manager. This recasting of the old heavenly world remains a fundamental motif in apocalyptic movies. A similar map occurs in Ridley Scott's *Blade Runner* (1982), an acknowledged classic of the genre that has recently been reissued in a revised director's version (1993). There the underworld/skyscraper map is imposed on Los Angeles. The city of the future is dominated by a soaring, glass skyscraper, rising like a ziggurat above the urban jungle at ground level, which is crowded, chaotic, dirty, and teeming with beastlike, foreign-appearing people. At the top of the skyscraper sits the Tyrell Company, lording it over the city below. In *Mad Max beyond Thunderdome* (1985), the third and best of the Road Warrior movies, the underworld/skyscraper map is less clear. Because the story takes place after an apocalypse, the earth is a desert and thus has no skyscrapers, only a cathedral-like tent floating in the sky from which an evil queen rules. Though the upper world lacks a strong symbol, a literal underworld provides power for the upper world, a recurring motif in these movies. This underworld derives its power from a methane gas made from pig feces. The significance of these fragments of a transcendent map and its reversal in modern apocalyptic will furnish an important element in our conversation.

These movies are not revelations, the third element in the Apocalypse Seminar's definition. With the demise of the two-storied universe, this option no longer exists, and so literally imagined revelation is impossible. Martin Scorsese faced this problem in *The Last Temptation of Christ* (1988). In a realistic movie he tried to depict Jesus speaking with God but he ended up with a Jesus who hears voices. In our society such people are thought to be demented. Thus, something that has verisimilitude in a book can lack it when projected on the screen.

Yet, from a metaphorical perspective, these movies certainly are revelations, although the sender and receiver are suppressed because of the very nature of film. Watching a movie is a type of voyeurism in which a viewer (receiver) looks in on a story and takes up a variety of points of view offered by the camera's eye. A camera's eye differs from a narrator's voice in a novel. It shows us what others see, yet often from a viewpoint that they cannot adopt, and at other times allows us to see into the past and/or future. Except for voice-narrated movies, the camera's eye is voiceless. Thus, insofar as we can see into the future, we are sharing the vision of another (a revelation), unnoted and hidden from our view.

In an ancient apocalypse the otherworldly narrator, the fourth aspect of the Apocalypse Seminar's definition, provides authority for the revelation. In a modern movie the camera's omniscient eye creates credibility of vision. The film creates a sense of presence that convinces us of its reality, its truth. At a deeper level, however, two related aspects undergird the real credibility of these movies about the future. First, the movie must present a convincing image of the physical world. Special effects make this easier and easier. A comparison of *Metropolis* with *Blade Runner* or *The Terminator* (1984) shows how far these techniques have come. *Metropolis* imagined the future in terms of the giant machines that dominated industry in the 1920s. The machines' gargantuan size indicates that the film's makers could only conceive of machines becoming larger. Miniaturization had not occurred to them. *Blade Runner* envisions a future with glass towers, neon signs, and compact cars that zip around in the sky.

Besides the physical vision of the future, the credibility of a film's revelation depends on whether its future is convincingly derived from the present. For *Metropolis* the future entails a more intense repression of labor and labor-management conflict on a grand scale. Laborers have literally become parts of the machine. In *Blade Runner*, the future results from current negative environmental trends—pollution and the despoiling of the environment continue unabated. In *Mad Max* the characters live in a world where nuclear weapons have destroyed civilization. The credibility of each of these movies comes from a scenario in which present trends play themselves out into the future.

Likewise, I suspect this accounts for the credibility of apocalyptic visions in the ancient world. We should hesitate to credit belief in these visions to the credulity of the ancients, as some scholars do (Collins 1984, 31). Rather, apocalyptic visions represent believable scenarios of current trends in the ancient world. Precisely for this reason apocalypses use traditional motifs and reuse older situations to forecast new situations. The Book of Daniel is a believable outcome for the future based on Israel's past experience. This explains why the apocalyptic seer invokes the past in disguised form to forecast the future. The seer in Mark invokes Antiochus IV's desecration of the Temple (167–164 B.C.E.) to forecast the outcome of Titus' entrance into the Temple in 70 C.E. Mark 13 in the first century derives its credibility from its believable scenario emanating from the destruction of the Temple. It follows out current trends.

Finally, the Apocalypse Seminar's definition specifies that the apocalyptic revelation is "temporal, insofar as it envisages eschatological salvation, and spatial insofar as it involves another, supernatural world." This aspect of the definition encompasses a vision of the future as eschatological salvation. Once again, this highlights a difference between ancient and modern apocalypse. Because ancient apocalypse uses the convention of the otherworldly revealer speaking to the recipient, it adopts the point of view of the past forecasting the future. Since modern apocalypses suppress this convention, for reasons we have already examined, they take the point of view of the future. The viewer looks into the future, visits the future. This, of course, is as much a fiction or convention as the convention of a seer from the past looking into the future.

The eschatologies, however, differ in a decisive way. A modern movie not only tells its story from a future point of view, but the action takes place after what Mad Max calls the " 'pokeelipse." In ancient apocalypses the trials will produce eschatological salvation; in modern apocalypses the breakdown produces a living hell. Now we can begin to see the price paid for the loss of transcendence. Without transcendence there is no relief from a continuing hell. Both God and Satan have disappeared from the movie world, but hell remains—here on earth. The very title of *Apocalypse Now* (1979) makes the point and indicates the difference. Hell cannot be escaped.

After apocalypse only comes more apocalypse. Yet *Metropolis, Blade Runner*, and *Mad Max* all hold out a type of salvation. The fragments of transcendence remain strong. In *Metropolis* the chief manager's son falls in love with Maria, the leader of the laboring masses, and mediates between his father and the laborers by offering his life. The father comes to his senses and all live happily ever after. In *Blade Runner* the hero falls in love with a replicant, a humanlike artificial person, whom he has been assigned to kill. In the end they ride off in a space car, invoking the conventional ending of many traditional Westerns. The space car leaves the city and shoots across green valleys and mountains, clearly indicating that they are arriving in paradise. But only this final scene displays anything pastoral.

Mad Max is more complex. Max's fate is ambivalent since he remains alone in the desert, his fate unnoted. In a series, killing off the hero eliminates the possibility of future productions (Jewett and Lawrence 1977, 186). Still Max has saved a group of children who previously had rescued him from the desert. In biblical style, they have a story of a savior, a Captain Walker, who will return and save them. When they mistake Max for Captain Walker, he disabuses them of any belief in a messianic Captain Walker, as one would expect in a nontranscendent movie. But hope does not die, and the film's final clip shows the oldest girl telling a new story of their salvation while holding a baby in her lap. The lap of this madonna promises a civilization reborn in a burned-out city of lights.

While the Apocalypse Seminar's definition contains many elements in the cluster of motifs that Koch identifies as characteristic of the apocalyptic attitude of mind, three do require a more careful look. Koch's first cluster is an "urgent expectation of the impending overthrow of all of earthly conditions in the immediate future" (Koch 1972, 28). "Eschatological" in the Apocalypse Seminar's definition probably implies this aspect, but given its prominence in Mark 13 we must deal with it explicitly. The movies indicate the future's immediacy by the date of story time. In *Metropolis* it is the twenty-first century; in *Blade Runner* the year is 2019; and in *Mad Max* the wars, as they are referred to, are in the immediate past of story time, thus not too far away from the present viewer looking into the future. Urgency also results because the viewer can easily believe that this tragic future has grown out of present conditions. This convention of deriving the imminent future from the immediate present gives apocalyptic its conviction and explains the continuing power of ancient apocalyptic in modern times. In Mark, the "present" for the apocalyptic scenario is the first century, not the twentieth. The author of that Gospel would have found our continued existence in the twentieth century quite surprising. Some modern readers, however, construe that "present" as the contemporary present, and so the apocalyptic scenario appears convincing once again.

Two of Koch's other clusters also call for comment. Apocalypticism views "the end as a catastrophe" and deals with history as "periodization and determinism" (Koch 1972, 29). Periodization is less evident in these films because they do not review history as the so-called historical apocalypses do. They take place in the future, not in the distant past looking forward. But determinism is evident not only in each of these movies individually, but also in the genre. Furthermore, the determinism leads to a tragic future. This feeds into the perception of why we see something as apocalyptic—it is determined and catastrophic. Essential to apocalypticism, although not unique to it, is the inevitable triumph of chaos over order without an extraordinary intervention. Because these movies lack such an extraordinary intervention, they are set after the breakdown, the catastrophe. Yet the transcendent is not lost, for all three movies find some hint of redemption. As one might expect, the earliest movie, *Metropolis* (1926), is the most hopeful. In that film the oppressors and the oppressed are reconciled. Society and the world are saved. The triumph over chaos is much less definitive in the two movies made during the 1980s. Here salvation is more individualistic or noncorporate, as one would expect in our individualistic culture. In *Blade Runner*, the saved couple escape into the sunset, while in *Mad Max* the children telling their story in a burned-out city imply an eschatological promise of new beginnings for society.

Thus far we have seen that these movies continue many aspects of the ancient genre apocalypse and the apocalyptic viewpoint, though with modifications to accommodate modern circumstances. Now I would like to focus on the chaos that overwhelms order.

[Computers] had already done so much—had so
thoroughly infiltrated advanced carbon-based culture—
that pulling the plug was not a realistic alternative. . . .
The symbiosis between man and computer has, within
an astonishingly brief span of time, become so intimate
that for a vast array of activities, pulling the plug would
be equivalent to social suicide.

—O. B. Hardison (1990)

METROPOLIS (1926) ON THE SURFACE LOOKS
like a German Marxist critique of emerging fascism, what today might
be called laissez-faire capitalism. The conflict between labor and
management drives the plot, and overcoming that conflict constitutes
resolution. Yet a more fundamental issue underlies the conflict, namely, what does it mean to be human? In the underworld that supports
Metropolis, laborers are pictured as parts of a machine. Not only do
they run the machines, they are actually parts of them. Maria, their
heroine, leader, nurse, and teacher of their children, is depicted as
a mother earth virgin. To destroy Maria, a scientist creates a robot
that duplicates her and leads the laborers in a revolt so the managers
can destroy them. The replacement of Maria with a robot and the
use of laborers as machine parts clearly indicate that the managers
view the workers as machines. When the manager's son falls in love
with Maria, he discovers the laborers' humanity. His love leads to
their liberation and reconciliation with the managers. The chaos that
threatens order has overturned it for a time and created the apocalypse by dehumanizing labor and turning humans into machines.
The solution is the age-old answer, love. Even though this solution
is a cliché, it should not necessarily be mocked. True humanity implies
authentic relationships between humans, the removal of alienating
and enslaving differences. Paul, himself an ancient apocalyptist,
reached a similar conclusion: "There is no such thing as Jew and
Greek, slave and freeman, male and female" (Gal. 3:28).

The question of what constitutes a human is even more crucial in
Blade Runner (1982). The story's hero, Deckard (Harrison Ford), is
a cop in the tradition of Dashiell Hammett or Raymond Chandler. By
trade he is a blade runner, a police officer who "retires" (kills) "replicants." The latter are powerful humanoids manufactured by genetic
engineers to serve as slaves in the "offworld" performing tasks too

dangerous for humans. Replicants are indistinguishable from humans except that they have no memory of their own; instead, someone else's has been implanted in them. Furthermore, they are programmed for a very short life span. The theme revolves around the question of what constitutes a human and in what sense humanoids are not human. Must you have your own memory to be human? Deckard becomes sickened at the killing of replicants and eventually falls in love with a replicant who has come to the end of her allotted life span. Eventually, he turns on his employer, Tyrell, and destroys him.

The similarity to *Metropolis* is obvious. Instead of managers enslaving laborers, a corporation enslaves humanoids and dehumanizes humans. In *Blade Runner* memory and love are the essence of a human. Tyrell, who has memory and parcels it out to the replicants, has no love—and so is inhuman. Likewise, when Deckard becomes repulsed at the killing and falls in love, even though with a replicant, he and she become human. An ecological breakdown launches the chaos in *Blade Runner*. This catastrophe replicates the disregard for humanity; Tyrell's treatment of both humans and replicants reflects his fundamental disregard for life and so also for the world and its environment.

There are no robots in *Mad Max beyond Thunderdome* (1985), and a greater and more destructive catastrophe has occurred than in either *Metropolis* or *Blade Runner*. The humans appear very inhuman—misshapen and dressed in bizarre costumes, many of which seem derived from the armor of the Roman legions. The semi-armor makes the wearers appear semihuman. People also wear odd contrivances as eyeglasses. Bartertown, the center of the action, is childless. One of the chief characters in Bartertown is called Master-Blaster. Master-Blaster is (are) two people. Master, a midget, is the brains while Blaster is the brawn. He is a giant whose face, concealed beneath a helmet, is that of an idiot child. The two make one person, but a very odd person indeed.

Bartertown is ruled by Auntie Entity, who lives in the cathedral-like tent that floats above the town. She describes herself as "nobody, except on the day after. I was still alive. This nobody had a chance to be somebody. Well, so much for history." This casual dismissal of history is telling, for without a history she becomes less human. She explains the meaning of Bartertown to Mad Max. "All this I built," she says, gesturing to the town below, a smoking, dirty, dusty collection of rock dwellings. "Up to my armpits in blood and shit. Where there was desert, now there's a town; where robbery, there's trade; where there was despair, there's hope, civilization. I'll do anything to protect it." She wants to hire Mad Max to kill the Blaster part of Master-Blaster. Auntie has a clear vision of how to bring order out of chaos. She employs controlled violence.

At the polar extreme of Bartertown is a group of abandoned children who live at the bottom of a canyon, a scar, a wound in the desert earth. In contrast to Bartertown, which is powered by the methane gas derived from pig feces, the children's world is an oasis, a place of water and trees in an otherwise barren desert. They are dressed like aboriginal natives, not in the garbled garb of the Roman Empire. The children represent an emerging civilization, while Bartertown exhibits all the degeneration of civilization. Even though the children appear like some primitive tribe, they are not uncivilized or barbaric as William Golding's *Lord of the Flies* (movie 1963) would have us believe is the inevitable fate of children left to their own devices. These children have a memory of what was, what happened, and therefore what might be, a memory they consciously keep alive by recitation. Unlike Auntie, they do not dismiss history. They stand behind a blank television frame and recite their story. Their leader, a teenage girl, has hope that they will yet find life. The movie ends with her and the children in a destroyed city of lights. Once again, she is telling the story of their deliverance, and on her lap is a baby, obviously her baby, although tribal life is without a hint of sexuality. Life and civilization go on. Life is reborn. Bartertown is a false civilization based on power. The children are a true civilization based on hope and memory. Paradoxically, *Mad Max beyond Thunderdome* insists that even after a nuclear apocalypse, true humanity is based on memory and hope. Even after all hope of a future has been given up, the future is the only hope.

> O Jerusalem, Jerusalem, city that murders the prophets
> and stones the messengers sent to her! How often have
> I longed to gather your children, as a hen gathers her
> brood under her wings; but you would not let me.
> Look! There is your temple, forsaken by God and laid
> to waste.
>
> *—Matthew 23:37-38 (REB)*

MY SELECTION OF ONE OF THE CONVERSATION
partners for modern films marks a departure from what has gone on
before. Even though 4 Ezra is not common Bible reading, it makes
an interesting companion to the much better known Gospel of Mark.
A catalyst for apocalyptic thinking in both 4 Ezra and Mark 13 is the
destruction of Jerusalem. Both take up an apocalyptic framework to
deal with the chaos that follows in the wake of Jerusalem's destruction. Their differing yet strikingly similar solutions to this problem
are instructive for our conversation.

Christians preserved the apocalypse in Greek by adding a suitable
beginning (2 Esdras 1–2) and ending (2 Esdras 15–16) and changing
its title to 2 Esdras. It never made it into the Hebrew canon and was
therefore rejected by both the reformers and the Council of Trent.
However, the Church of England has normally printed it in the Apoc-
rypha as 2 Esdras (Suter 1985).

Even though New Testament scholars generally date the Gospel
of Mark around 70 C.E. because of the sense of urgency associated
with the destruction of Jerusalem, 2 Ezra belongs at the end of the
first century. The beginning of the first vision indicates the date of
the writing: "In the thirtieth year after the fall of Jerusalem, I, Salathiel
(who am also Ezra), was in Babylon" (3:1 REB, all translations of 2
Esdras are from the REB). Even though the author places the seer
Ezra in a position to reflect on the destruction of Jerusalem by
Nebuchadnezzar in 586 B.C.E., as Metzger observes, "it becomes obvious when one begins to study the book that this statement is intended to refer cryptically to the fall of Jerusalem in A.D. 70 (3:2; 6:19;
10:48)" (Meztger 1983, 520; so also Stone 1990, 10).

At the very beginning of the first vision, the author clearly states
the apocalypse's motivation: "Lying on my bed I was troubled and
my mind filled with perplexity as I reflected on the desolation of Zion
and the prosperity of those who lived in Babylon." (3:1b-2). The same

basic structural situation that provokes 4 Ezra occurs in all classic, ancient apocalyptic literature—the disparity between the pain of God's chosen people and the blessings of those who persecute them. In modern apocalyptic the element of "God's chosen people" is absent because of the transcendent's disappearance. These movies portray the disparity between what is and what ought to be. In ancient apocalyptic God sanctions this "ought-to-be," while in modern apocalyptic a vision of true humanity derived from the surviving fragments of transcendence serves the same function.

Ezra's reflection on the suffering of Israel and the prosperity of its enemies starts off a cycle of visionary dialogues between the prophet Ezra and the angelic emissary Uriel. Uriel is a substitute for God, and often the angel's voice blends into that of God. Adding to the acuity of Ezra's perplexity is his charge that God sanctions these events: "Those who reject your promises have trampled on the people who put their trust in your covenant. If you are so deeply displeased ("hate" RSV) with your people, yours should be the hand that punishes them" (5:29-30). This argument occurs frequently in the apocalypse, as in the initial vision in a phrase that echoes the opening line: "But when I arrived here, I saw wickedness beyond reckoning, and with my own eyes I have seen evildoers in great numbers these thirty years. My heart sank because I observed how you tolerate sinners and spare the godless, how you have destroyed your own people but preserved your enemies" (3:29-30).

Yet Ezra's concern is not just with Israel, but also with the Gentiles. Because the apocalyptic crisis results from the belief that God the creator is the Most High, a title that occurs sixty-eight times in the apocalypse, Ezra senses a fault in creation itself. According to the angel Uriel, "A man corrupted by the corrupt world can never know the way of the incorruptible" (4:13). To which Ezra responds, "Better never to have come into existence than be born into a world of evil and suffering we cannot explain!" (4:12). Arguing from analogy, as he often does, the angel claims that "Just as the land belongs to the trees and the sea to the waves, so dwellers on earth can understand earthly things and nothing beyond; only he who lives above the heavens can understand the things high above the heavens" (4:21). This argument fails to satisfy Ezra, and he raises two objections to the angel's dualistic distinction between heaven and earth. First, "Why have I been given the faculty of understanding?" (4:22; see also 7:62-68; 7:116). If God has created humankind with a mind, why is that mind incapable of understanding its fate? As was the case with modern apocalypticism, to question the nature of God is to question the nature of humanity. Next, Ezra objects that he is asking not about the things of heaven but of the earth:

> My question is not about the distant heavens, but about what happens every day before our eyes. Why has Israel been made a byword among the Gentiles? Why have the people you loved been put at the mercy of godless nations? Why has the law of our fathers been brought to nothing, and the written covenants made a dead letter? We pass from the world like a flight of locusts, our life is but a vapour, and we are not worth the Lord's pity. What then will he do for us who bear his name? Those are my questions. (4:23-25)

Ezra's question actually has two aspects; one is specific to Jewish apocalypticism but the other is more general. The first part of his question deals with the fate of Israel—why does this discrepancy exist between the promise and the reality? The second part concerns the general fate of humanity, a question reminiscent of Job. It is this latter aspect of the question that provokes Ezra's identification with the fate of humanity.

In an effort to resolve Ezra's dilemma, the angel employs the analogy of the farmer planting seeds: "The farmer sows many seeds in the ground and plants many plants, but not all the seeds come up safely in due season, nor do all the plants strike root. It is the same in the world of men: not all who are sown will be saved" (8:41). Since Ezra's complaint had been that "The truth is, no one was ever born who did not sin, no one alive is innocent of offence" (8:36), the analogy is meant to suggest that for the seed to survive it must be fortunate, all the conditions must be perfect, as indeed was the case in ancient agronomy where the rate of seed germination was low. Thus, the analogy appeared to fit the case "I repeat what I have said again and again: the lost outnumber the saved as a wave exceeds a drop of water" (9:14, from a speech of Ezra).

But the seer, being a smart dialectician, spots the logical breakdown in the angel's analogy: "The farmer's seed may not come up, because you did not give it rain at the right time, or it may rot because of too much rain; but man, who was fashioned by your hands and

called your image because he is made like you, for whose sake you
formed everything, will you really compare him with seed sown by
a farmer? Do not be angry with us, LORD; but spare your people and
show them pity, for it is your own creation you will be pitying" (8:43-
45). Ezra senses that the analogy implies determinism, that God has
willed the people's destruction. If this is the case, then creation is
perverted. The ancient apocalyptist cannot fall back on the modern
filmmaker's option of no transcendence. Like much apocalyptic literature that wrestles with the question of theodicy, 4 Ezra verges on
atheism, except that the atheistic option is unavailable to the ancients.
As Robert Lane Fox has argued, there were no atheists in our sense
of the word in the ancient world: "Atheists were either Epicureans
who denied the gods' providence, but not their existence, or Jews
and Christians who worshiped their own God, while denying everyone else's" (Fox 1989, 10). Both here and in a number of other places,
the evident logic of Ezra's argument would blame God for the Jewish
predicament, but to do so would deny God's goodness or existence
or the chosen character of the Jewish people. Thus, another answer
must be found.

In approaching Ezra's questions, the angel's strategy is to separate
Ezra from the rest of humanity and then turn him against those with
whom he has sympathized. First, he separates Ezra from the rest of
humanity. The angel begins by questioning Ezra's motives: "It is not
possible for you to love my creation with a love greater than mine—
far from it!" (8:47). Then the angel maintains that Ezra is not to
identify himself with the rest of creation: "But never again rank
yourself among the unjust, as so often you have done. . . . But you
should direct your thoughts to yourself and look to the glory awaiting
those like you" (8:47, 51). Since Ezra had maintained that "no one
was ever born who did not sin," on what basis can the angel differ-
entiate Ezra from the rest of humanity? The answer lies in what the
others did with the freedom that God gave them: "For when they
[the many who are lost] were given freedom they used it to despise
the Most High" (8:56). This constitutes a clear distinction. Even more
significant is the second part of the response: "What is more, they
trampled on the godly" (8:57). This reverts to the question that initiated Ezra's distress, "the desolation of Zion and the prosperity of
those who lived in Babylon" (3:2), that is, Rome. To maintain Ezra's

righteousness and justify God's condemnation of the wicked Gentiles, the angel severs Ezra's solidarity with creation by reminding him that these Gentiles have persecuted his people. The only remedy becomes intervention by the Most High: "Yours, then, will be the joys I have predicted, theirs the thirst and torments already prepared" (8:59). As the outcome of this position, the world was created for Israel (Stone 1990, 188).

To protect God's control of creation and the election of Israel, Ezra must break his tenuous identification with the Gentiles, his persecutors, and agree with the angel. "Ask no more questions, therefore, about the many who are lost" (8:55).

What then will the owner of the vineyard do? He will come and destroy the tenants and give the vineyard to others. Have you not read this scripture: "The stone that the builders rejected has become the cornerstone; this was the Lord's doing, and it is amazing in our eyes." When they realized that he had told this parable against them, they wanted to arrest him, but they feared the crowd.

—Mark 12:9-12

BURTON MACK IN HIS *A MYTH OF INNOCENCE* produces a challenging and brilliant reading of Mark 13. He observes that without chapter 13 no one would think to interpret the Gospel in an apocalyptic sense (Mack 1988, 325). Accordingly, chapter 13 becomes decisive for an understanding of Mark, and the destruction of Jerusalem becomes a pivotal point in a deterministic timetable that (1) blames the Jews for the death of Jesus and (2) exonerates the Christian community as innocent. For Mack, Mark was impelled to construct a myth of origins by a conflict with the synagogue that resulted from the failure of the Christian community's efforts to re-form the synagogue. When the reform movement had failed and the synagogue had turned on the Marcan community, Mark adapted the apocalyptic myth to explain the situation. The anger in Jesus' debates with the Jews in the Temple (chap. 12) really reflects the community's anger at the synagogue, while the destruction of the Temple represents God's vengeance on Israel for its participation in Jesus' death. After the community's rejection and persecution by the synagogue, the apocalyptic myth vindicates the community. As Mack summarizes: "Vindication was achieved by shifting the locus of conflict from the synagogue to the temple in Jesus' time (by narrative device), in order to claim the destruction of the temple in Mark's time as the judgment upon those who rejected Jesus's words" (Mack 1988, 245). The cursing (11:12-14) and withering of the fig tree (11:20-25), which form a sandwich for Jesus' cleansing of the temple, make this point clear. Mark 13 is the linchpin in this apocalyptic schema for it identifies the destruction of the Temple as the punishment. At Jesus' death the veil of the Temple is torn in two, foretelling its destruction (Mark 15:38). In Mark's view, just as the Jews were punished for crucifying Jesus, so the righteous who suffer now will be vindicated when the Son of man comes to power.

The apocalyptic myth has a similar function and outcome in 4 Ezra and the Gospel of Mark. The myth serves to separate the community from the larger society. In Ezra's case it separates Israel from the nations, and for Mark it separates his community from Israel (or, in Mack's phrase, the synagogue). In both cases this separation leads to a condemnation of the other and the announced innocence of the offended party. Ironically, the author of 4 Ezra and the author of the Gospel of Mark view the same historical events—the capture of Jerusalem and the destruction of its Temple—and employ the same myth, yet they see God active in a functionally similar but historically different way. For Ezra, the destruction threatens the election of Israel, so he needs reassurance of God's future vindication for Israel. For Mark, the destruction vindicates Jesus' death and the community's rejection by Israel.

Both Mark and 4 Ezra likewise argue that the unjust have failed in their use of the freedom God has given them, and the sign of this is their persecution of the chosen. Consequently, both ancient and modern apocalypticism diagnose the chaos threatening humanity as inhumanity. Yet the transcendence infusing ancient apocalypticism provides it with an option—the total destruction of the enemy. God as almighty, 4 Ezra's primary title for the transcendent, blocks an ultimate human solidarity and demands a mythical vengeance. Such vengeance in modern apocalypticism carries a heavy price because not just the unrighteous will be destroyed. The lack of an option of transcendent hope forces the modern movie into a sense of solidarity, even if only among individuals. When overwhelming violence is invoked as in the Terminator movies, it produces not a new transcendent reality but *Terminator II*. As *Mad Max* indicates, surviving the apocalypse is not an enviable fate.

Mack sees this apocalyptic transformation of Mark's heritage as disastrous not only for Mark but also for subsequent Christianity (and by implication for Judaism, for here lies the root of the Holocaust). What had originally started out as a program "for social reform, open borders, the presence of the new social spirit, the affirmation of plural pasts," was "sacrificed to the new desire for self-justification" (Mack 1988, 311).

Mack interprets Mark's apocalyptic drama as a desire and need for self-vindication and vengeance. Mack quotes the advice of Mark 13:11 about not worrying about what to say "when they arrest you to lock you up . . . it is not you who are speaking, but the holy spirit," as evidence that the community has nothing to say to the world (Mack 1988, 331). They have nothing to say because they have been vindicated by the destruction of the Temple and the sure coming of the Son of man in power. But self-vindication and vengeance are precisely what Mark 13 and the death of Jesus withhold from the reader. They will have something to say, and it will be the spirit. Even more the watch word of Mark 13 is "Watch, stay alert." The world undergoing the apocalyptic catastrophe is a dangerous place and not one in which the believer will be vindicated. At this point, Mark 13 and modern apocalyptic movies agree.

Mack is surely right that the Temple's destruction is punishment for Jesus' death in the Gospel of Mark. The tearing of the Temple curtain makes that connection. However, another issue is also at stake in Jesus' death. The centurion's confession has confounded interpretation for centuries. The centurion, who was in charge of the death of Jesus, witnesses the despairing Jesus in death and confesses, "This man really was God's Son" (15:39). This verse calls into question the whole meaning of transcendence—what does transcendence mean in the face of such a witness? The watchful and alert reader has witnessed not a Jesus of power, but a Jesus of weakness as God's true manifestation. The ultimate chaos that threatens Mark's word is a false humanity that demands of God a power the narrator deems demonic. Such power brings upon itself the destruction of its world.

In the complex of materials in chapter 8, Mark has laid out his program. Sandwiched between the narration of the feeding of the four thousand and the disciples' worry in the boat that they have only one loaf of bread is Jesus' short, isolated confrontation with the Pharisees in Dalmanoutha district. The construction of this scene indicates its importance. Surrounding the scene with bread stories and a trip across the lake for a single question and answer is a way of setting the stage. The narrator reports, "to test him, they demanded a sign in the sky" (8:11 SV). The sign requested is not just any sign (see 2:11), but an apocalyptic sign that will show that God is about to vindicate Israel's enemies (Gibson 1990). Jesus' response must be a shock not just to the fictional Pharisees but especially to the reader: "I swear to God, no sign will be given this generation!" (8:12 SV). No explanation is offered; no softening of the response as in Matthew (16:4) and Luke (11:29). Rather, he abruptly departs: "And turning his back on them, he got back in the boat and crossed over to the other side" (8:13 SV).

This same theme recurs in the confession at Caesarea Phillipi. When Peter finally confesses Jesus as the Messiah (8:29), he is attributing to Jesus the fulfillment of the messianic signs as demonstrated by his powerful activity in the first eight chapters (Weeden 1971, especially 54–56). In the boat Jesus had recalled the two feeding miracles for the disciples and warned them against the leaven of the Pharisees and Herodians. But now that Peter and the disciples have finally seen the light after all their confusion, "He warned them not to tell anyone about him." The silencing echoes the exorcisms as does Jesus' rebuke of Peter for rejecting his open claim "that the son of Adam was destined to suffer a great deal, and be rejected by the elders and the ranking priests and the scholars . . ." (8:31 SV). The rejection of the messianic pretension comes full circle with Peter's identification with Satan (8:33), completing the pattern of the exorcism. Thus, the messianic claim to exercise apocalyptic power presents a demonic temptation.

Jesus reaffirms this message to the crowd when he tells them to "pick up their cross, and follow me" (8:34), and God's voice in the transfiguration not only acknowledges Jesus as "my son" but also commands, "Listen to him!" What Jesus has just said concerns his death and suffering as well as that of his followers and the rejection of the satanic temptation toward a Messiah of power.

At the death scene the same paradigm persists. The priests and scribes taunt him with the titles Messiah and King of Israel and demand that he "should come down from the cross here and now, so that we can see and trust for ourselves!" (13:32 SV). The leaders persist in their request for a sign. But the centurion, seeing only Jesus' death in despair, joins the heavenly voice in confessing Jesus as God's son. Mark ironically undercuts his own use of the destruction of the Temple as a sign of God's punishment of Israel for its involvement in Jesus' death. In sanctioning Mark's story, the reader and author fall guilty to requesting and finding a sign. In the profound effort to understand the death of Jesus as the act that eliminates all violence, Mark was mythically seduced so that unintentionally it has become a death that has led to the death of many. Likewise, Ezra proposes a solidarity with all humanity, but the angel cuts it off. The apocalyptic myth of God's power demands the avenging of his chosen ones.

This conversation between two ancient apocalyptic texts and three modern movies shows that apocalypticism's value lies not in its predictive powers, which have proven less than reliable, but in its diagnostic ability. The apocalyptic myth risks separating humanity into the chosen and rejected. The movies demonstrate that we no longer can afford this option. Paradoxically, many movies contemplating the war in Vietnam have opted for precisely this mythical demonizing of the other. Both ancient and modern apocalypticism agree on the evaluation of present trends: they are leading toward catastrophe. They also agree on the diagnosis: the threatening chaos is our inhumanity. For ancient apocalypticism inhumanity derives from a false use of God-given freedom, a failure to calculate our place in reality correctly. In modern apocalypticism inhumanity results from a failure to allow others to exercise their basic human freedoms. Thus, by enslaving others, we set ourselves up as gods in our own version of reality. But how do the movies know what constitutes true humanity? The measures of true humanity are those fragments of transcendence that have survived from the ancient stories, fragments that allow us to envision what ought to be. Both ancient and modern apocalypticism agree on the centrality of memory in the definition of humanity. For the ancient, the memory of God's past dealings with the people defines true humanity and offers hope, while in modern apocalypticism memory recalls who we are, giving depth to the human person. Milan Kundera reminds us of the centrality of memory in freedom's contest with totalitarianism. He tells the story of a famous photograph of the founders of Czechoslovakian communism. It was a cold day and the leader had no hat, so one of his comrades offered him his cap. Subsequently, the comrade was eliminated in a purge. He was then airbrushed from the photo. Only the blank space remained and the hat he had given to the leader. Authoritarianism attempts to control our memory. What is real is what we remember. But those fragments persist. As Kundera says, "the struggle of man against power is the struggle of memory against forgetting" (Kundera 1981, 3).

But Woody Allen also reminds us that time is the enemy of memory. In *Crimes and Misdemeanors* (1989) Judah Rosenthal (Martin Landau), a very wealthy and successful doctor, arranges for the murder of his mistress. At first he is plagued by guilt and remorse, which he calls "little sparks of his religious background." He nearly has a mental breakdown. But in his own words, "And then one morning he awakens and the sun is shining and his family is around him and mysteriously the crisis is lifted. . . . And as the months pass he finds that he is not punished; in fact he prospers. All returns to normal. Maybe once in a while he has a bad moment, but it passes and with time it all fades." And Judah was a good man. It is, as he says, a chilling story made especially pungent by being told by and to a Jew in the light of the Holocaust. If time is the enemy of memory, it is the ally of myth. Remembering the right story is all-important.

Both modern and ancient apocalypticism see love as the solution to chaos. For the ancient, the love of God restores true humanity and allows the human to respond in a truly human fashion. For the modern, loving and bonding with another restore true humanity. Though often mocked as romantic sentimentalism, love is one of the few publicly available symbols of transcendence, of something beyond ourselves. The true human comes to birth with the rupture of the isolation created by alienation. Yet both ancient and modern apocalyptic have an undertow. The logic of Ezra's and Mark's critique of God as almighty demands attention to block the temptation to vengeance. Only in imagining the weakness of God can we avoid the temptation to destroy the other in God's name. Similarly, the modern should follow out those fragments of transcendence that memory remembers in its understanding of what constitutes a true human.

WORKS NOTED

BULTMANN, Rudolf. 1961.
New Testament and mythology. In *Kerygma and myth: A theological debate*, 1–44. Edited by Hans Werner Bartsch. New York: Harper Torchbooks.

COLLINS, John J. 1979.
Apocalypse: The morphology of a genre. Semeia 14. Missoula: Scholars Press.

———. 1984.
The apocalyptic imagination: An introduction to the Jewish matrix of Christianity. New York: Crossroad.

ELIOT, T. S. 1943.
Little Gidding. In *Four quartets*, 49–59. New York: Harvest Books.

FOX, Robert Lane. 1989.
Pagans and Christians. New York: Alfred A. Knopf.

GIBSON, Jeffrey. 1990.
Jesus' refusal to produce a "sign" (Mk 8.11-13). *Journal for the Study of the New Testament* 38: 37–66.

GOLDING, William. 1954.
Lord of the flies. New York: Aeonian Press.

HARDISON, O. B. 1990.
Disappearing through the skylight: Culture and technology in the twentieth century. New York: Penguin Books.

JEFFERSON, Thomas. 1984.
Thomas Jefferson: Writings. New York: Library of America.

JEWETT, Robert, and John Shelton Lawrence. 1977.
The American monomyth. Garden City, N. Y.: Anchor Press/Doubleday.

KOCH, Klaus. 1972.
The rediscovery of apocalyptic. Studies in Biblical Theology, 2nd ser. Naperville, Ill.: A. R. Allenson.

KUNDERA, Milan. 1981.
The book of laughter and forgetting. Translated by Michael Henry Heim. New York: Penguin Books.

MACK, Burton L. 1988.
A myth of innocence: Mark and Christian origins. Philadelphia: Fortress Press.

METZGER, Bruce. 1983.
The fourth book of Ezra. In *The Old Testament Pseudepigrapha*, 517–60. Vol. 1: *Apocalyptic literature and testaments.* Edited by James H. Charlesworth. Garden City, N.Y.: Doubleday.

PATTERSON, James, and Peter Kim. 1991.
The day America told the truth. New York: Prentice-Hall Press.

STONE, Michael Edward. 1990.
Fourth Ezra. Hermeneia. Minneapolis: Fortress Press.

SUTER, David. 1985.
Esdras, the second book of. In *Harper's Bible dictionary*, 278–79. Edited by Paul J. Achtemeier. San Francisco: Harper & Row.

WEEDEN, Theodore J. 1971.
Mark: Traditions in conflict. Philadelphia: Fortress Press.

WOODWARD, Kenneth. 1992.
The final days are here again. *Newsweek*, March 18, 55.

Judy Benjamin (Goldie Hawn) joins the U.S. Army in Howard Zieff's *Private Benjamin* (1980). (Photo courtesy of Archive Photos)

MALE AND FEMALE

Male and female he created them.

—Genesis 1:27

There is no longer male and female.

—Galatians 3:28

The wife-taking always results in the embedding of the female in the honor of her husband. She, in turn, symbols the shame of the new family—its sensitivity to public opinion and for its own self-image. . . . Hence divorce means the process of disembedding the female from the honor of the male, along with a sort of redistribution and return of the honor of the families concerned.

—Bruce J. Malina (1981)

ON THE BASIS OF THE REAL DIFFERENCES BE-tween women and men, myth has drawn an imaginary line that has served to divide reality. A form of this myth that has had a strong influence on America derives from Mediterranean cultures. In ancient Mediterranean society, the male occupied public space and the female private space. For example, even the house, which is normally the place of women, was divided into a public part, where men could entertain other men, and the private part where the women, children, and slaves went about their domestic routine. The elaborate architecture of the Roman house expressed this division. The ornate front door with its vestibule faced the street. Then came the formal court-yard (the peristyle) and dining rooms (triclinia), all part of the public space. The architecture in the rest of the house—the bedrooms, kitchens, and workrooms—was much less distinctive (Thébert 1987, 378). These were the private, female parts of the house.

This division between public and private may well go back to the way in which traditional societies represent the genitalia. The male sexual organs are external (public), while the female are internal (private) (Malina and Neyrey 1991, 42), and this arrangement is replicated in other aspects of Mediterranean life beyond architecture. The Mediterranean notion of *machismo* "is a male-centered ideology that encourages men to be sexually aggressive, to brag about their sexual prowess and their genital attributes" (Carroll 1986). Women are supposed to be sexually defensive, while males are aggressive. Thus, women should protect their purity, while men sow their seed.

This public/private division finds expression in the traditional understanding of conception. The male begets the child by planting his seed in the field of the woman. Although women contribute to the process, their contribution "does not carry the essential, eternal identity of the person, nor is it generative. . . . that is the quality of seed that allies men with the creative ability of God" (Delaney 1987, 38). This last point is very telling because viewing the female's contribution to conception as passive leads to the identity of god with the male, generative member. Thus, the male becomes the symbol of the divine, the creator. It is important to recognize the logic. There is a real biological difference between females and males, but a faulty understanding of biology allows myth to represent and symbolize reality in terms of the public male and private female. Though the logic is clear, it is impossible to know whether the faulty understanding of biology gave rise to the myth or the myth to the understanding of biology.

Anthropologists refer to Mediterranean woman as embedded in a male, first in her father, then in her husband, and finally in a son. By "embedded" they mean that a woman in such a culture receives her status, protection, worth, and identity from those males with whom she is aligned. The Bible witnesses to this embeddedness from cover to cover. When Adam and Eve are expelled from the garden, God quotes a verse to the woman:

> I will greatly increase your
>   pangs in childbearing;
>   in pain you shall bring forth children,
> yet your desire shall be for your husband,
>   and he shall rule over you. (Gen. 3:16)

Likewise the author of Ephesians offers the traditional advice to wives, "be subject to your husbands" (Eph. 5:22). In the genealogy of Matthew's Gospel, the men beget sons, and occasionally it is mentioned that they are "from" or "out of" a woman. But in the genealogy's description of Joseph and Mary, the text literally reads "Jacob begot Joseph the man [husband] of Mary, out of whom was begotten Jesus." Mary does not beget Jesus; he is begotten out of (from) her. She is the receptacle or field for the male, divine seed.

This notion of embeddedness summaries the mythical overlay that seeks to interpret and direct male/female relations. What is the appeal of this myth? From the male's point of view, the conception of children entails two fundamental conflicts, and the myth solves them both. The act of intercourse can be viewed as an engulfment of the male, and the male can never have full security about the child's paternity, whereas the female's maternity is certain. The myth of embeddedness compensates for and hides the male's fear and insecurity. It reverses the male embeddedness by symbolizing the male apart from intercourse. In myth the woman is embedded. One can even represent this male dominance through the more elaborate architecture of the public (male) rooms. The male's disembedded insecurity is reassured by making him the contributor of the essential element (his seed). Myth builds on a real difference between male and female, but it fuses this reality with its own interpretation. Although it is possible to distinguish between biology and interpretation analytically, myth prefers to fuse them and makes that fusion appear necessary and natural. Once analysis separates the layers, however, the arbitrariness of the interpretation appears, and myth loses its power. From the Mediterranean basin, we in the West have inherited the myth of female embeddedness as a primary mythical structure. We have employed this myth not only as a way of making sense of male/female relations, but also as a way of mythically ordering the world.

Embeddedness is buried deep in the myths of Mediterranean culture. The Adam and Eve story exemplifies this. Eve comes from the rib/body of Adam: "The rib he had taken out of the man the LORD God built up into a woman, and he brought her to the man. The man said: 'This one at last is bone from my bones, flesh from my flesh! She shall be called woman, for from man was she taken.' That is why a man leaves his father and mother and attaches himself to his wife, and two become one" (Gen. 2:22-24 REB). While the man is described as leaving home, in reality the woman left home and became something of a stranger in her husband's house. She attached herself and became dependent on and subordinate to him, all of which is symbolized in God making her from the rib of the man. But if the myth of embeddedness demands that a man possess a wife and that she be embedded in him, the woman is also a threat to the man. Adam blames Eve for his eating the forbidden fruit (Gen. 3:12).

In ancient times the model of the faithful wife was Penelope who waited for Odysseus throughout his nineteen years of war and wandering. During those years she employed various schemes to resist the advances of her suitors who insisted Odysseus was dead. She first put them off by saying that she could not make a decision until she had finished a robe in which to wrap Odysseus's father at his death. During the day she would weave, but at night she would unravel what she had woven, so that the robe remained tantalizingly unfinished. By such stratagems the wise Penelope, as she was called, imitated the wily Odysseus.

But if Penelope is the model of the faithful wife, Homer's tale also contains the contrary model, the treacherous wife. When Odysseus goes down to Hades, he meets his former commander Agamemnon, the leader of the Greek forces against Troy. When Odysseus asks how he came to be there, Agamemnon reports that his own wife, Clytaemnestra, plotted to kill him upon his arrival home. Significantly, the narrative blames Agamemnon's death not on the man who actually killed him, but on Clytaemnestra who plotted with her lover. Agamemnon describes her as a harlot, indicating that the origin of her crime is the violation of his sexual rights over her.

> But the harlot turned her face aside, and had not even the grace, though I was on my way to Hades, to shut my eyes with her hands or to close my mouth. And so I say that for brutality and infamy there is no one to equal a woman who can contemplate such deeds. Who else could conceive so hideous a crime as the deliberate butchery of her husband and lord? Indeed, I had looked forward to a rare welcome from my children and my servants when I reached my home. But now, in the depth of her villainy, she has branded not herself alone but the whole of her sex and every honest woman for all time to come. (*Odyssey* 11.424–34 [1946, 182–83])

Not only is Clytaemnestra solely responsible for the crime, but her crime stains all women, just as Eve's is said to have stained all women in Christian interpretation (Pagels 1989, 68). Odysseus's response associates Clytaemnestra with Helen: "It was for Helen's sake that so many of us met our death, and it was Clytaemnestra who hatched the plot against her absent lord" (*Odyssey* 11.438–39 [1946, 183]). Clytaemnestra and Eve both betray their husbands into the hands of death, and like Helen, all women pose a potential death threat to men. Hence no woman can be trusted after this original sin because she can betray her lord.

Accordingly, Agamemnon warns Odysseus, "Let this be a lesson to you also. . . . Never be too gentle even with your wife, nor show her all that is in your mind. Reveal a little of your counsel to her, but keep the rest of it to yourself" (*Odyssey* 11.440–43 [1946, 183]). Agamemnon assures Odysseus that his wife, the wise Penelope, would never betray him, but nevertheless advises, "Do not sail openly into port when you reach your home-country. Make a secret approach. Women, I tell you, are no longer to be trusted" (*Odyssey* 11.455–56 [1946, 183]). And Odysseus follows this advice exactly. Penelope is the last person to whom he reveals himself, and she must pass a test of recognition before they are reconciled. As Marilyn Katz has argued in her study *Penelope's Renown*, Clytaemnestra's crime is the frame for Penelope's faithfulness and remains a trajectory that she could and might follow: "The praise of Penelope and the assurances of her faithfulness are enclosed on either side by a warning, and inserted into a general framework of betrayal and mistrust. Agamemnon concludes his discourse with the all-encompassing warning to Odysseus that 'women are no longer to be trusted' " (Katz 1991, 52). Even after the suitors have been killed by Odysseus and gone to Hades, women continue to receive the blame. The suitors in Hades report to Agamemnon, "In the prolonged absence of Odysseus we began to pay our addresses to his wife. These proved distasteful to her, but instead of refusing us outright or taking the final step, she schemed to bring about our downfall and our death" (*Odyssey* 24.124–27 [1946, 354]). The suitors blame their fate on Penelope as though she were Clytaemnestra because all women are betrayers.

> Within a sexist ideology and a male-dominated cinema,
> woman is presented as what she represents for
> man. . . . It is probably true to say that despite the
> enormous emphasis placed on woman as spectacle in
> the cinema, woman as woman is largely absent.
> —*Claire Johnston (1977)*

IN THE 1970s A SERIES OF FILMS CHALLENGED this traditional myth of female embeddedness. *Diary of a Mad Housewife* (1970), *Up the Sandbox* (1972), *A Woman under the Influence* (1974), *Alice Doesn't Live Here Anymore* (1974), *The Turning Point* (1977), *An Unmarried Woman* (1978), and *Private Benjamin* (1980) all feature women who leave home to find their freedom, often separately from a man. Among the most popular of these films were *An Unmarried Woman* and *Private Benjamin*, which, though quite different in genre, attack the myth of female embeddedness in a similar way. *An Unmarried Woman* is a serious drama or perhaps melodrama, and *Private Benjamin* is a comedy.

Paul Mazursky's *An Unmarried Woman* (1978) was well received by both audiences and critics. It garnered Academy Award nominations for best picture, best screen play, and best actress. Jill Clayburgh's performance as Erica, the protagonist, stands out as an intelligent portrayal. In many other films the plot would have been treated as tragedy or pure melodrama, which ironically it became in the made-for-television film *A Married Woman* (1988), also starring Jill Clayburgh. Erica, an upper-class New York wife in her late thirties, finds herself suddenly alone when her stockbroker husband announces that he is in love with a younger woman. The film observes her negotiating the aftereffects: finding a job, dealing with the neighborhood Romeos, dating, and coping with sex for singles. Her friends offer her a variety of well-meaning advice, and a female psychologist helps her regain her self-respect. Finally, she meets an artist (Alan Bates), who embodies the sensitive male, and forms a warm, loving relation with him. But in the end she does not go off with him. The film's final cut shows her walking down the street with a large painting he has given her. She has become an independent, self-sustaining woman, whose identity is not based on a male.

The army made a man out of me.

—Marching song

JUDY BENJAMIN (GOLDIE HAWN), THE HEROINE
of *Private Benjamin*, actually makes a reference to *An Unmarried
Woman*. Following her husband's sudden death on their wedding
night, she goes into a depression and secludes herself in a motel. She
tells the host of an all-night talk show, "Well, I didn't get it. I'd been
Mrs. Alan Bates so fast." Judy Benjamin epitomizes the myth of female
embeddedness. Before the credits, the screen proclaims:

> When Judy Benjamin was eight years old, she confessed her life's desire
> to her best friend.
>
> "All I want," Judy whispered, "is a big house, nice clothes, two closets,
> a live-in maid, and a professional man for a husband."
>
> Today, all of Judy's dreams come true.

The opening scene is her wedding to a Jewish accountant.

Judy embodies the princess myth. After she joins the army, the
female captain in charge of her basic training coos to the sergeant,
"Ooo, what do we have here?" and then condescendingly addresses
her as "Princess." Judy has been raised to be an accessory to a man,
to be concerned only with her house and its decorations. When the
army posts her to Brussels, Belgium, as a purchasing agent, she
remarks that it is "a job I have trained for my whole life." Earlier her
father complains, "The girl is twenty-nine years old and trained to
do nothing." To which she mutters under her breath, "I'm twenty-
eight," an indication of how little real connection he has with her.
Indeed, her father treats her like a servant—as if she were invisible
except when attending to his wants. He asks her for a cigarette and
match, but when she tries to talk, he ignores her and concentrates
on a football game on television. He treats his wife exactly the same
way. Judy's new husband treats her similarly, sending her off during
the wedding reception to get him a Perrier with a twist of lemon and
forcing her into oral sex in the back of the limo during the party.

The death of Judy's second husband on their wedding night, appropriately while he was forcing her to have sex on the bathroom
floor, is the catalyst that forces her to change. As she accurately
remarks, "I've never not belonged to somebody—never." An army

recruiter convinces her to sign up by persuading her that the army is a kind of Club Med. At first she resists basic training and tries to resign. Meanwhile her parents are appalled that she has joined the army, believing it is well below their social status. Her father accuses her of going temporarily insane, and they tell their friends she has had a breakdown. He protests, "Didn't we give you everything? A car on your sixteenth birthday . . . bailed you out of your first marriage." She evidently has heard the litany before. When her parents arrive at boot camp to "save" her, her father attempts to reassert control: "You're obviously incapable of making your own decisions. Starting tomorrow, I'm not letting you out of my sight." Her choice is simple, either the army or her father—the latter choice would keep her embedded in a male forever. Despite her efforts to leave, she chooses the army.

The army makes a man out of her. Basic training, as they say, shapes her up. Yet she is not a man's man. The image is more complex and her transformation more gradual. In the war games that conclude basic training, her squad is assigned to guard the swamp, a signal of the low esteem in which the captain holds them. During the evening they swap stories around the camp fire and in the morning are hopelessly lost. By accident they stumble on the enemy's headquarters. To this point they have behaved in a stereotypical female fashion. But now they jump into high gear and by female charms manage to trick the entire enemy army into surrendering, thus winning the war games and becoming heroes. Judy's acceptance in the male world is symbolized by her appointment to the elite Thornbirds, a previously all-male group of paratroopers.

Now her relations with males revert to an old and familiar pattern. Or, to put it more accurately, though Judy Benjamin has changed, the male world has not. Colonel Thornbush (Robert Webber), who had encouraged and supported her in her army career, attempts to rape her, telling her throughout that she really wants it. She escapes by parachuting out of the plane. Next, she becomes involved with a French gynecologist, Henri (Armand Assante). When he proposes to her, he insists that she sign a prenuptial agreement, written in French, that protects his ancestral property. Then he begins to make her over, changing her hair and clothes and turning her back into the old Judy. Meanwhile he continues to dally with various former girl friends, including the maid. When Judy arrives at the altar to take her wedding vows, all the men in her life pass before her, and instead of saying "I do," she calls off the wedding. Henri attacks her as ungrateful, pointing out that she was "in the army" when he met her. She returns the compliment, telling him "you're such a schmuck." After he calls her stupid (something her father had hinted at), she slugs him and walks out. As she walks down the road, throwing her veil to the winds, an army march plays quietly in the background.

Both *An Unmarried Woman* and *Private Benjamin* attack the myth of female embeddedness. A woman can be a self-existent person without and apart from a man. Ironically, *Private Benjamin* the comedy is in the end the more pessimistic of the two films. At the end of *An Unmarried Woman*, there is a strong hint of an eventual marriage between Erica and the artist, and he does represent the ideal male for the new female. In *Private Benjamin* all the men are unsuitable and appear incapable of change. This film ends with Judy in a wedding dress triumphantly celebrating her escape from embedment. As a prophecy of female/male relations, *Private Benjamin* paints a dark picture and foretells continuing conflict. Movies since that time have developed along two tracks. The overwhelming majority and the most financially successful have returned to the myth of female embeddedness, while a small group of films have tried to explore new versions of the female story.

Women's history, the lived experience of servitude, must be fought for, however painful its recollection. For without the knowledge of our own suppression, without the humiliation of our own exclusion, the dominant culture offers us nothing but the prefabricated structures and categories of male thought.
—*Elizabeth Fox-Genovese (1991)*

MYSTIC PIZZA (1988) IS A COMING OF AGE STORY, a genre frequently employed for men but seldom for women. Though a low-budget film, or what's sometimes referred to as a little film, it was well received by the critics and has done well in the rental market. The writing and acting are strong, and it was Julia Roberts's (of *Pretty Woman*) first major role.

The film is set in the Portuguese immigrant fishing community of Mystic, Connecticut. The movie's title refers to the Mystic Pizza Parlor where the three heroines work. Each represents a different version of the female stereotype, and they play both with and against type.

Jojo (Lili Taylor) opens the movie by fainting at her own wedding and then calling it off. She wants to maintain her independence, keep her options open, and is not ready for commitment. Yet she aggressively pursues Bill (Vincent D'Onofrio). His lines normally belong to the female: "I love you. I think we should make a commitment. I think we ought to get married." She replies that if he says that word one more time, she's going to scream and promptly does so, bringing her parents into the living room at an embarrassing moment. On another occasion when Jojo wants Bill to go away with her for a few days, he refuses, "I'm telling you, Jo, that I love you and all you love is my dick. Do you know how that makes me feel?" This graphic complaint certainly plays against our expectations of standard male/female behavior.

Daisy (Julia Roberts) plays the vamp, a slut as she calls herself, or the bad girl. She contrasts with her sister Kat (Annabeth Gish), the good girl. Daisy knows she is attractive and is willing to use her appeal to get ahead. She picks up Charlie Winsor (Adam Storke), a rich law student who's using his parents' summer home during the winter. Initially, he tells her he's taking a vacation from law school, but eventually it turns out that he has been expelled for cheating.

Charlie and his father are locked in combat. He is angry because of his dependence on his father, who in turn sees his son as a failure. As the romance develops, Charlie invites Daisy to dinner to meet his family. They serve lobster, a delicacy for them but not for the daughter of a fisherman whose refrigerator is stuffed with lobster. The maid turns out to be one of her friends, and some disparaging remarks are made about the quality of the help. In a misguided effort to defend Daisy, Charlie asks for beer instead of wine and taunts his father, much to Daisy's embarrassment. When Daisy and Charlie are leaving, he remarks on his father's bad behavior, but Daisy comes to the father's defense, saying, "He was only being himself." Rather, she accuses Charlie of using her to get at his father. "I would never use you to get at somebody. Your father didn't cheat his way out of law school. You did that all on your own. You're not even good enough for me," she exclaims as she storms away.

Kat, the final member of the trio, has won a scholarship to Yale. To earn enough money for college, she takes a second job babysitting the daughter of a young architect, whose wife is in England. Kat, the good girl and the innocent, is overwhelmed when the sophisticated architect appears to be interested in her. He too is a graduate of Yale. What begins innocently goes too far. When the architect's wife comes back, he abandons Kat without a word. Near the film's end he does offer her a check to help out with school, but she tears it up without even opening it, much to Jojo's dismay when she pieces it together and discovers the amount.

The Mystic Pizza Parlor serves as the locus of action that allows the young women to interact. It is presided over by Leona (Conchata Ferrell) who serves as their substitute mother. Daisy and Kat's own mother is so busy working that she has little time to interact with them, although there is one touching scene with Daisy. After the mother expresses strong reservations about Charlie, Daisy responds that she's a bad girl and will never go to Yale like Kat. Her mother remarks that she doesn't expect her to go to Yale, she's just scared for her. Daisy replies that she's scared too. Leona comforts the young women through their various trials. But her pizza is the film's real metaphor for life. She claims it is the best pizza in the world and the recipe is a secret. It's all in the spices she says. "My grandfather taught my father and my father taught me and one of these days when I retire I just might teach one of you. It's tradition," and all the girls join in the refrain, "and you don't monkey with tradition." The TV Gourmet vindicates her claim when he gives the pizza four stars. The movie hints that the recipe for life, like Leona's pizza, is a secret that must be handed down, and you don't monkey with tradition.

Just as the movie began with an aborted wedding ceremony, it ends with a wedding reception. Jojo agrees to marry Bill insisting all the while that she needs to maintain her independence. Charlie comes to the party and tells Daisy that what she said about him and his father was right. "I owe you an apology," he says. She puts him to work dishing out the ice cream. A little later, Kat remarks, "You had some company in there," and Daisy shrugs, "Who knows?" Finally, Leona gives Kat a check to help with her college expenses.

One might take this rounding off in the conclusion as a return of the myth, since myth likes order and completion. But that is not quite what happens. In the film's final cut the three women are alone and

Jojo gets the final word. "What the hell do you think Leona really puts in that pizza?" she says, and they all laugh. This film is trying to wrestle with the old myth of female embeddedness by giving these young women a new future independent of that myth, yet it still respects tradition. Can men and women relate without the myth of female embeddedness? Bill plays the traditional female part demanding love and commitment, Jojo maintains her independence, Daisy discovers her self-worth, and Kat loses her innocence without losing her integrity. All three women learn to respect and bond without competing with each other. The story rejects the myth of female embeddedness and begins to sketch out a new blending of tradition. But the recipe remains a mystery.

> For some people today the Bible supports female slavery and male dominance in culture, while for others it offers freedom from sexism. Central in this discussion are such passages as the creation accounts in Genesis, certain laws in Leviticus, the Song of Songs, the wisdom literature, various Gospel stories about Jesus and the powerless, and particular admonitions of Paul and his successors.
> —*Phyllis Trible (1978)*

FEMINIST ANALYSIS OF BIBLICAL TEXTS HAS been expanding and developing in recent years. Such analysis has pointed out that the Bible is both an enslaving and a liberating book for women. As a part of Mediterranean culture, the Bible partakes in the myth of female embeddedness. For the most part it does not seriously challenge that myth, although it does at times call many of the myth's implications into question, as we saw earlier in chapter 4 in the story of the Samaritan Woman (John 4). While Jesus in that story repudiates the myth as replicating the boundary between God and humanity, he does not attack the embeddedness *per se*. The story of the Samaritan Woman offers important implications for our conversation between the movies and the biblical text. But first, several caveats are in order. Although there are strong similarities between the status of women in the ancient world and ours, the differences are vast. The social liberation of women was not a concern in the ancient world. Even where we find women acting in independent roles, we must take care to avoid the anachronism of seeing our situation in theirs.

At the same time that we avoid anachronistic thinking, we should likewise disavow a hermeneutics that mistakes social construction for the will of God. I admire the honesty of Elisabeth Schüssler Fiorenza's hermeneutics since she admits that her criteria for liberation are the product of female experience and are not drawn explicitly from the Bible (Schüssler Fiorenza 1983, 33). Others are less honest and selectively employ the text to enforce conservative social structures as the revealed will of God because they appear in the Bible. By the same argument, a whole range of activity that the Bible endorses, such as slavery, would have to be reinstituted. Hermeneutics is more complicated than simply determining what the Bible has to say. One needs a more sophisticated sorting method.

Finally, it is extremely difficult to determine what Jesus' view of women was. Because of the time span between Jesus' ministry and the writing of the gospels, we often cannot determine whether a piece of material is from Jesus, and frequently there is good reason to believe it is not. Virtually no scholar would maintain that the story of the Samaritan Woman represents a verbatim account of a historical event or even that it is based on an actual conversation between Jesus and a Samaritan woman. It has all the earmarks of a Johannine dialogue in that it contains so much of his special vocabulary, symbolism, and concepts. Thus, it is much more likely to be a later product of the Johannine community. Even more we must be careful not to make Jesus the advocate of our position. Doing so is a real temptation. If we can show that Jesus agrees with us, then we have a weapon that we can use to coerce other Christians into a similar belief or practice. To give in at this point is to fall victim to the authoritarian myth and turn Jesus into an authoritarian superhero. Such tendencies were already underway in the formation of the New Testament, but as we have seen in the case of the Philippians' hymn and the death scene in Mark, such a view of power was repudiated by many early Christians as incompatible with their understanding of what had happened in Jesus.

On what grounds, then, might we develop a conversation between the New Testament and the movies about the myth of female embeddedness? If we observe the way in which women were viewed at various moments in the history of the early community, a pattern will emerge. I will focus on a specific issue from Jesus and another from Paul that raise the issue of female embeddedness. For Jesus the issue is divorce and for Paul the baptismal confession that there is neither male nor female. In both cases we will follow up with a brief look at how these issues were received in subsequent generations of early Christianity.

> It is not that sexual differentiation and sexuality do not exist in the "world" of God, but that "patriarchal marriage is no more," because its function in maintaining and continuing patriarchal economic and religious structures is no longer necessary. This is what it means to live and be "like the angels" (Mark 12:25) who live in "the world" of God.
> —*Elisabeth Schüssler Fiorenza (1983)*

DIVORCE EXPLICITY BRINGS THE MYTH OF FE-male embeddedness to the surface. The question of divorce was a live issue in first-century Judaism. The Hebrew Bible text to which any debate in Judaism must refer is Deuteronomy 24:1: "If a man has taken a woman in marriage, but she does not win his favour because he finds something *offensive* in her, and he writes her a certificate of divorce, gives it to her, and dismisses her . . ." (REB). The debate revolves around the meaning of the Hebrew word translated "offensive." The NRSV translates the word as "objectionable" (RSV "indecency"), while the NAB translates it as "indecent." Just as modern translators cannot decide on the Hebrew word's meaning, so the rabbis debated its meaning. The schools of Shammai and Hillel represent the two main options. A quotation from the Mishnah summarizes their positions:

A. The House of Shammai say, "A man should divorce his wife only because he has found grounds for it in unchastity.
B. "since it is said, Because he has found in her indecency in anything (Dt. 24.1)."
C. And the House of Hillel say, "Even if she spoiled his dish.
D. "since it is said, Because he has found in her indecency in anything."

E. R. Aqiba says, "Even if he found someone else prettier than she.
F. "since it is said, And it shall be if she find no favor in his eyes (Dt.
24:1)" M. Git. 9:10. (Neusner 1988, 487)

Both Shammai and Hillel were active during the time of Jesus, so
they probably represent the opinions of his day. Shammai takes the
more conservative position that narrows the grounds for divorce to
"unchastity," along the lines of the NAB or the RSV, while Hillel holds
that it can be for as simple a reason as that she is a poor cook. Aqiba,
an important rabbi of a later period, elaborates on Hillel's interpretation, indicating that it became the dominant position in a
later period.

The technical debate about the meaning of Deuteronomy is missing in the New Testament except perhaps in the exception clause in
Matthew (5:32; 19:9) where he seems to side with Shammai. A number
of sayings about divorce all ascribe an extreme position to Jesus.
These would seem to indicate that Jesus did take such a stand forbidding divorce. If we sort through these sayings, we can see the
shape of the tradition and ask how the early communities
interpreted it.

The New Testament preserves five sayings in which Jesus forbids
divorce. The earliest is in 1 Cor. 7:10-11. Paul is responding to a series
of questions raised by the Corinthians who have asked his advice
about whether a man can touch a woman. In this context he addresses
married persons about the issue of divorce. Unlike Shammai and
Hillel who envision a Jewish context in which a woman may not
divorce a man, Paul is writing in the Roman legal context where a
woman may divorce a man; therefore, he must address both sides of
the question. This saying to the married is parallel to and placed
between a saying to the unmarried and one "to the rest." In the latter
two sayings, Paul "says" to them, whereas in the saying to the married,
he "orders" or "instructs." Furthermore, he emphasizes that "not I,
but the Lord" commands this (Conzelmann 1975, 120). Paul obviously
has in mind a saying of Jesus as the basis for his "command." Paul
does not directly quote Jesus' saying, but implies its existence. Two
aspects of this saying are important for our discussion. Paul takes a
male point of view. When speaking of the female, he employs the
passive voice: "a woman is not to be separated from a husband, but
if she has been separated" (my translation). When Paul speaks of the

male, he employs the active voice and uses another term: "A man should not send away his wife" (my translation). The term for "send away" is frequently found in the sense of "to release someone from a legal relation" (Bultmann, 509). Furthermore, even though Paul uses command language to introduce this saying, he does not view it as being without absolute exception for he immediately says, "if she has been separated," thus implying that separation does take place. Paul does not view this as divine law.

In the Synoptic Gospels, a saying in which Jesus forbids divorce occurs four times: once each in Mark and Luke, twice in Matthew. One Matthean passage (19:3-12) parallels Mark (10:2-12), while the other Matthean passage (5:31-32) parallels Luke (16:18). Thus, we actually have two different sayings, one for which the primary source is Mark and the other for which the source is Q (the Synoptic Sayings Source):

Q (Synoptic Sayings Source) = Luke 16:18

Anyone who divorces his wife and marries another commits adultery, and whoever marries a woman divorced from her husband commits adultery.

The Matthean parallel has two interesting variations. First, Matthew has an exception clause, "except on the ground of unchastity." Matthew repeats the exception clause at 19:9 whereas the Marcan parallel 10:11 has no exception clause. Since the parallels in both cases lack the exception clause, scholars think this clause is an insertion by Matthew (Luz 1989, 304; see also pp. 304–10 for a excellent discussion of what the phrase might mean and the history of its influence). Matthew's addition further demonstrates that the saying circulated in early Christianity neither as unchangeable, divine law nor as an absolute proscription of divorce.

A second difference between Matthew and Luke concerns who commits adultery. In Matthew, by divorcing his wife a man "causes her to commit adultery," while in Luke the husband commits adultery. Some have argued that Matthew's version at this point is earlier (Davies and Allison 1991, 528). There is much to support this because Matthew's version interrupts the male point of view that dominates both the Q saying and the Pauline saying. But the Marcan saying goes even further in this regard:

Mark 10:11-12

Whoever divorces his wife and marries another commits adultery against her; if she divorces her husband and marries another, she commits adultery.

Mark's double form, in which both husband and wife are forbidden to divorce, clearly reflects a gentile, Roman situation, since a woman could not initiate a divorce under Jewish law. Thus, the second part of the saying must be an adaptation to meet the changing situation of the early communities. But the most significant and striking phrase occurs in the first part of the saying. Mark alone states that when a man divorces his wife and marries another, he "commits adultery *against* her." This is unprecedented. As Craig Keener remarks, "the husband could not legally commit adultery against his own wife; he could only commit it with another man's wife. This is a widely rec ognized feature of the Old Testament and Jewish law" (Keener 1991, 35). A whole tractate of the Mishnah and subsequently of the Talmud is devoted to "The Straying Wife" (*Soṭah*). A husband who suspected his wife of adultery could even force her to submit to an ordeal to prove her faithfulness. As Judith Wegner has argued, "[l]ike marriage and divorce, this is a unilateral procedure, which cannot be invoked by a wife against her husband, for although she is *his* exclusive sexual property, he is not *hers*" (Wegner 1988, 52). While a woman incurs a penalty for adultery, "a married man incurs no penalty for extramarital relationships unless his mistress happens to be another man's wife" (Wegner 1988, 52). Adultery, in other words, is a sin *against* a man; he is always the offended party because he has property rights to his wife.

Even though the other sayings about divorce in Paul and Q originate from this saying, the male point of view so dominates that they cannot conceive of a man committing adultery *against* a woman. Thus, they reshape the saying so that the man commits adultery. The original saying was not concerned with forbidding divorce but with the detrimental effect of embedding a woman in a man. In such a system the woman becomes a symbol of shame and the man a symbol of honor. But by using *adultery* in such an unusual, provocative, and scandalous sense, Jesus makes the woman a symbol of honor. He attacks the "androcentric honour whose debilitating effect went far

beyond the situation of divorce. It was also the basis for the dehu-
manization of women, children, and non-dominant males" (Kloppenborg 1990, 196).

The saying was not originally a legal saying, a sentence of holy
law, but more like a riddle or parable. Such is the way Mark also
understands it since he has Jesus withdraw into a house to discuss
the saying with his disciples, a clear signal he has used elsewhere to
denote a parable or riddle (Mark 4:10; 9:28, 33). Matthew also situates
the saying among the so-called antitheses in his Sermon on the Mount.
Robert Tannehill has defined these sayings as "focal instances":

> The focal instance, then, is characterized by 1) specificness and 2)
> extremeness. Extremeness means that it stands in deliberate tension
> with a basic pattern of human behavior. Specificness means that there
> is a surprising narrowness of focus due to the desire to present an
> extreme instance. No attempt is made to encompass a major area of
> human behavior under a general rule or to cover such an area by
> systematic discussion of the legal and ethical problems of different
> classes of situations. Thus consideration of an area of behavior seems
> to be incomplete, and yet the specific instance is directly suggestive
> for many other situations. (Tannehill 1975, 72)

This saying meets Tannehill's definition of a focal instance. The
specific situation is the setting aside of a wife and the taking of
another. Likewise it is extreme, since it is unprecedented in Judaism
for a man to commit adultery *against* a woman. Had Jesus' design
in forbidding divorce been legal clarity, he could simply have forbade
it. Rather, by means of this saying, he focuses attention on a whole
field of human behavior, relations between women and men, and
calls that organization into question without offering a specific plan
of reorganization. Like *Private Benjamin* and *Mystic Pizza*, this
saying focuses our attention on what is wrong with female embeddedness without offering a specific remedy.

The subsequent New Testament and Christian tradition has ignored
this critique of female embeddedness in favor of maintaining the
embeddedness of the female in the male. The saying became a statement of divine law used to enforce female embeddedness because
they could not conceive of how a man could commit adultery *against*
a woman. Therefore the saying became one in which divorce was
equated with adultery. Since adultery is wrong, so also is divorce.

In a society [Greco-Roman] where women are in short
supply due to female infanticide and death at childbirth
and are therefore married young and remarried quickly
when widowed, many Christian women have withdrawn
from sexual relations ([1 Cor.] 7:1-40).
—Antoinette Clark Wire (1990)

PAUL'S VIEW OF WOMEN HAS BEEN A BATTLE-
field in recent years, with some claiming Paul as a champion of
women's rights while others employ him to continue the subjection
of women. I suggest that we will never get to the bottom of this issue
both because we lack sufficient evidence and because Paul himself
was conflicted about female freedom. The classic text espousing
female freedom is the baptismal confession in Galatians 3:28. The
confession employs a six-line arrangement:

1. For you are all sons of God, through faith, in Christ Jesus.
    2. For as many of you as were baptized into Christ have put on
    Christ
    3. There is neither Jew nor Greek;
    4. there is neither slave nor freeman;
    5. there is neither male and female.
6. For you are all one in Christ Jesus. (Betz 1979, 181)

Lines 1 and 6 are parallel, repeating the same idea in different
words. The phrase "through faith" is probably a Pauline comment to
tie the confession to his argument in the Letter to the Galatians. Line
2 notes the setting, Christian baptism, while lines 3-5 denote baptism's
outcome. Betz summarizes the liturgical function of the sayings as
follows: "In the liturgy, the saying would communicate information
to the newly initiated, telling them of their eschatological status before
God in anticipation of the Last Judgment and also informing them
how this status affects, and in fact changes their social, cultural, and
religious self-understanding, as well as their responsibilities in the
here-and-now" (184). In sacramental action, this becomes a performative statement that accomplishes a change by its pronouncement.
Things are different after such a performative statement, even if they
do not appear to be different. For example, when the bride and groom
say "I do" under the proper circumstances, they are married. Their
status has changed legally and socially, even though no external

change is apparent. Wayne Meeks has powerfully described this language's performative character:

> A resident of one of the cities of the province of Asia who ventured to become a member of one of the tiny Christian cells in their early years would have heard the utopian declaration of mankind's reunification as a solemn ritual pronouncement. Reinforced by dramatic gestures (disrobing, immersion, robing), such a declaration would carry—within the community for which its language was meaningful—the power to assist in shaping the symbolic universe by which that group distinguished itself from the ordinary "world" of the larger society. (Meeks 1974, 182)

While understanding this language as performative helps us to understand its power within a liturgical and religious context, does this language have a function outside a religious context? The terms originate not from the religious sphere but from the political and social spheres of life. The first set of relations, "neither Jew nor Gentile," probably parallels the common Hellenistic distinction between Greeks and barbarians. Paul uses this phrase in Rom. 1:14 where he states his indebtedness "both to Greeks and to barbarians, both to the wise and to the foolish." This example illustrates that the first term dominates or determines the point of view and represents the positive value in the old world. The new world created by baptism destroys the coordinates of that old world. In the baptismal confession, the first term is "Jews," indicating that the point of view is Jewish Christianity and that the formula emerged during the period when Jewish Christianity was accepting gentile converts. Paul understood this affirmation to represent an empirical reality. The Gentiles have now been brought into the promises of Israel. Because there is one God, humankind is unified. "Or is God the God of Jews only? Is he not the God of Gentiles also? Yes, of Gentiles also, since God is one; and he will justify the circumcised on the ground of faith and the uncircumcised through that same faith" (Rom. 3: 29-30). While Paul had to struggle to assert the reality of unity of this first polarity in his Letter to the Romans, in the end the Christian church accepted that position. The Gentile church, however, has had a hard time accepting Paul's argument that Israel is the natural olive branch and that the Gentiles are grafted in unnaturally (Rom. 11:24), even at times doing our own pruning of the tree.

The second confession announces the abolition of the institution of slavery. The status of this confession is more problematic than the first because literally supporting such a statement would have undermined the economic system of the Roman Empire, which depended on slave labor, and brought the church into direct conflict with the political authorities. In 1 Cor. 7:21-24 Paul writes to the Corinthians to advise them to remain "in whatever condition you were called" (7:24), obviously not encouraging them to revolt. To a slave Paul's argument might appear demeaning. "For whoever was called in the Lord as a slave is a freed person belonging to the Lord, just as whoever was free when called is a slave of Christ" (7:22). Such a comparison trivializes the slaves' aspirations for freedom as the numerous slave revolts and inscriptions of manumission testify. Nor would slaves necessarily be persuaded by an eschatological argument that the end of the world is approaching when the eschatological promise of baptism will be fulfilled. That argument offers hope, but one suspects that a slave would respond to Paul that such an argument is all right for Paul because he's already free, but what about us slaves?

Yet for Paul slave language functions as a primary description of his own ministry. He is both a slave and a son of God to be, an heir. In many of his letters, the opening address contains a reference to himself as a slave, frequently toned down in translations with the less offensive euphemism "servant" (see Rom. 1:1; Phil. 1:1, Gal. 1:10). Though a free man, he has made himself a slave for all (1 Cor. 9:19). Such language represents Paul's understanding of the cross and resurrection. Now we are under the cross and like Jesus, a slave; then we shall be raised like Jesus and be a son of God. We have already seen this dynamic in the Philippians' hymn (Phil. 2:6-11; see chap. 4 above).

If Christians are not to attempt to rid themselves of their status as slaves, but the social distinction between slave and free is made irrelevant by baptism, how then is a Christian master to behave toward a Christian slave? This question comes to the fore in the Letter to Philemon. Unfortunately, the letter is a request written in an indirect style, and we do not know its outcome. But Norman Petersen's brilliant book on the letter enables us to make some informed guesses. The clear difference between Onesimus's status before and after he ran away has to do with his conversion while with Paul. In the before state, he was Philemon's slave and a nonbeliever. Though believing that in Christ there was neither slave nor freeman, Philemon apparently felt no pressure to free his slave. From Petersen's reconstruction, "we can infer further that Philemon was able to compartmentalize his life in such a way as to be both a good churchman and a good man of the world" (Petersen 1985, 265). But after Onesimus's conversion the situation is different. Now that Onesimus is a believer, he is a brother of Philemon. In the Letter to Philemon, Paul refers to Onesimus as "my child . . . whose father I have become" (10) and tells Philemon that he should take Onesimus back as "no longer a slave but more than a slave, a beloved brother" (16). The family character of the community denotes it as a brotherhood based on the selfless love of its members. For Paul, what is good is what builds up the body (1 Cor. 8:1; 10:23). Paul seeks to create a crisis in Philemon's double life as a churchman and a man of the world. "Paul suggests that being a fellow worker and a master over a brother are as mutually exclusive as being both the slave and a brother of a brother" (Petersen 1985, 267). Paul does not attack the institution of slavery itself, but Philemon's participation in it in the case of two believers. One cannot be a slave and a brother simultaneously. But since Paul himself treated Philemon as his brother, he does not command his behavior, although the promised visit is a veiled threat in case Philemon does not do right. Paul wants Philemon to determine what builds up, what his proper response to Onesimus should be. As a result, the conclusion must be inferred. The tradition missed the point, and Paul's remarks about slavery were used for centuries to reinforce the institution of slavery in Christian nations.

The first two aspects of the baptismal formula indicate that for Paul they are not merely "spiritual" statements. They have a reality in the world. Yet Paul is not a utopian. He understands the difference between the world and the community. But he also understands that the baptismal confession undermines the world. The confession eschatologically foretells what is to be, as well as what is now coming about. The destruction of these oppositions destroyed the world as they experienced it.

The final parallel concerns male and female: "there is neither male and female." The Greek text does not exactly parallel the other two statements. First, the connective is not "neither" but "and." This echoes the Septuagint translation of the Genesis statement, "God made them male and female" (Gen. 1:27), thus signaling a new creation in which the old distinction disappears. Betz also maintains that the use of the neuter instead of the masculine as in the other two statements "indicates that not only the *social* differences between man and woman ('roles') are involved but the *biological* distinctions" (Betz 1979, 195).

This statement has no parallel in the New Testament or in Greek or Roman culture (Betz 1979, 197). Certain groups of early Christians, principally Gnostics and ascetics, understood the abolition of sexual difference in terms of androgyny, the unity of male and female. The *Gospel of Thomas* 22 presents a clear parallel: "When you make the two into one, and when you make the inner like the outer and the outer like the inner, and the upper like the lower, and when you make male and female into a single one, so that the male will not be male nor the female be female . . . then you will enter [the <Father's> domain]" (SV). But the androgyny solution seems unlikely here because the other two confessions do not refer to the unity but to the irrelevance and abolition of the difference.

A group of Christian prophetesses in Corinth appear to have radically disembedded themselves by withdrawing from sexual relationships. Their action creates a dilemma for Paul because while he agrees that celibacy is the ideal in theory, he believes that in practice marriage helps solve the problems of immorality. Celibacy is the ideal because it testifies to the elimination of the distinction between male and female. As Petersen says, "perhaps the most profound example of Paul's status as a son of God-to-be is his celibacy (1 Corinthians 7), for it anticipates the erasure of sexual distinctions that characterizes the form of the sons of God" (Petersen 1985, 262).

In 1 Corinthians 7, Paul writes about a number of issues that the Corinthians have raised. The argument is measured and careful. He sets out what appears to be a slogan, although whether it is his or the Corinthians' is unclear: "It is a good thing for a man not to have intercourse with a woman" (1 Cor. 7:1 REB). But in light of the immorality detailed in the letter's previous chapters, Paul cautions that each man should have a wife and each wife a husband. Paul is caught in a vise of his own principles. On the one hand, the baptismal confession denies sexual differentiation—and some in Corinth have taken this literally—and he desires that all be celibate like him (1 Cor. 7:7), but on the other hand, the community must maintain order.

For a woman in Greco-Roman society, to be married is to be subject to a man. Thus, to recommend that those women who have disembedded themselves return to their husbands is to recommend that they lose the very freedom that made Christianity so attractive. In an effort to finesse this problem, "Paul goes far beyond what is required in Greek to make the point that men and women have the same responsibilities to each other. . . . There is no question that Paul is rhetorically accentuating the equal and reciprocal nature of sexual responsibilities" (Wire 1990, 79–80). Not only is a husband to have a wife, but a wife is also to have a husband. Grammar does not demand this careful balancing, so its purpose must be to emphasize that what is true of one is true of the other. Furthermore, we who speak English are likely to overlook the little word "have" that denotes possession and property rights in Greek. John the Baptist had told Herod, "It is not lawful for you to *have* your brother's wife" (Mark 6:18). It is not lawful because she is the possession, property, of Phillip. Likewise, the so-called parable of the Prodigal Son begins with the note "There was a man who *had* two sons" (Luke 15:11). "Had" denotes the *potestas patris* (the power of the father), which in Roman society was nearly absolute. Thus, for Paul to parallel a man having a wife with a wife having a husband creates a mutuality or equality between husband and wife unprecedented in the ancient world (Wire 1990, 82). He accents this reciprocity in the very next verse: "The husband should fulfill his duty toward his wife, and likewise the wife toward the husband" (1 Cor. 7:3, NAB). Given the context, duties include sexual duties, and putting the man's duties to the wife first is also unprecedented. The statement about the wife's duties parallels the statement about the husband's but in elliptical style. The woman's duties would have been taken for granted in this culture, but the duties of a husband would have been assigned a much more secondary place, if alluded to at all.

Paul proceeds in a similar vein in dealing with a variety of situations. If the disembedding continues, then Paul fears immorality will become rampant throughout the community. Marriage is the concession (1 Cor. 7:6) that controls immorality. Yet he appears not to want to surrender the freedom of men and women in baptism, so he reconstitutes marriage as an act not of property possession, but of equality, of balanced relations. The case turns out to parallel that of slavery. While baptism eliminates the distinction, that way of relating still continues in the political world, so Paul attempts to work out a compromise. But just as in the case of slavery, Christianity used the Pauline letters to justify a contractual understanding of marriage. The deutero-Pauline letters to Ephesians and Colossians clearly retreat from the Pauline compromise in which eliminating the distinction leads to equality and reciprocity. "Wives, be subject to your husband as you are to the Lord" (Eph. 5:22; Col. 3:18) is not balanced by a similar statement about the husband; instead, the husband is told to love his wife "as Christ loved the church" (Eph. 5:25) or, in the case of Colossians, not to treat her harshly (Col. 3:19) as one would a slave. The hierarchical model is restored, the husband is the head, and equality and reciprocity are forgotten. As Peter Brown has argued, this step was a decisive one in the transformation of Christianity into a religion capable of dominating late antiquity. "Other pseudo-Pauline writings made clear that this order, though gentle, was to be quite as hierarchical as that praised in his *Advice on Marriage* by Plutarch, the exact contemporary, we should remember, of Paul's later follow-ers" (Brown 1988, 58). Brown quotes 1 Timothy 2 as a parallel to Plutarch:

> Let a woman learn in silence with full submission. I permit no woman to teach or to have authority over a man; she is to keep silent. For Adam was formed first, then Eve; and Adam was not deceived, but the woman was deceived and became a transgressor. Yet she will be saved through childbearing, provided they continue in faith and love and holiness, with modesty. (1 Tim. 2:11-15)

Eve and Clytaemnestra are the archetypal women, not to be trusted, who introduced evil and betrayal into the world. The freedom of the Jesus movement has given way to a perfect match of the assumptions of Greco-Roman society's hierarchical pattern by identifying Eve and Clytaemnestra.

The history of the noble claims of the Galatians' baptismal formula is tragic and discouraging. The first claim was succeeded by pogroms; not until modern times was a Christian defense of slavery abandoned, and many Christians continue to justify segregation and discrimi-nation; only now are we beginning to deal with the last claim.

But surely the recent pain and struggle of woman's self-
exploration has yielded more fruit and taken her farther
than those feeble overtures offered by the film industry
would have us believe and this is the real scandal. At
present, the industry, such as it is, is giving women
the same treatment that it gave blacks for the half-
century after *Birth of a Nation:* a kick in the face or a
cold shoulder.

—*Molly Haskell (1973)*

SUSAN FALUDI HAS LOOKED AT THE WOMEN'S
movement in America and sees a recurring cyclical pattern in which
as soon as women make social advances, an inevitable backlash sets
in and attempts to reverse the gains: "An accurate charting of American women's progress through history might look more like a cork-
screw tilted slightly to one side, its loops inching to the line of freedom
with the passage of time—but, like a mathematical curve approaching
infinity, never touching its goal" (Faludi 1991, 47). Faludi finds a
conspiracy rising up each time and repressing women. For her, the
1980s were a period of backlash in which government, media, aca-
demia, and religion conspired to repress women, to drive them back
to the home and out of competition with men. She sees the origins
of this conspiracy in the New Right "where it first took shape as a
movement with a clear ideological agenda. The New Right leaders
were among the first to articulate the central argument of the backlash—that women's equality is responsible for women's unhappiness"
(Faludi 1991, 230).

But there may be another way to look at this issue. The disembedding of women is a massive attack on myth and its ability to order
reality. For millennia, humans traditionally have used an imaginary
line between male and female to symbolize more complex realities
in a society. Changing the relation between male and female changes
what they symbolize and alters the way a society understands and
orders itself. It also threatens chaos because the mythical order has
been undercut. What Faludi sees as backlash is real enough, but myth
is a major component in it. Furthermore, a conspiracy theory demands
a villain and a victim, thus reinforcing the myth of female embeddedness. But as the New Testament makes evident, attacking a myth
is not sufficient. That only produces chaos and reaction toward order.
A new mythical realignment is necessary.

We have touched on the theme of female embeddedness in discussing the films in other chapters. Marian in *Shane* is still playing the traditional female role. The demarcation between the male and female worlds is clear and strong. Her place is in the house; often she appears in the kitchen, with the top half of the Dutch door open so that she can look out on the male world. When Shane initiates Joey into the male world of the gun, she appears in her wedding dress, drawing a strong contrast between the aggressive male world of violence and the virgin/domestic female world. She remains embedded in the male and derives her identity from her husband. Marian must be protected from male violence, which supposedly defends her world of peace. Between the first-century Mediterranean and *Shane*, little has changed in the myth of female embeddedness.

Although on the surface male/female roles appear stable in *Shane*, a revolution had been shaking the foundations for over a hundred years. Because of changes brought on by the Industrial Revolution and the American and French Revolutions, in the nineteenth century women began to organize to attain and increase their rights and freedoms. In a series of waves, always resisted and temporarily turned back, women have expanded their role in public life and gradually have been establishing their independence. Usually, the beginnings of the feminist movement in the United States are dated to the Seneca Falls Convention of 1848, which was organized by Elizabeth Cady Stanton and Susan B. Anthony. Around the turn of the century, the cycle reached another peak with the drive for the vote, an equal rights amendment, and labor rights. In 1910 the International Ladies' Garment Workers Union was founded, and Margaret Sanger began her work for Planned Parenthood. Ironically, 1920 marked not only the enfranchisement of women but also the establishment of the Miss America Contest. In the 1940s women entered the workplace in unprecedented numbers to replace the men who had gone off to war.

Following the involvement of women in public life during World War II, the 1950s saw a concerted effort to return to more traditional roles, a movement that *Shane* both represented and reinforced. But by the 1970s and 1980s, even movies with strong, aggressive, traditional males had to come to terms with the emerging assertiveness of women and their growing involvement in public life. Both the Duke persona and its successor Dirty Harry began to make a place for this public female. In *Rooster Cogburn* Miss Goodnight challenged the marshall's worldview, while proudly affirming that she did not quite measure up to the traditional view of women. And a series of women, beginning with Inspector Kate Moore, forced a similar reconsideration in Dirty Harry 's world. But, as we noticed in both cases, the woman was still required to acknowledge the male's superiority. Miss Goodnight's parting words testify to the male embodied in Rooster Cogburn, and Kate Moore's dying words request Harry to get her killer. Not only do the women have to acknowledge the superiority of the male world, in important ways they have to become male and enter the male world of violence to be accepted. To my mind, perhaps the most devastating image of the female in any of the movies we have viewed is the final, silent scene of *The Shootist*. As Gillom walks away from the saloon after killing a man and seeing his hero shot, his mother walks behind him, unable to console or enter this male world on which he has just embarked.

In *Working Girl*, a film with pretensions of representing the newly liberated working woman, Tess McGill achieves her new status at the expense of another woman. A woman plays the villain in this film, not the men who still get to play hero to the damsel in distress. Tess plays the Horatio Alger hero part, but in the end her two male patrons rescue her and banish her opponent. The male myth is capable of adjusting to the presence of a woman; the female can play a male role, but only by becoming malelike. As Tess says of herself, she has "a bod for sin and a head for business." Katharine, her nemesis, stands as a warning that one can become too male, too aggressive, and thus forfeit the prize (a male). In the end, Tess steals Jack from Katharine.

Although Goldie Hawn and Julia Roberts have starred in movies that rejected the myth of female embeddedness, some of their more recent films have reinforced it. In *Overboard* (1987), Goldie Hawn plays a spoiled, childless heiress who falls overboard from her yacht and wakes up with amnesia. As a result, she ends up with a carpenter and his three sons. Claiming that she is his wife to get even with her for not paying his bill, he remakes her into an obedient and dutiful housewife. When she regains her memory, she confesses that all she wants in life is to have his baby. Thus, after disengaging herself from embeddedness in *Private Benjamin*, Goldie Hawn goes to being totally embedded in *Overboard*. Similarly, Julia Roberts's character in *Mystic Pizza* is based on playing against the expectations of type, whereas her later film *Pretty Woman* makes the fairy tale of the princess in the tower come true.

Movies of the late 1980s reinforced this move toward the myth of female embeddedness. In *Mr. Mom* (1983), produced by Lynn Loring and Lauren Shuler, a husband and wife switch roles; she becomes the breadwinner and he the homemaker. But ultimately the switch doesn't work, and the movie argues that a woman can't have it all. Perhaps the most devastating view of working women in the movies of this period came in *Fatal Attraction* (1987). In a tactic we have already seen in *Working Girl*, two women are pitted against each other, while the man escapes unscathed. Alex (Glenn Close) is a single career woman who has a weekend affair with Dan (Michael Douglas). When she doesn't want the affair to end and attempts suicide, the plot shifts to portray her as the dangerous pursuer and destroyer of his perfect family life. His wife Beth (Anne Archer) is depicted as Alex's polar opposite. Beth is the devoted mother and wife, warm and caring, the perfect Beth of *Little Women*. The casting conforms to type. Alex is cold and blond, Beth warm and brunette; Alex's name sounds masculine, Beth epitomizes the female. After Alex's outrageous attacks on her family escalate, Beth kills Alex. The truly embedded woman must attack and kill the one not embedded. Even more, Alex is depicted as demented, a true *femme fatale*. It is as though Penelope and Clytaemnestra are doing battle. To be disembedded is so disturbing that the woman becomes not liberated but dangerous to society and must therefore be eliminated.

Few movies that reinforce the myth of female embeddedness take a view as extreme as *Fatal Attraction*. Most reflect the social conflict between tradition, the bonding and pairing of women and men, and the economic necessity compelling many women to enter the workplace. While many women moved from the home to the pink ghetto, fewer moved into the executive suite. *Baby Boom* (1987) deals with an aspirant to the executive suite who has no intentions of being a mother. The movie begins with a voiceover describing J. C. Wiatt (Diane Keaton): "First in her class at Yale, M.B.A. Harvard; six-figure income; works five to nine; married to her job and lives with an investment banker married to his." The initials J. C. are probably no accident; she has a messianic complex. She wears tailored suits with ties and has a male assistant. Her nickname is the Tiger Lady, and she is proud of it. At another point in the film she remarks, "I went to Harvard and Yale and I don't have babies." This defines her self-view.

Her boss raises the implied conflict when he discusses her possible promotion to a partnership in the firm. "How many hours do you work?" he asks. She answers, "Seventy to eighty." "As a partner," he continues, "it gets worse. Normally, I don't think of you as a woman. But in this case I have to think of you as a woman/partner. But what if you and Steven decide to get married and he wants a wife?" One can see where the conversation is leading. The role of wife/mother conflicts with the demands of being a partner in a high-powered management firm. J. C. is ready: "I understand what it takes to make it."

He continues to push the point, comparing his situation to J. C.'s: "But do you understand the sacrifices you're going to have to make? I mean, a man can be a success and still have a personal life, a full personal life. My wife is there for me whenever I need her. She raises the kids, she decorates, [pausing] I don't know what the hell she does [laughing]. I mean, I'm lucky. I can have it all." It never occurs to him that J. C. could get a husband who would perform these duties for her or that the system that makes such demands is sick. After all the ultimate reality in America is business. What's good for General Motors is good for the country. To be a wife is to be embedded. J. C.'s reply is straightforward, "Forget it. I don't want it all."

After J. C. renounces the conflict, the plot proceeds to challenge her decision. The improbable undoing of J. C.'s resolution is an inheritance. After her English cousin and his wife die in an auto accident, she inherits their child, Elizabeth (Kristina and Michelle Kennedy). The film follows J. C. through her various efforts to cope with a child. First, she puts Elizabeth up for adoption; then she decides to keep her and find a nanny, but loses her live-in companion because he could not adjust to the child; finally, J. C. attempts to balance baby and career. As her boss had prophesied, work cannot adjust to the demands of a baby. The male world of business is antagonistic to the child. A call from the nanny interrupts J. C.'s presentation to a client's board of directors. She is demeaned and made to feel out of place. When her boss decides to postpone her partnership and demotes her to a less demanding and prestigious account, she quits and buys a farm in Vermont.

Once in Vermont, she tells Elizabeth her version of Sleeping Beauty as a bedtime story: "Thank you for waking me prince because I overslept and have an important medical exam and I'm going to be an important doctor like all women can be today. And then after graduation they made a date to meet."

But the Vermont plan doesn't work out. J. C.'s house is a money pit, and in a fit of hysteria she decides to get out: "I'm a career woman, not a mother." When she is unable to sell the house, she stumbles by accident on an idea for gourmet baby food. Having made hundreds of jars of baby food applesauce from the surplus apples in her orchard, she begins to sell it in the local market where yuppie couples from New York spot it and start buying it up. Thus begins Country Baby, which she quickly builds into a successful business.

In the meantime a romance has developed between J. C. and Dr. Cooper (Sam Shepard), a strong, silent type who is the local veterinarian. When her car gets a flat tire, he stops to offer help. She appears to be incompetent, but struggles to change the tire without his help. "You kinda remind me of a bull terrier," he says. She's highly insulted and tells him that she is not interested in him but only wants to get out of town. He grabs her, kisses her, and says, "See you around." This treatment reduces her to putty and her only comment is "wow." When a true man enters the scene, as opposed to the wimp investment banker, the liberated woman dissolves into the passive, embedded woman.

When the management consulting firm she used to work for hears about Country Baby's success, they arrange for J. C. to be bought out by a larger company. She returns in style to the scene of her former disgrace, arriving in a stretch limo and looking up at the skyscraper where she used to work. The offer is very generous, $3 million in cash for Country Baby, plus about $1 million a year in salary and bonuses. She tells them that she wants to think about it for a few minutes and goes out to the ladies' room. Initially, she is very pleased with herself and looks into the mirror saying, "I'm back, I'm back." But on the way back to the boardroom, she pauses and finally announces to everyone's dismay that she is going to refuse the offer. Country Baby is not for sale. "I was really excited about this offer. You know, I don't think I really thought about what it meant. And you see, I'm not the Tiger Lady anymore. I have a crib in my office and a mobile over my desk and I really like that." Then she refers back to the conversation when her boss spelled out the conflict between career and family: "Fritz [her former boss], do you remember that night when you told me all the things I was going to have to give up, the sacrifices I was going to have to make? Well, I don't want to make those sacrifices, and the bottom line is, I don't think anybody should have to. . . . I just think the rat race is going to have to survive with one less rat." This speech involves a certain sleight of hand, a characteristic common to the hiding technique of myth. On the one hand, J. C. is withdrawing from the rat race, and on the other, she declares that nobody should have to make the choice. She is saying that a woman cannot be a high-powered executive and a mother, but her solution, her own successful Country Baby, is an option that is not open to many women. Furthermore, if Country Baby grows, will she be able to keep the mobile over her desk?

She concludes, "I really think I'd miss my sixty-two acres in Vermont. And Elizabeth is so happy there." Now comes the punch line. In a shy and coy manner, she says, "And well, you see, there's this veterinarian there that I'm seeing." In the end the myth of female embeddedness wins out. The conflict has been set up in such extreme terms that only one choice is possible. Furthermore, by mythical sleight of hand, J. C. gets to have her cake and eat it too.

> Woman may have to be returned to her place so that order is restored to the world. In classic Hollywood cinema, this recuperation manifests itself thematically in a limited number of ways: a woman character may be restored to the family by falling in love, by "getting her man," by getting married, or otherwise accepting a "normative" female role. If not, she may be directly punished for her narrative and social transgression by exclusion, outlawing or even death.
> —*Annette Kuhn (1982)*

WHILE *BABY BOOM* ATTEMPTS TO WRESTLE with the conflict between career and motherhood, though a little disingenuously, other movies take a bleaker view of female embeddedness. A lawyer tells the story of *The War of the Roses* (1989) as a morality tale to a client contemplating divorce. Oliver Rose (Michael Douglas) was an up-and-coming workaholic Washington lawyer. His wife, Barbara (Kathleen Turner), a former gymnast, threw her intense energy into raising their two children and renovating and restoring a stately old house. When she finished those tasks, she realized her marriage was a fraud and turned her energies to a catering business. As her emerging feminism came up against his sexism, the husband refused to change, and so she sued for divorce. The divorce floundered over the house. She said she should have it because she had found it, got it for a cheap price, and devoted herself to renovating it. He said he should have it because he had bought and paid for it with his work. No compromise was possible. They fight *The War of the Roses* over the house, and the film ends with them both dead on the marble floor of the foyer. They were so deeply embedded in each other's lives, so dependent on the common symbol of the house for their self-worth, that only death can separate them.

The film has a double message. By telling the story of the Roses, the lawyer successfully persuades his client not to go through with the divorce—the price is not worth it. Thus, as a morality tale about divorce, the movie fits the social conservatism of the 1980s. On the other hand, it paints a picture in which only an embedded wife can ensure a happy marriage. Barbara Rose's move to independence provokes the outbreak. While the movie initially presents her sympathetically, the tone shifts so that in the end the husband is the more sympathetic partner. She becomes another Clytaemnestra who demonstrates how dangerous a woman can be to her husband. The film cannot envision a new way to develop a relationship between men and women. It's either the old myth of female embeddedness or death.

Thelma and Louise (1991) plays out this same theme, but as the mirror opposite of *Baby Boom*. Children are nowhere in evidence, the heroines are blue collar, and their lives are headed unrelentingly downward. Louise (Susan Sarandon) works as a waitress in a coffee shop, and Thelma (Geena Davis) is a housewife married to an overbearing, insensitive, couch potato carpet salesman.

While on their way to a friend's cabin to enjoy a few days' vacation, they stop at a honky-tonk for a few drinks. Thelma flirts with one of the local Romeos, and when he attempts rape in the parking lot,

Louise shoots and kills him. Thelma suggests they should call the police, but Louise refuses, arguing that no one would believe their story. With this decision they're on the lam and eventually decide to head to Mexico to escape the law.

During the first part of the film, Louise plays the older sister who takes charge and makes the plans. Thelma goes with the flow and is out to have a wild time. In Oklahoma City, Thelma picks up a drifter and, after a night of wild sex, is a transformed person. Like much else in the plot, it strains belief that a woman who had almost been raped the evening before now has sex with a stranger. The next morning Thelma confesses to Louise that she finally understands what the fuss is all about. "I'm glad you finally got laid proper," Louise gushes. This becomes a transforming moment. But when they discover that the drifter has made off with all their money, Louise becomes the passive one and Thelma goes on the offense. To replace the lost money, she robs a convenience store. Now they are wanted for armed robbery as well as murder. As Thelma says, "I know it's crazy, but I think I got a knack for this shit." Once again we see the ghost of Clytaemnestra.

The detective assigned to the case eventually begins to put the pieces together and develops a sympathy for Thelma and Louise. He sees the murder for what it was—defense against rape. After he picks up the drifter, he accuses him of forcing them into robbery by taking their money. The detective also finds out that Louise had been raped in Texas years before and the case dismissed. As the police are massing for the final pursuit, he attempts to de-escalate the violence and tries to find another option for them. "How many times do these girls have to be fucked over?" he protests in vain.

As the chase progresses, Thelma and Louise sense that their options are running out, both in the chase and in life. As Thelma says, "Something crossed over in me." The final scene literally boxes them in. Behind them are the police, ready to shoot; in front is the Grand Canyon. "Let's don't get caught," says Thelma. "What do you mean?" asks Louise. "Let's keep going." Louise floors the accelerator, and over the cliff they go holding hands.

This film generated considerable debate among feminists. Some saw it as a triumphant statement of feminist resolve while others argued that it betrayed women. If it had been a male movie, they argued, the women would have escaped into Mexico. A comparison with *Stagecoach* (chap. 4) illustrates the point. Though relentlessly pursued, the Ringo Kid never runs out of options. He always triumphs over his enemies, and in the end, the marshall lets him escape to Mexico. Ridley Scott, the director of *Thelma and Louise*, also directed *Blade Runner* (chap. 8). So he knows the *Stagecoach* version of the tale. In *Blade Runner* the hero Deckard faces overwhelming odds, yet in the end he escapes into the sunset. But in *Thelma and Louise*, the canyon where they end their lives is a metaphor for their options—they're out of them. Deckard's space car rises through the canyon to escape; Thelma and Louise's car plunges to the depths below. Thus, some feminists argued that the movie was delivering a negative message. If women attempt to break out, they will be punished. But from the perspective of the myth of female embeddedness, the film demonstrates the lengths to which some women will go to break out of embeddedness. Just as the law has betrayed them in the past, it will not rescue them now. Even geninue male support is rejected because the myth of embeddedness hides it. Faced with the choice of being re-embedded after the freedom of lawlessness, they choose death.

Conversation between the biblical texts and the modern movies finds several points of contact. A regular pattern emerges in myth's response to efforts to dismantle it, both in the New Testament and in modern American movies. The initial insight created by the liberation from the myth of female embeddedness leads both to an effort to understand how it relates to traditional values and to an attack on female freedom as destructive of society. *Private Benjamin* and Jesus' charge of adultery against a man who sets his wife aside have much in common. Both see the embeddedness of women as abusive of their true selves. Like Judy Benjamin, the Corinthian women have tossed away the wedding veil, and like Thelma and Louise, they will appear lawless to some and willing to drive over the cliff. But Paul and *Mystic Pizza* are trying to figure out the recipe. Both want to maintain freedom without alienating men and women, to be descriptive and not prescriptive. It is a difficult and frustrating effort. As more than one scholar has noted, Paul has a double-edged effect. He supports Christian freedom and the mutuality of women and men in marriage. "On the other hand, he subordinates women's behavior in marriage and in the worship assembly to the interests of Christian mission, and restricts their rights . . . as 'women,' for we do not find such explicit restrictions on the behavior of men qua men in the worship assembly" (Schüssler Fiorenza 1983, 236). But as we have seen, this same charge can be leveled against *Mystic Pizza*. The deutero-Pauline letters, like *Baby Boom*, give lip service to female freedom while obliterating it in practice. There is no mobile over the desk, only subjection for wives. Their formula is that of the majority culture.

Another aspect of the conversation is Jesus' challenge of the focus on the myth of female embeddedness. As long as the argument involves some aspect of the myth of embeddedness, the myth will win. Miss Goodnight will have to salute the fine example of a man in Marshall Cogburn. The saying about committing adultery against a woman focuses on the woman and her integrity. Once the myth is seen for what it is—a myth—then we can understand that it is not a necessary interpretation of reality, but an arbitrary one. We are then free to begin to envision that women and men are, in the words of the saying, people who can be sinned against.

Finally, this conversation is important because when we see that the same dynamic is active in both the New Testament and modern American movies, we can begin to view the biblical text in a different way. The Bible, as a sacred text, has been important in transmitting and enforcing the myth of female embeddedness in the West. Yet we can now understand how the myth of female embeddedness has distorted the freedom proclaimed by the text. The Bible does not speak with a unified voice, but it engages the reader in conversation and invites us to experiment with the recipe for freedom.

WORKS NOTED

Betz, Hans Dieter. 1979.
  Galatians. Hermeneia. Philadelphia: Fortress Press.

Brown, Peter. 1988.
  The body and society: Men, women and sexual renunciation in early Christianity. New York: Columbia University Press.

Bultmann, Rudolf. 1965.
  "ἀφίημι." In *Theological dictionary of the New Testament* 1:509-12.

Carroll, Michael P. 1986.
  The cult of the Virgin Mary: Psychological origins. Princeton: Princeton University Press.

Conzelmann, Hans. 1975.
  1 Corinthians. Translated by James W. Leitch. Hermeneia. Philadelphia: Fortress Press.

Davies, W. D., and D. C. Allison. 1991.
  A critical and exegetical commentary on the Gospel according to Saint Matthew. Vol. 2. International Critical Commentary. Edinburgh: T. & T. Clark.

Delaney, Carol. 1987.
  Seeds of honor, fields of shame. In *Honor and shame and the unity of the Mediterranean*, 35–48. Edited by David D. Gilmore. Washington, D.C.: American Anthropological Association.

Faludi, Susan. 1991.
  Backlash: The undeclared war against American women. New York: Crown Publishers.

Fox-Genovese, Elizabeth. 1991.
  Feminism without illusions: A critique of individualism. Chapel Hill: University of North Carolina Press.

Haskell, Molly. 1973.
  From reverence to rape: The treatment of women in the movies. New York: Holt, Rinehart & Winston.

Homer. 1946.
  The Odyssey. Translated by E. V. Rieu. London: Penguin Books.

Johnston, Claire. 1977.
  Myths of women in cinema. In *Women and the cinema*, 407–11. Edited by Karyn Kay and Gerald Peary. New York: E. P. Dutton.

Katz, Marilyn A. 1991.
  Penelope's renown: Meaning and indeterminacy in the Odyssey. Princeton: Princeton University Press.

Keener, Craig S. 1991.
  . . . *And marries another: Divorce and remarriage in the teaching of the New Testament*. Peabody, Mass.: Hendrickson Publishers.

KLOPPENBORG, John S. 1990.
Alms, debt and divorce: Jesus' ethics in their Mediterranean context. *Toronto Journal of Theology* 6:182–200.

KUHN, Annette. 1982.
Women's pictures: Feminism and cinema. London: Routledge & Kegan Paul.

LUZ, Ulrich. 1992.
Matthew 1–7: A commentary. Translated by Wilhelm C. Linss. Minneapolis: Fortress Press.

MALINA, Bruce J. 1981.
The New Testament world: Insights from cultural anthropology. Atlanta: John Knox.

———. 1990.
Mother and Son. *Biblical Theology Bulletin* 20:54–64.

MALINA, Bruce J., and Jerome H. Neyrey. 1991.
Honor and shame in Luke-Acts: Pivotal values of the Mediterranean world. In *The social world of Luke-Acts: Models for interpretation*, 25–66. Edited by Jerome H. Neyrey. Peabody, Mass.: Hendrickson.

MEEKS, Wayne. 1974.
Androgyne. *History of religions* 13:165–208.

NEUSNER, Jacob. 1988.
The Mishnah: A new translation. New Haven: Yale University Press.

PAGELS, Elaine. 1989.
Adam, Eve, and the serpent. New York: Vintage Books.

PETERSEN, Norman. 1985.
Rediscovering Paul: Philemon and the sociology of Paul's narrative world. Philadelphia: Fortress Press.

SCHÜSSLER FIORENZA, Elisabeth. 1983.
In memory of her: A feminist theological reconstruction of Christian origins. New York: Crossroad.

TANNEHILL, Robert C. 1975.
The sword of his mouth. Semeia Supplements. Philadelphia: Fortress Press; Missoula: Scholars Press.

THÉBERT, Yvon. 1987.
"Private" and "public" spaces: The components of the domus. In *A history of private life*, Vol. 1: *From Pagan Rome to Byzantium*, 353–82. Edited by Paul Vegne. Cambridge, Mass.: Belknap Press of Harvard University Press.

TRIBLE, Phyllis. 1978.
God and the rhetoric of sexuality. Overtures to Biblical Theology. Philadelphia: Fortress Press.

WEGNER, Judith Romney. 1988.
   Chattel or person? The status of women in the Mishnah. New York and
   Oxford: Oxford University Press.

WIRE, Antoinette Clark. 1990.
   *The Corinthian women prophets: A reconstruction through Paul's rhet-
   oric.* Minneapolis: Fortress Press.

Peter Finch as newscaster and "mad prophet of the airways" Howard
Beale in Sidney Lumet's *Network* (1976). (Photo courtesy of Archive
Photos)

10 I'M DREAMING OF A WHITE CHRISTMAS

Then we must first of all, it seems, control the story
tellers. Whatever noble story they compose we shall
select, but a bad one we must reject. Then we shall
persuade nurses and mothers to tell their children
those we have selected and by those stories to
fashion their minds far more than they can shape
their bodies by handling them. The majority of the
stories they now tell must be thrown out.

—*Plato,* Republic

All the world's a stage,
And all the men and women merely players:
They have their exits and their entrances;
And one man in his time plays many parts.

—*Shakespeare,* As You Like It

THE NEW TESTAMENT SITS ON THE BLURRED
edge between orality and literacy. A peasant culture nurtured the
early Jesus movement, and its initial elaboration was oral. The earliest
traces of Jesus' sayings show a heavy indebtedness to orality. The
Gospel of Thomas and Q (the Synoptic Sayings Source) are collections
of sayings structured in a proverbial form like the Book of Wisdom.
The Gospel of Mark, the first written gospel built around a narrative
outline, sports orality's signals. The patterned form of its miracle
stories, for example, betrays an oral origin. The Gospel of Matthew,
written in the last half of the first century, still evidences oral forms
in the elaborate sermons it constructs for Jesus. The Sermon on the
Mount imitates the patterned units of oral speech, unlike Paul's Ath-
enian speech (Acts 17:22-31) with its highly abstract connectives.

Since we have always known a printed Bible, we find it difficult
to either see or appreciate orality's vestiges in our printed text. Actually, our assumption that these people were like us, that they wrote

259

for the same reasons that we write, is highly misleading. In a culture of nearly universal literacy, writing functions much differently than in an ancient culture where only about 5 percent of the population could read and write. We write to disseminate and read to learn. They wrote to preserve, read to recite. They learned by apprenticeship. A writer wrote to be recited, not to be read. As Harris says about book publication at Rome, "it is assumed to be the *recitatio*, not the book, which will make a man celebrated" (Harris 1989, 226). Private, silent reading, our normal practice, is nearly unattested until the time of Bishop Ambrose (d. 397).

In the first century C.E., the division between orality and literacy was not watertight. As Vernon Robbins has so forcibly argued, a manuscript culture is a rhetorical culture in which

> speech is influenced by writing and writing is influenced by speaking. Recitation, then, is the base of a rhetorical culture. People know that certain traditions exist in writing. They also know that all traditions, whether oral or written, need to be composed anew to meet the needs of the day. Each day as they spoke, they were interacting with written traditions: whenever they wrote, they were interacting with oral traditions. This interaction characterized their thinking, their speaking, and their writing. (Robbins 1993)

The model of a rhetorical culture helps us understand both the world of the New Testament and, by analogy, our own world. Increasingly, print is being subsumed into an electronic, visual culture, just as orality was absorbed into a manuscript culture. Just as writing dominates in the rhetorical culture, so electronic media dominate our culture.

Plato replaced Homer's tales with logic, science, and rationality. The truth becomes what is written, and one learns by analyzing what was written. Plato attacks the poets for precisely this reason:

> Clearly the imitative poet does not relate naturally to this [rational] part of the soul, nor is his cleverness directed to please it if he is to attain high repute among the many, but he relates to the excitable and varied character because it is easy to imitate. . . . So we are right not to admit him into a city which is to be well governed because he arouses this part of the soul and strengthens it, and by so doing he destroys the reasonable part . . . he sets up a bad government in the soul of every private individual by gratifying the mindless part which

cannot distinguish the small from the large but thinks that the same things are at one time small, at another large. He is a maker of images that are very far from the truth. (Plato, *Republic* 605, a–c [1974, 249])

Plato is right. In an oral culture the tale itself is the thing, to paraphrase Shakespeare. The tale is its own sufficient reason and needs no analysis, as anathema as that may seem to us literates who write books of analysis. In a rhetorical culture the rational contests the tale itself, just as today the graphic image competes with analysis.

All the tales we possess from the oral tradition of early Christianity have been preserved in writing and thus reformulated to meet the demands of writing. In the beginning, the parabler tells the story. The audience laughs, grieves, puzzles over the story, or even argues. Later, a scribe copies the story and analyzes the parts. The story becomes less important—words, meaning, truth overrule it. An example from an unfamiliar text can illustrate the process:

Parable
There was once a poor woman who dwelt in the neighborhood of a landowner. Her two sons went out to gather gleanings, but the landowner did not let them take any. Their mother kept saying, "When will my sons come back from the field; perhaps I shall find that they have brought something to eat." And they kept saying: "When shall we go back to our mother, perhaps we shall discover that she has found something to eat." She found that they had nothing and they found that she had nothing to eat. So they laid their heads on their mother's lap and the three of them died in one day.

Commentary
Said the Holy One, blessed be He: "Their very existence you take away from them! By your life! I shall make you, too, pay for it with your very existence!"
    And so indeed it says, Rob not the weak, because he is weak, neither crush the poor in the gate; for the Lord will plead their cause, and despoil of life those that despoil them. (Prov. 22:22-23; *Fathers according to Rabbi Nathan,* 38 [1955, 158])

We can observe three distinct moves in this parable. In the parable itself a peasant voice protests against the abuses of the wealthy. It registers a strong protest against life's inequality. Perhaps the voice is female, that of a mother appealing to the compassion of other mothers. The tale's tragic plot is driven by the landowner's failure to allow for gleanings contra Leviticus: "When you reap the harvest of your land, you shall not reap to the very edges of your field, nor shall you gather the gleanings of your harvest; you shall leave them for the poor and for the alien: I am the LORD your God" (Lev. 23:22; see also 19:9).

The parable achieves its effect implicitly. It depends on the situation's innate tragedy and the hearer's pathos for mother and sons. Its condemnation is likewise implicit; it never refers to the landowner's failure to follow Torah's demands.

When the story was written down, the epistemology changed, and scribes began to comment on the story. First, the voice shifted: "*you take away from them.*" The scribe who added this comment assumed that the reader/hearer and the landowner shared the same social position, and so the tale became a warning for the social elite, to which scribe, landowner, and reader all belong.

Also, God entered threatening future judgment: "Said the Holy One, blessed be He." Unlike the parable, which employed protest, sympathy, and solidarity, an elite accustomed to power assumes that some Power will set things aright. So the scribe invoked the apocalyptic myth. When chaos threatens to overwhelm order, God will respond. The solution is in the future; the solution is power.

That scribe or another made a second addition to the tale by quoting Prov. 22:22-23, a proof from scripture (a writing). Writing, not human experience, proves the point. Like Plato, the scribe trusts rationality; the tale belongs to the lower levels of both society and the soul. In parable, the story's concreteness proves its truth, its insight; in a scribal culture, texts prove truth: it is written.

New Testament parables were preserved and interpreted in ways very similar to the rabbinic parable of the widow and her sons. The so-called parable of the Good Samaritan, which we examined in chapter 2 in the discussion of hero stories, exhibits the same stages, an original oral story and an interpreting scribal commentary. The parable itself is easy to spot and distinguish from its scribal context. It is the story of a man traveling on the road from Jerusalem to Jericho who is robbed and then rescued by a Samaritan. The narrative context of the Gospel dictates that the scribal commentary be included in a dialogue between Jesus and a lawyer, unlike the parable of the widow and her sons, which was part of a midrash. As befits a rhetorical culture as described by Robbins, the dialogue itself is borrowed from another writing, which in turn probably adopted it from an oral form. Mark preserved this dialogue with the lawyer in the context of Jesus' Temple debates. So the author of Luke's Gospel, like the anonymous scribe of the commentary on the widow and her sons, has created the context in which the parable of the man traveling from Jerusalem to Jericho is now preserved.

Luke's commentary shifts the parable's effect. As we noticed in chapter 2, the initial shift from a Jewish point of view to a gentile one transforms the Samaritan into a "good fellow," as the traditional title "Good Samaritan" indicates, instead of a hated enemy. The story becomes a hero story, encouraging the reader/hearer to do likewise, instead of an antihero story in which the pretensions of heroism are questioned by making one identify with the victim instead of the hero. Even more, the commentary narrows the story to a legal point and thus the parable becomes an interpretation of the law on how to gain eternal life.

This shift from an oral culture to a manuscript, rhetorical culture involves a loss for the parable, what Robert Funk has termed its sedimentation. In making this point, I am not passing judgment on the Lucan commentary or the commentary of the scribe on the parable of the widow and her sons. An oral culture is not more or less moral than a manuscript culture. The loss is in hermeneutical potential in that the story is narrowed. As Funk notes, "[i]t is inevitable that world-gain be freshly institutionalized or sedimented as it becomes established as tradition. In phenomenological parlance, tradition houses the 'received world,' the circumspective horizon of all inter-pretation" (Funk 1975, 69). But there is gain, not the least of which is the parable's preservation. Without the scribal impulse, the parable would have been lost. The interpretation has also served as a powerful motivating factor in creating an admirable ideal of altruistic behavior. In this way a tradition of interpreting the parable begins. Tradition makes the parable part of sedimented language.

The parable and its commentary can serve as a paradigm of the kind of shift that we are dealing with in this chapter and that has underlaid the conversations in this book. The shift from one medium to another, whether from oral to manuscript, manuscript to print, or print to electronic, as is occurring today, involves both a loss and a gain. Things do not remain the same because hermeneutical and epistemological assumptions shift. The term *sedimentation*, which Funk has used for the shift from oral parable to written interpreted parable, has a pejorative connotation, but it need not be interpreted in this sense. The cultural shift enables the parable to find a home, a place to dwell, without which it would be lost. The sedimentation of the parable is part of the battle with myth over the issue of awareness. The sedimentation attempts to silence the parable and prevent it from breaking through the forgetfulness that allows myth to operate. But the parable remains like some forgotten fossil to disturb the sedimented layers and astonish the imagination. Through historical imagination we now have the ability to understand the parable not only as preserved in Luke's Gospel, but also as part of an oral culture. The historical imagination, a hermeneutical tool created by the printing press, must be maintained and enhanced in the new electronic culture. We must not surrender it to the engulfing present of the television tube.

> It is fair to say that in Pauline theology the ear triumphs over the eye.
> —*Werner H. Kelber (1983)*

PAUL EXPERIENCED THE TENSION BETWEEN orality and literacy and employed the distinction as part of his basic hermeneutical reflection. Yet we tend to misread the clues because of both our insensitivity to the issue and our picture of Paul. Although we know that Paul's letters are not the writings of a systematic theologian, but the occasional pieces of a pastor, we cannot help seeing in these letters a great thinker whose effect on Christian theology is incalculable. We therefore imagine Paul as highly educated and belonging to the educated elite of his day. And yet there are reasons to doubt this image.

Even Paul's writing skills are in doubt. References to his own writing in his letters always appear at a letter's end. When he tells Philemon to charge Onesimus's debts to his account, he notes that he is writing with his own hand (Philemon 19). At the conclusion of Galatians Paul notes, "Look how big the letters are, now that I am writing to you in my own hand" (Gal. 6:11 REB). Adolf Deissman thought the large letters might be a reference to Paul's untrained handwriting, although more recent scholarship has preferred to see it as a form of emphasis (Betz 1979, 314). By writing the last part of a letter in his own hand, Paul was probably trying to assure the reader that the letter was authentic; 2 Thessalonians (3:17) and Colossians (4:18), both pseudo-Pauline letters, make such a reference in an effort to gain authenticity.

Unique in the Pauline letters is the reference in Romans 16:22: "I Tertius, who took this letter down, add my Christian greetings" (REB). The REB prints the comment in parentheses, which is appropriate since it interrupts the Pauline voice that is relating greetings to the community from others, "Greeting to you from. . . ." The REB interprets the Greek text to mean that Tertius was Paul's secretary, whereas the NRSV maintains a more literal translation: "I Tertius, the writer of this letter. . . ." The interpreted translation of the REB is surely correct, but it raises an interesting question. How much freedom did Paul permit his secretaries in the composition of his letters? We do not know the answer to this question, although that has not stopped speculation.

Paul's letter writing was a substitute for his own presence and in his letters he developed a formal convention that has been identified as the apostolic *parousia*. The form has three recurring elements: "he (a) implies that the letter is an anticipatory surrogate for his presence. . . ; (b) commends the emissary who is to represent him in the meantime; and (c) speaks of an impending visit or a visit for which he prays. Through these media his apostolic authority and power are made effective" (Funk 1982, 100).

Though the Corinthians complained that he was a weak speaker, but a powerful writer (2 Cor. 10:10), and we remember him as a letter writer, that is not the way he understood himself. In Paul's autobiographical reference in Gal. 1:16, metaphors of speaking and hearing dominate: "But then in his good pleasure God, who from my birth had set me apart, and who had *called* me through his grace, chose to *reveal* his Son in and through me, in order that I might *proclaim* him among the Gentiles" (NEB). As Krister Stendahl has argued, Paul employs call language, not conversion language in describing his Damascus experience, as the reference to Isaiah 49:1 indicates (Stendahl 1976, 7–22). The call model is also reinforced with speaking/hearing language: call, reveal, proclaim. *Call* obviously belongs to an

oral hermeneutics since speaking, calling, and hearing are tied together in an oral web uniting speaker and hearer. For us *reveal* is a
content term. Some content, a message or doctrine, is revealed. But
as scholars have long noted, spelling out the content of revelation
for Paul is nearly impossible, a problem we will also encounter with
gospel. For Paul, the content of revelation is a person, "his Son,"
favoring the concrete (orality) rather than the abstract (writing). The
NEB nicely catches the double meaning of Paul's Greek text with the
expansive translation "in and through me." Revelation is not "in me"
in the sense of "inside of me." Revelation is not something that is
seen or some internal (psychological) activity. Instead, revelation is
a dynamic activity made manifest by means of Paul's preaching. The
final oral term, to preach (*euaggelizesthai*), is in Greek the verbal
form of the noun *gospel* (*euaggelion*), literally to gospelize. Thus,
Paul's autobiographical reference to his own "conversion" belongs
to a metaphorical system (Lakoff and Johnson 1980, 7–9) of the mouth
and ear—speaking and hearing—not of the eyes. His own self-understanding depends on orality, not scribalism. This metaphorical
system of speaking and hearing undergirds his hermeneutics.

The term *gospel* is a core metaphor in Paul's metaphorical system.
For us, *gospel* designates either a written gospel, a narrative of the
life of Jesus, or the Christian message. Again, it indicates content,
something expressible in writing. For Paul, *gospel* belongs to an oral
matrix, and writing the gospel turns out to be problematical for him.
In Greek *euaggelion* (gospel) has as its root sense the announcement.
As we noticed, one word commonly used by Paul for preaching,
euaggelizesthai, belongs to this same root. The accent falls not on
content or message, but on the act of announcing. The gospel is an
announcement between two people. The gospel is "the power of God
for salvation" (Rom. 1:16), a dynamic activity. Paul can speak of it
as the gospel of God (Rom. 1:1), the gospel of God's Son (Rom. 1:9),
and my gospel (Rom. 2:16), since oral speech tends to fuse speaker,
hearer, and content.

Furthermore, the word (*logos*) of God is interchangeable with
gospel, as, for example, in 1 Thessalonians where Paul parallels "we
preached (*ekēruchsamen*) to you the gospel of God" (2:9) with "you
received the word of God which you heard" (2:13). Thus, preaching
parallels hearing, and gospel parallels word. *Logos* (word) is speech
that makes something happen, "which is at work [literally energizing,

energeitai] in you believers" (1 Thess. 2:13). Like *dabar*, Hebrew for word, *logos* is God's creative activity. In speaking of those in Christ as a new creation, Paul remarks that this "is from God, who through Christ reconciled us to himself and gave us the ministry of reconciliation" (2 Cor. 5:18). He goes on to rephrase this confession: "In Christ God was reconciling the world to himself, not counting their trespasses against them, and entrusting to us the message of reconciliation" (2 Cor. 5:19). This last phrase, "message of reconciliation," is *logos* in Greek, and the "of" modifying phrase does not mean a word *about* reconciliation, but a word that *effects* or creates reconciliation. Thus, a better translation than "message of reconciliation" would be "the speaking that brings about reconciliation." Since Paul parallels the ministry of reconciliation with the *logos* of reconciliation, his ministry is speaking (preaching) that effects reconciliation. The emphasis is not on content, but on the effect of the gospel or God's word. This is performative language, like the baptismal language we observed in the previous chapter.

When we ask about the content of the gospel (or the word/message), we discover the pairing of the death and resurrection of Jesus. Although the classic elaboration is 1 Cor. 15:3-4, perhaps the earliest formulation is 1 Thess. 4:14: "For since we believe that Jesus died and rose again, even so, through Jesus, God will bring with him those who have died." This pairing occurs in every genuine Pauline letter. As Kelber notes, "The very core of Paul's gospel, the rhythmic thematization of death and resurrection, can thus be considered a product of mnemonic, oral dynamics: it is eminently memorable, repeatable, and orally usable" (Kelber 1983, 148).

This oral dynamic at the core of Paul's Gospel explains the close association of faith and hearing. In a complex argument in Romans 10, the contrast between writing and hearing becomes central. Paul contrasts Moses, who *writes* about the righteousness from the law, with the righteous of faith, which *speaks*. Most scholars in trying to explain this text employ an eschatological model, arguing that Moses represents the old age and righteousness the new one. But this leads to a confusing exegesis that cannot explain why the contrast is between Moses and righteousness instead of Christ. As James Dunn's recent commentary tellingly notes, "in contrast Paul put forward another speaker—not Christ, but 'the righteousness from faith'" (Dunn 1988, 611–12). Paul has carefully contrasted Moses as a writer and righteousness by faith as a speaker. Furthermore, the letter states that Moses *writes* (present tense), not *has written* (past tense). What righteousness says accentuates the writing/speaking contrast. The heart, which is "the main organ of psychic and spiritual life, the place in man at which God bears witness to Himself" (Hauck 1965, 611), should not *say*, " 'Who will ascend into heaven?' (that is, to bring Christ down)" (Rom. 10:6). To bring Jesus down is wrong because it treats Jesus as an object like a written thing. But what the heart does *say* is, "The word (*hrēma*) is near you, on your lips and in your heart" (Rom. 10:8). Dunn misses the point by failing to see the dominant metaphor: "Paul would regard Moses as the author of the second quotation as well as of the first. Paul must mean therefore to identify the old epoch with Moses, not unnaturally since, 'the law' and 'Moses' would be obvious correlates in his thought (cf. 2 Cor. 3). It is less clear what motivates his personification of 'righteousness' as the opposite side of the antithesis" (612). Being the honest scholar that he is, Dunn notes that his eschatological model does not explain why the contrast is righteousness and not Christ. But righteousness is the contrast because it is what results from speaking the word of faith. Paul makes it clear that the word that is near you is "the word of faith that we proclaim (*kērussomen*)" (10:8) or, perhaps better, the speech that effects faith. Paul goes on to explain "because if you confess with your lips that Jesus is Lord and believe in your heart that God raised him from the dead, you will be saved" (10:9). He elaborates this metaphorical system of speaking/hearing in a series of questions arranged in a step pattern: "How are they to *call* on one in whom they have not *believed*? And how are they to *believe* in one of whom they have never *heard*? And how are they to *hear* without someone to *proclaim* him? And how are they to *proclaim* him unless they are *sent*?" (Rom 10:14-15). The metaphorical matrix of calling, believing/faith (*pisteuein*), hearing, proclaiming (*kērussein*), and sending (*apostellein*) clearly ties Paul's preaching and apostolic mission into what Kelber describes as an oral synthesis: "At its optimum, apostolic preaching may thus promote the solidarity of the speaker with the audience, and an equation of the knower with the known" (Kelber 1983, 147).

Paul's opposition to writing comes out when he attacks those superapostles with letters of recommendation. His letter is the Corinthians, written on his heart to be seen by all (2 Cor. 3:2). This contrast between the written letter and the letter on the heart suggests the contrast between tablets of stone and the spirit of the living God. Spirit is a critical part of the metaphorical system of speaking/hearing because of its connection to breath and life. For Paul, the new covenant is not of the letter but of the spirit, "for the letter kills, but the Spirit (breath) gives life" (2 Cor. 3:6). The semantic play on breath/spirit is inevitable in Greek since the primary sense of *pneuma* is breath and by extension spirit. Breath is the metaphor for spirit. Writing is cold and dead; speech is warm and breathing. "We also constantly give thanks to God for this, that when you received the *word of God* that you *heard* from us, you accepted it not as a human word but as what it really is, *God's word*, which is also at work (energizing) in you *believers* (*pisteuein*)" (1 Thess. 2:13).

Despite the strong line that he drew between speaking and writing, ironically writing preserved Paul for us—we remember him as a writer. He himself lived on the edge of a media shift, and he feared that the new medium, writing, signaled death. Yet in the end he was wrong; it meant life for his spoken words. In a sense we lost Paul the preacher, but gained Paul the letter writer.

The only truth you know is what you get over this tube. Right now there is a whole, an entire generation that never knew anything that didn't come out of this tube. . . . This tube is the gospel, the ultimate revelation. This tube can make or break presidents, popes, prime ministers. This tube is the most awesome goddamn force in the whole godless world. And woe is us if it ever falls into the hands of the wrong people. . . . When the twelfth largest company in the world controls the most awesome goddamn propaganda force in the whole godless world, who knows what shit will be peddled for the truth on this network. So you listen to me, listen to me! Television is not the truth. Television is a goddamn amusement park. Television is a circus, a carnival, a traveling troop of acrobats, storytellers, dancers, singers, jugglers, side show freaks, lion tamers, and football players. We're in the boredom killing business.

—*Howard Beale, Mad Prophet of the Airways* (Network)

THE EFFECT OF THE ELECTRONIC MEDIA ON our culture has not gone unnoticed nor without debate, yet its power seems to grow regardless of the protest. A part of this debate has been a series of movies that have examined the impact of the new media on our lives. It is important to pay attention to the movies' critique because they were produced by people who know and understand the media and are trying to reflect on them. Furthermore, the pattern the movies create indicates how our culture is adapting to the new media.

One of the earliest films of this type was *Fahrenheit 451* (1966), François Truffaut's adaptation of a Ray Bradbury story. Produced by a British film company with American backing, it marked Truffaut's first film in English as well as his first one in color. It came at a time when major directors were beginning to take the science fiction genre seriously, a trend that culminated with Stanley Kubrick's *2001: A Space Odyssey* (1968). *Fahrenheit 451* is seriously flawed, but its image of a future age addicted to and manipulated by television is chillingly prophetic.

The movie is set in the indefinite future, which it sees not so much in terms of technological grandeur, as in the dark gray spirit of George Orwell's *1984*. Society has been leveled, and people look and behave alike and live in similar gray buildings. They are emotionless and hedonistic, tripped out on drugs and wall-screen televisions. Television so dominates this society that reading and writing have been abolished and forbidden.

Television serves as the control mechanism for a totalitarian society organized as a family. People refer to each other as cousins and have no last names, thus eliminating any sense of family history. Instead, television provides the familial glue that creates their sense of belonging. In one episode, Linda (Julie Christie), the wife of Montag (Oskar Werner), the story's protagonist, announces that she has a part in a television show "The Family." The female announcer opens the show with "Come, play with us. Come in, cousins. Be one of the family." Two men discuss how to seat dinner guests and at various points stare out from the wall screen to ask, "What do you think, Linda?" The television beeps to signal that it's her turn. Her answer is always the same, "yes." Linda believes that she alone is playing this part. When Montag suggests that the government calls all the Lindas in the country, she shoots back, "That's not true, and even if it is, you shouldn't have told me. That was very mean." She sulks and withdraws to listen to her own music through an earplug, technology that seemed futuristic in 1966, but is common today.

Montag is a fireman and firemen burn books. Very early in the film Montag meets Clarisse (likewise played by Julie Christie), who appears suspicious in several ways. First, she approaches him on the monorail to talk. In this society, individuals are isolated and conversation is rare. Second, she lives in an old-fashioned, English cottage-style house, not one of the identical, nondescript tract houses in which everyone else lives. Clarisse asks Montag about the number 451 on his uniform, and he explains that it is the temperature at which book paper catches fire and begins to burn. Then she asks whether it is true that "a long time ago, firemen used to put out fires and not burn books?" He thinks this is a very strange idea—"Houses have always been fire proof." But her house is not fireproof, so she knows better. Montag has no sense of history. He thinks things have always been this way, but she understands differentiation.

Clarisse then asks him why he burns books. He responds that it's a good job: "There's lots of variety. Monday, we burn Miller; Tuesday Tolstoy; Wednesday Walt Whitman; Friday. . . ." Obviously, no disgrace is attached to his profession, and he can hardly believe her question. Though Montag thinks Clarisse is indeed very strange, he is intrigued and continues the conversation. She asks why he thinks some people continue to read books although it is dangerous. "Precisely because it's forbidden," he answers. But she presses on, asking why it is forbidden. "Because it makes people unhappy," he replies. When she questions whether he really believes that, he insists that he does. "Books disturb people. They make them antisocial." To which she asks rhetorically, "Do you think I'm antisocial?"

Finally, she asks Montag whether he ever reads the books he burns. "Why should I?" he answers. "First, I'm not interested; second, I have better things to do; and third, it's forbidden." By now they have reached her house, and the viewer has all the clues: Clarisse is different, she lives in an unusual house, and she reads books. She must therefore be a subversive, an enemy of the family.

Many of these themes are elaborated in a conversation between the captain (Cyril Cusack) and Montag in a secret library that has been discovered in an old house. One wonders, by the way, why the firemen don't burn down all the old houses since there are so few of them and they all seem to harbor books. The captain remarks that only once before has he seen so many books in one place. Now he says, "Listen to me, Montag. Once to each fireman, at least once in his career, he just itches to know what these books are all about, he just aches. Isn't that so?" The captain acknowledges the temptation to which Montag has already given in. After Clarisse's suggestion, Montag has begun to steal books and read them at night. He began with Charles Dickens's *David Copperfield* whose opening is appropriate: "Chapter 1. I am Born. Whether I shall turn out to be the hero of my own life or whether that station will be held by another, these pages must show." When Montag reads at night, he dresses like a monk, preserving culture in another dark age.

The captain continues, "Well take my word for it, Montag, there's nothing there. The books have nothing to say." With his voice rising in anger, he sweeps a shelf of books onto the floor. "These are all novels, all about people who never existed. The people who read them, it makes them unhappy with their own lives, makes them want to live in other ways that they can never really be." Thus, reading makes people antisocial. For the captain, books are like the apple in the Garden of Eden. To give into this temptation will bring chaos. "All this philosophy, let's get rid of it, it's even worse than the novels," he says, sweeping another shelf of books onto the floor. "Thinkers, philosophers, all of them saying exactly the same thing, 'Only I am right. The others all are idiots.' One tells you that man's destiny is predetermined; the next says he has freedom of choice. It's just a matter of fashion, that's all philosophy is, just like short dresses this year, long dresses next year." How can one belong to the family, be happy, and play in the midst of violent disagreements provoked by the philosophers? Such thinking only makes the truth unknowable. Picking up a copy of Aristotle's ethics, the captain drives his real point home: "The ethics of Aristotle, now anyone who read this must think he's a cut above everyone else who hadn't. It's no good, Montag.

We've got to be alike. The only way for everyone to be happy is for all to be made equal. So we must burn the books, Montag. All the books." The captain has turned Jefferson's great declaration on its head and homogenized it into an anti-intellectual, totalitarian formula. *Fahrenheit 451* paints a picture in which one of the driving ideologies of the Western liberal tradition, the equality of all humans, becomes in the hands of the new media a tool for leveling and controlling society. Instead of inducing freedom, it produces tyranny.

The film's ending returns to the theme that we are entering a dark age and that only the monastic dedication of the few will preserve culture for the future. Linda, upset by the way reading has changed Montag, turns him in at the fire station for harboring books. A chase ensues, and the cousins are called on to report the whereabouts of the "criminal Montag." While the chase becomes a videodrama, followed avidly on television, Montag actually escapes upriver to the book people. But the television drama cannot conclude with such an unsatisfactory ending. "They must find a victim, anybody will do," one of the book people explains to Montag. So Montag gets to see "himself" being hunted down and shot on television. The mythic tale demands that evil be destroyed.

The book people are the new monks; they live peacefully in the outlands, careful never to do anything that would give the authorities an excuse to attack them. Each person memorizes a book; indeed, they so become the books they have learned that they use book titles as personal names. As one book person tells Montag, without them all human knowledge would come to an end. They have an eschatological vision that echoes a famous biblical quotation. As "*The Diary of Henri Boulard* by Stendhal" tells Montag, outwardly they look like tramps, but inwardly they are libraries: "We're a minority of undesirables crying out in the wilderness. But it won't always be so. One day we shall be called on one by one to recite what we've learned and then books will be printed again."

Montag becomes "*The Tales of Mystery and Imagination* by Edgar Allan Poe." The last line we hear from him is, "I'm going to relate a tale full of horror," a fitting balance to his first reading from *David Copperfield.*

The television drama of Montag has a different ending. As the camera shows "Montag" being gunned down, the announcer reports, "A crime against society is avenged." Everyone in the family is still equal. The tale of the new man ends more ambiguously. The tramps in the country have surrendered their own identity and become books, the very things that cause antisocial behavior. The film ends with the tramps/monks walking around, reciting their books in different languages, creating a babble of words and phrases. But this is no tower of Babel but monks reciting their breviaries. This story seeks a happy ending, but one that is happy only in the sense of eschatology. The day will come when they will be called on to recite their books.

In *Fahrenheit 451* books and television are at war, but the movie's eschatology holds out the promise that the books will eventually triumph. In *Being There* (1979) reading and writing have moved to the background, and the hero is illiterate. Chance (Peter Sellers) is a middle-aged, mentally retarded gardener who has spent his whole life in an old, secluded town house in Washington, D.C. Chance is a *tabula rasa*, a blank slate. He has been isolated in his garden with a television as his only companion. All he knows is gardening; all he knows about the outside world is from television. From it he has learned how to comport himself—to be pleasant, smile, and be calm. He is the perfect television guest. He also responds to the outside world as though it were a television. When confronted by a group of thugs, he tries to make them disappear with his remote control. He watches life the way he watches television, passively. Peter Sellers plays Chance within a very narrow emotional range, with a tight, controlled style.

When his benefactor dies, Chance must leave his town house refuge, but he is soon hit by an automobile driven by the chauffeur of Eve Rand (Shirley MacLaine), the wife of Benjamin Rand (Melvyn Douglas), a wealthy industrialist and a confidant of the president. Seeing Chance's expensive clothes (he is dressed impeccably in the hand-me-downs of his former employer), the Rands take Chance the gardener for Chauncey Gardiner and welcome him into their home.

Chance/Chauncey always speaks literally in a slow monotone, but his hearers translate his literal statements into wise sayings. When the president (Jack Warden) asks Ben for advice during an economic slump, Ben brings Chauncey to the meeting. When the president asks Chauncey for his opinion, he ponders a while and then says, "As long as the roots are not severed, all is well and all will be well in the garden." The president looks puzzled. "In the garden?" he asks. "Yes," replies Chauncey, and he continues in his precise monotone, "In a garden growth has it seasons. First comes spring and summer, but then we have fall and winter and then we get spring and summer." The president looks even more puzzled and slightly exasperated. But suddenly Ben's face lights up and he translates, "I think what our insightful young friend is saying is that we welcome the inevitable seasons of nature, but we are upset by the seasons of our economy." Later in a speech, the president quotes Chauncey: "To quote Mr. Gardiner, a most intuitive man, 'As long as the roots of industry remain firmly planted in the national soil, the economic prospects are undoubtedly solid.'" Of course, he is not quoting Chauncey, but translating Chance's literal words into the metaphorical speech befitting Chauncey Gardiner.

As a result of the president's speech, Chauncey becomes an instant celebrity and is invited to appear on the "Gary Burns Show," a late night talk show. Chauncey turns out, of course, to be a natural on the television, because it has been his education; it has literally formed him. When Gary asks if he agrees with the president's view of the economy, Chauncey responds hesitantly, softly, and in his deadpan monotone, "Oh? a, a, which view?" at which the audience breaks out in laughter and applause. Gary brings up the president's image of the stages of growth. "Yes," replies Chauncey, "it is possible for everything to grow strong and there is plenty of room for new trees and new flowers of all kinds." "And so you're saying, Mr. Gardiner, that this is just another season in the garden, so to speak." Gary clearly is speaking metaphorically, but Chance is speaking literally as a gardener. The interview continues in this vein, with Chance's literal statements being interpreted as the wisdom of Chauncey Gardiner.

While the television interview is running, the movie cuts away to a variety of people watching it, creating a complex time sequence and contrasting points of view. Among the viewers is Louise (Ruth Attaway), the black maid who had cared for Chance. "It's for sure a white man's world in America," she exclaims, shaking her head in disbelief. She is the only person in the film who raises the question of reading and writing, which so dominated *Fahrenheit 451*. "And I say this, he never learned to read and write. No sir. Had no brains at all. Stuffed with rice pudding between the ears. Short changed by the Lord and dumb as a jackass." She ends by exclaiming, "Gobbledygook," a comment not only on the television show but on the whole society that supports it. By contrast the wife of the lawyer who had turned Chance out of the town house now considers him brilliant, while the lawyer, who should know better, thinks Chance must have tricked him. He remarks how clever Chauncey is to keep his comments at a third-grade level that everyone can understand.

Throughout the film, Ben has been dying and his funeral concludes the film. The president eulogizes Ben by reading some of his one-liners, an appropriate touch for a television age. They are all trite, but catchy. "I have no use for those on welfare, no patience whatsoever. But if I'm to be honest with myself, I must say that they had no use for me either."

While the pallbearers are bearing the casket to a mausoleum that looks like the pyramid on the dollar bill, we overhear them plotting the nation's future. These old, gray eminences do not want to lose their power and can no longer back a losing president. One suggests Chauncey Gardiner. To which another responds, "But what do we know of the man? Absolutely nothing, we don't have an inkling of his past." But the response is positive, anticipating the emergence of "stealth nominees" like David Souter, plucked from obscurity to assume high positions. "Correct, that could be an asset. A man's past cripples him. His background turns into a swamp and invites scrutiny." Another joins in, "Up until this time he hasn't said anything that could be held against him. The mail and telephone response from that Burns show was the highest they've ever had. And it was 95 percent pro." After agreeing that they can no longer stand by the president, another one adds, "That is exactly why I agree with Ben's final wishes." We are left in the dark as to what these were until another one concludes, "I do believe, gentlemen, that if we want to hold onto the presidency, our one and only chance is Chauncey Gardiner." As incredible as this may seem, the film's final image suggests that it is possible. Chance walks away during the funeral, just as he constantly changes channels when watching television. At the lakeside, always the gardener, he stoops to straighten a sapling; then he walks out across the water indicating that all things are possible, as the president reads the last of Ben's one-liners, "Life is a state of mind."

This last view of Chance walking across the water, so seemingly out of place, is reminiscent of a scene in *Fahrenheit 451*. The firemen in that movie slide up the pole as well as down it. But when Montag begins to read, he can no longer slide up the pole. His captain even asks if there's something wrong between him and the pole. Those who do not read are not only blithely ignorant but are also apparently unaffected by the laws of gravity. Likewise, both films end with the first snow of winter, signaling the onset of a dark age. But there the similarities break down. The tone of the two films is completely different. *Fahrenheit 451* mounts a strident protest; *Being There* accepts the situation. Only the black maid, excluded by society, protests. The only other person who realizes that Chauncey Gardiner is Chance the gardener is the doctor who cares for Ben Rand, but he tells no one. A wry, sardonic observer, he knows better, but he allows the illusion to stand. *Fahrenheit 451* has an eschatology; this dark age will end. But the eschatology of *Being There* is realized. The characters live in the present, the now, and their attention span lasts as long as it takes to change channels.

Broadcast News (1987) is James L. Brooks's witty look at network television journalism cast in the form of a love story. Aaron Altman (Albert Brooks) is a reporter with high standards and ambitions of becoming an anchorman. Jane Craig (Holly Hunter) is an intelligent, compulsive, hard-driving news producer. Aaron and Jane are best friends and Aaron loves Jane. Tom Grunick (William Hurt) forms the triangle's third member. The network's golden boy, he admits that he sometimes doesn't even understand the news that he is reading on the air. Jane summarizes his experience for his job as, "So you're not well educated, you have almost no experience, and you can't write." To which he responds, "And I'm making a fortune." Tom is Chauncey Gardiner as a television anchor/personality. Jane loves Tom, but we are not sure whom Tom loves or whether he's sincere or a fake.

Tom represents the values of the new media whereas Aaron and Jane hark back to the old values of a print culture. But unlike *Fahrenheit 451* where the two cultures are at war, in *Broadcast News* television is the only remaining player. Both Aaron and Jane work for television and cannot envision another option. Tom is clearly the future and they must learn to fit in.

A triangular love story is an appropriate vehicle for displaying this clash of cultures and values because it allows a resolution that fits the individualistic demands of television. Aaron makes an impassioned and reasoned speech to convince Jane that she cannot marry Tom and in the process exposes the underlying mythological struggle. The speech is even cast in overt mythical terms. He begins by telling her that she cannot end up with Tom "because it totally goes against everything you're about." This has been evident from the beginning. Tom personifies flash over substance. In their first meeting, Jane is attracted to him, but she also tells him that it is hard to advise someone whom "I truly think is dangerous." In Tom's first big, on-air appearance, where he anchors a special report that she produces, she must feed him every line. When he must ad-lib for a brief moment, he degenerates into trivia.

Yet when Aaron tells her that she cannot end up with Tom because that is not what she is about, she responds, "Yeah, being a basket case." This response should be taken seriously, not treated as a throwaway line, because it indicates the way this film resolves larger issues: it reduces them to the personal. What she is about is reduced to her psychological tics.

Aaron continues, "Don't get me wrong when I tell you that Tom, while being a very nice guy, is the devil." She stomps out angrily and shouts that he's crazy. But Aaron persists. "What do you think the devil is going to look like when he's around. . . . Nobody's going to be taken in by a guy in a pointy bright tail. What do you think he's going to sound like?" he asks with fiendish groans. "No, I'm semiserious here. He'll be attractive, nice, and helpful. He'll get a job where he influences a great God fearing nation. He'll never do an evil thing, he'll never deliberately hurt a living thing. He'll just bit by little bit lower our standards where they're important. Just a tiny little bit, just coast along, flash over substance, just a tiny little bit. And he'll talk about all of us really being salesmen." After a slight pause, with a sense of despair and resignation, he adds, "And he'll get all the great women." Even though Aaron says that he is only semiserious in calling Tom the devil, his speech is serious and marks an important turning point in the narrative. In the Holocaust the twentieth century has seen the banality of evil, in the phrase of Hannah Arendt (1963); now Aaron has found evil in yet another guise, that of the nice guy, the attractive guy. The devil is so nice, so good looking, it is nearly impossible to work up the appropriate moral horror.

Aaron's reference to everyone being a salesman suggests that the desire to sell products is what has reduced standards in the new technology. The commercialization of American broadcasting has relentlessly driven it toward the lowest common denominator. This point recalls a speech from *Network* (1976). In this earlier movie, Howard Beale (Peter Finch), the anchor of the network evening news, has gone mad and become an on-air prophet. He begins by urging everyone to go to the window and shout, "I'm mad as hell and I'm not going to take it anymore." Beale becomes an instant success, and the nightly news is turned into a type of game show, while the entertainment division takes over the news division, an unthinkable development in 1976, but the blurring of news and entertainment today points to the problem. When Beale attacks the attempted take-over of the network by Saudi Arabian businessmen, Mr. Jensen (Ned Beatty), chairman of the board, calls him to the boardroom. Jensen puts his arm around Beale and walks him quietly into the boardroom. On the way he tells Beale that he started out as a salesman and people say he can sell anything. "And I'm going to try to sell you something, Mr. Beale." At the center of the paneled boardroom is a long table with a green light before each director's chair. Beale sits at one end, Jensen stands at the other, and the lights on the table form a runway connecting them.

In contrast to his previous quiet demeanor, Jensen speaks in a booming voice, like a divine messenger: "You have meddled with the primal forces of nature, Mr. Beale, and I won't have it. Is that clear? You think you merely stopped a business deal? That is not the case. The Arabs have taken billions of dollars out of this country and now they must put it back. It is ebb and flow, tidal gravity, it is ecological balance." Like some ancient god, Jensen proclaims the new order of reality. Nature has been replaced by economics. "You are an old man who thinks in terms of nations and peoples. There are no nations, there are no peoples, there are no Russians, there are no Arabs, there are no third worlds, there is no West. There is only one holistic system of systems, one vast and immense, interwoven, interacting, multi-varied, multi-domain of dollars, petrol dollars, electro dollars." Not only has nature been superseded, but the nation-states—those tributes to the printing press—have themselves been superseded. "It is the international system of currency that determines the totality of life on this planet. That is the natural order of things today. That is the atomic and subatomic and galactic structure of things today." In one of his early prophetic ravings on television, Beale had proclaimed that the tube was the new gospel, the new revelation. Now, in Jensen's proclamation, we hear the content of that new gospel. Jensen proceeds in a calm voice: "There is no America. There is no democracy.

There is only IBM and ITT and AT&T. . . . Those are the nations of the world today. . . . The world is a business, Mr. Beale."

As Jensen confronts Beale, the backlighting obscures his features and creates a halo effect. Beale thinks he has seen God and asks why he has been given this message. "Because you're on TV, dummy," Jensen shoots back. Paddy Chayefsky's screenplay exposes the dirty little secret—the driving force of the media is business.

In *Broadcast News*, Aaron's devil speech is only semiserious, like the movie itself. It cannot bring itself actually to protest against the evil it sees. It is, after all, a love story, and movies are entertainment, like the news. But the love story is frustrated because Jane catches Tom unethically staging a news event. While interviewing a woman for a report on date rape, a tear wells up in Tom's eye, a very sentimental gesture. But Jane discovers that the tear was produced later and was not a natural reaction to the woman's story. It is appropriate that Tom's staging deals with emotion and draws attention to himself. Though Jane confronts him and breaks off with him, she does not report him to the network.

At the film's conclusion, Tom is named the new network anchor, and true to form, not trusting his own ability, he asks Jane to be the managing news director. But the love triangle has broken down. Aaron is an anchor in Portland, happily married with a family. Jane is seeing somebody, and she and Aaron remain best friends. Tom has a beautiful blond wife. There is no revolt, no walking on water, and no raving mad man as in *Network* to symbolize the absurdity of it all, just a quiet retreat into individual lives as Tom continues what Aaron calls the longest running success story in history. Is he really the devil or only a good guy who has gone far with minimal talent?

> When a paradigm shifts, everyone goes back to zero.
> —*Joel Arthur Barker (1992)*

MOVIES ABOUT THE NEW MEDIA PRESENT US with a rather chilling picture. Are we anesthetizing ourselves and slipping off into a dream world, devoid of community, where our own pleasure becomes the driving force? The shift in tone between *Fahrenheit 451* and *Broadcast News* would indicate that although we fear the new media, we have already accepted their inevitable triumph. The election of Ronald Reagan and our recent political campaigns are sufficient proof of the media's conquering might. Do we like Aaron retreat to Portland and make a life of our own? Are the Christian churches to retreat into the desert like Benedict and his monks at the approach of another dark age? Do we cede the field to Tom? Or do we work out a compromise like Jane? Or are these movies only the reflection of a paranoia, so there is no reason to be concerned? Is it merely future shock, the inevitable tension of living in an age of change?

The church historian Walter Bauer in his seminal study *Orthodoxy and Heresy* (1971) has argued for a more complex picture of the relation between orthodoxy and heresy in early Christianity. The early church assumed that Jesus revealed the pure doctrine, which was preserved by the apostles and corrupted by the heretics, but that in the end the truth triumphs. As Bauer showed, the winners imposed this pattern later. Bauer's study forces us to come to terms with several myths. In early Christianity what would later be identified as orthodoxy and heresy lived together, both as Christian. In many areas, what became the "heretical" position represented the majority position, while in some others the opposite was true. Even more important, Bauer has shown that the definition of orthodoxy is always preceded by heresy, that heresy is necessary in order to define what is orthodoxy.

Bauer's study of early Christianity has important implications for our current position. With Christianity rapidly fragmenting along fault lines of conservative and liberal, Bauer's conclusions become more significant. Numbers mean nothing. Counting Christians in the second or third century would have given no indication of the outcome. So success in preaching and church growth ought not to be criteria. The preaching of the gospel is a sign of contradiction that contradicts the pleasing blandness of the television host or Chauncey Gardiner. But we must be careful here; the corollary is likewise true. Rejection does not make one a prophet, nor is success a sure sign of a false prophet. As Bauer's study indicates, numbers are irrelevant.

Even more, a fight over preserving a pure gospel is a vain argument. There is no pure gospel. We must finally abandon the myth of a pure, original gospel revelation because heresy precedes orthodoxy. We must avoid the Platonic temptation to view the gospel as a pure essence that is encapsulated in different historical garb. The gospel is not pure essence, but a living expression—the speech as Paul would have it—of historical communities and thus must constantly be worked out anew. This makes conversation an even more important method for ferreting out our situation. In conversation, the Bible is not so much the "revealed truth," a Platonic understanding of the scriptures. Rather, in the terms of David Tracy, the Bible is a classic. For Tracy, "the classics, therefore, are exemplary examples" (Tracy 1987, 12). The Bible as a classic expression of Christianity exemplifies what it means to be Christian and provides a critical conversation partner for us. It cannot represent the totality of Christianity nor even be the essential element, unless we are willing to admit that Christianity did not exist until very late in the second century when the Christian Bible came into existence (Coote and Coote 1990). The Christian communities must engage in conversation with the Bible, their traditions, each other, and the cultures in which they are incarnated. The gospel, revelation, is found in all of these.

Although there is little direct reflection in the New Testament on the shift from an oral gospel to a written gospel, that shift had a profound effect on the development of Christianity, and we are still discovering its contours. Even though Paul feared the letter and favored the spirit/breath, writing did not destroy the gospel, but only allowed it to continue the incarnating process. The rise of Protestantism occurred during another major shift in media. Although we may not ordinarily view the division between Roman Catholicism and Protestantism in terms of the differences between a manuscript culture and a printing culture, these differences go a long way toward defining the characteristic accents of the major divisions in Western Christianity. Now it appears that the electronic media are causing yet another shift. The rise of televangelists probably represents a new form of Christianity adapting to the media's new requirements. The genius of the televangelists is the pretense that they represent the old-time religion, as in the name of Jerry Falwell's "Old Time Gospel Hour." They have claimed to be traditional Christians and usurped the title "Christian." Yet they represent a complete accommodation to the needs of the new media—they are shaped and defined by the media. This shaping does not extend simply to matters of format, although one should not underestimate the impact of format (remember McLuhan's aphorism that the medium is the message).

The televangelists have created an entrepreneurial religion, built around a charismatic, telegenic host. The minister is an entertainer, a dominant model in the electronic imagistic culture. The minister in Steve Martin's *Leap of Faith* (1993) claims he puts on a professional show for a lot less than a ticket to a Broadway play. The new American religions are ahistorical and stress presence, the now. Their Christianity is reduced to bite-size bits and a few readily grasped hot buttons. Like the television news, they are better at the sensational than the analytical. They were able to make this transition so quickly because they had already dehistoricized themselves in the struggle over the legitimacy of a historical critical approach to the Bible. Thus, they forced themselves to live in an eternal present. This allows them to use the myth of traditionalism as a guise for radical change. As Harold Bloom has charged, these religions represent a post-Christianity and a new Gnosticism (Bloom 1992).

Walter Bauer's study assures us that heresy does indeed precede orthodoxy. That should not lull us into believing that we know what orthodoxy is, however. Only the myth of a pure gospel allows us that luxury. A media shift would indicate that we will have to work out a new definition and vision of Christianity.

Perhaps we should take a page from business where studies of paradigm shift have flourished in response to questions about survival. No company is large enough to assume that it can continue doing business the way it always has. The sudden collapse of IBM, once a symbol of the computer, indicates the problem. Whole industries can disappear overnight. Joel Barker, drawing on Kuhn's *Structure of Scientific Revolutions* (Kuhn 1970), defines a paradigm as "a set of rules and regulations (written or unwritten) that does two things: (1) it reestablishes or defines boundaries; (2) it tells you how to behave inside the boundaries in order to be successful" (Barker 1992, 32). Barker constructed his definition to help businesses identify successful strategies, but his definition of a paradigm covers what we have termed a media shift. By comparison, a media shift is a mega-paradigm, because it involves something much more than a shift in manufacturing technology.

Barker in his study of paradigm shifts concludes that "the single most important lesson is captured in what I call the going-back-to-zero rule. When a paradigm shifts, everyone goes back to zero" (1992, 140). Baker's paradigmatic case study is the Swiss watch industry, which long dominated world watch manufacturing. The Swiss manufacturers were the best at producing precision watch parts, and their names were synonymous with quality and accuracy. Yet the emergence of the electronic quartz movement, ironically invented by Swiss engineers but rejected by Swiss watchmakers, made all their expertise irrelevant. Actually, their success blinded them to the importance of the new development. With a new paradigm, the rules change and everyone is back to zero. Past accomplishments are irrelevant. Barker's going-back-to-zero rule is a warning to the churches. Past successes do not guarantee future success. Even more, the past may turn out to be a poor guide to the present.

In the past the Christian church has coped with two mega-paradigms. The Roman Catholic church followed the paradigm of the Roman Empire so successfully that it became the successor to that empire and even superseded it. Yet when the rules changed, when a new paradigm came, it could not adapt and so retreated into a ghetto. It is still debating whether it can leave that ghetto, or in the phrase of John XXIII, whether the windows should be thrown open to let in fresh air and light. The Protestant churches became protestant because they successfully responded to the mega-paradigm shift of the printing press. They too adapted to the rules of the reigning paradigm, as evidenced, for example, in the various models of the minister that have circulated. The minister initially was modeled on the professor, and preaching was a form of a university lecture. In more recent times, the professional model has dominated sometimes under the guise of a therapist, at other times in the guise of a counselor or a CEO. We have already seen that the new American religions view the minister as entertainer and entrepreneur.

The churches will continue to adapt to the prevailing paradigm, whether by wholesale acceptance, gradual accommodation, or resistance. The two examples we examined from the New Testament are still instructive. In the case of the parable, the shift involved both loss and gain. With writing, meaning narrowed to a point, but there was also gain in that the parable and tradition remained in contact and thus potentially in conversation. The parable could and did question its context, and its context was actually a conversation with the parable suggesting many other potential conversations. Paul, as we have seen, responded negatively to writing, identifying it with death and speaking with life. Yet his judgment turned out to be wrong.

Writing, ironically, gave his gospel (and by extension God's) life. But again what is important in Paul is the conversation. The gospel is a conversation that creates life. Conversation implies partners, us, the parable, God, Paul, and our culture.

If we engage in a conversation, then one partner cannot dominate. Howard Beale's proclamation that the tube is the new gospel, the new revelation, should be taken seriously. Heresy is always the wholesale surrender to the culture. As the Johannine Christ remarks, we are sent into the world but do not belong to it (John 17:14-16). Thus, conversation demands the establishment of independent yet dependent poles.

In *The Purple Rose of Cairo* (1985), Woody Allen, another prophet of the new media, has created a parable of the new media's temptation. The movie is set during the Great Depression; Cecilia (Mia Farrow) spends all her time watching light romantic movies because her own life is so miserable. At one point in the movie, a character comes off the screen because he has fallen in love with Cecilia. This development raises a wonderful series of epistemological questions about the status of our electronic creations. In one conversation Tom (Jeff Daniels) tells Cecilia that he enjoys his freedom and doesn't want to go back onto the screen. Cecilia replies that times are tough, "People get old and sick and never find true love." Her response blends the real world, where people get old and sick, and the filmic world, where they find true love. She sets up the contrast between reality and a dream world of true love. Tom protests that in the movies people are always consistent and never disappoint. "Y-you don't find that kind in real life," replies Cecilia. "You have," Tom assures her. You can have the dream, as the commercial cries out. But, of course, she can't. In the end, Tom is only an illusion, and Cecilia is left with her real life and the narcotic dream of the romantic movie.

How do we distinguish between a narcotic dream of escape and the promise of future redemption? Woody Allen's *Purple Rose of Cairo* and Howard Beale's proclamation of the tube as the new gospel warn us of the media's power to overwhelm and dominate our experience. The media become reality. The engagement of the gospel with this powerful new force demands we heed Karl Marx's charge that Christianity is an opiate. What keeps eschatology from being a vain dream of escape? In the parable of the widow and her sons, the story's redeeming character is its protest, which affirms the value of their lives. The parable cannot stop their deaths, but its ability to create pathos ensures their worth and will perhaps prevent the deaths of other real widows and their children. Likewise, were the scribe only to hold out the promise of God's eventual revenge, his eschatology would be a vain dream. But the warning calls the elites to task by placing God on the side of the weak rather than the powerful. The redemptive claim in the parable of the man journeying from Jerusalem to Jericho is its critique of the crippling demands of always playing the hero and the implicit identification of God with the outcast and downtrodden. The eschatological dream opposes the narcotic dream because it is not an escape from reality but a claim to redeem it. The eschatological dream is redemptive when it provokes a conversation on the meaning of reality rather than providing an escape from it. Chauncey Gardiner provides not redemption, but the illusion of well-being. The book people in *Fahrenheit 451* discover their true selves in becoming another.

The myth of the happy ending demands that I tie up into a neat package the Pandora's box of problems that I have opened. Like all myths, in the end it turns out to be an illusion that tries to think for us. Don't worry, all will be OK. Paradoxically, we cannot live without myth. It is a primary way in which we put order into our lives. The myth of the happy ending has driven me to try to understand our current situation. Yet we cannot live with merely myth. Such a life is the dead life of a television sitcom. As Paul reminds us, the word of God is speech, and all speech demands a conversation partner. We must go on conversing, seeking to sort out the babble of sound and images that surround us. Only in this way will we begin to speak the gospel in an electronic world.

WORKS NOTED

ARENDT, Hannah. 1963.
Eichmann in Jerusalem: A report on the banality of evil. New York: Viking Press.

BARKER, Joel Arthur. 1992.
Future edge: Discovering the new paradigms of success. New York: William Morrow.

BAUER, Walter. 1971.
Orthodoxy and heresy in earliest Christianity. Translated by Philadelphia Seminar on Christian Origins. Edited by Robert A. Kraft and Gerhard Krodel. Philadelphia: Fortress Press.

BETZ, Hans Dieter. 1979.
Galatians. Hermeneia. Philadelphia: Fortress Press.

BLOOM, Harold. 1992.
The American religion: The emergence of the post-Christian nation. New York: Simon & Schuster.

COOTE, Robert B., and Mary P. Coote. 1990.
Power, politics and the making of the Bible. Minneapolis: Fortress Press.

DUNN, James D. G. 1988.
Romans 9–16. Vol. 38b. Word Biblical Commentary. Dallas: Word Books.

FUNK, Robert W. 1975.
Jesus as precursor. Semeia Supplements. Philadelphia: Fortress Press.

———. 1982.
Parables and presence. Philadelphia: Fortress Press.

GOLDIN, Judah, trans. 1955.
The Fathers according to Rabbi Nathan. Yale Judaica Series. New Haven: Yale University Press.

HARRIS, William V. 1989.
Ancient literacy. Cambridge, Mass.: Harvard University Press.

HAUCK, Friedrick. 1965.
καρδία. *TDNT* 3:605–13.

KELBER, Werner H. 1983.
The oral and the written Gospel: The hermeneutics of speaking and writing in the synoptic tradition, Mark, Paul, and Q. Philadelphia: Fortress Press.

KUHN, Thomas S. 1970.
The structure of scientific revolutions. 2nd ed. International Encyclopedia of Unified Science, Vol. 2, No. 2. Chicago: University of Chicago Press.

LAKOFF, George, and Mark Johnson. 1980.
Metaphors we live by. Chicago: University of Chicago Press.

PLATO. 1974.
Plato's Republic. Translated by G. M. A. Grube. Indianapolis: Hackett Publishing Company.

ROBBINS, Vernon. 1993.
Progymnastic rhetorical composition and pre-Gospel traditions: A new approach. Edited by Camille Focant. BETL. Leuven: Leuven University Press.

STENDAHL, Krister. 1976.
Paul among Jews and Gentiles. Philadelphia: Fortress Press.

TRACY, David. 1987.
Plurality and ambiguity: Hermeneutics, religion, hope. San Francisco: Harper & Row.

SCRIPTURE AND ANCIENT SOURCE INDEX

Hebrew Scriptures

Genesis
1:27—*219, 241*
2:22-24—*221*
3:12—*222*
3:16—*220*
3:28—*219*
18:1-5—*147*

Leviticus
19:9—*262*
23:2—*261–62*

Deuteronomy
24:1—*232*
32:35—*113*

2 Samuel
7:2—*25*
7:3-7—*25*

Isaiah
49:1—*265*

Habbakuk
2:5—*144*

Psalms
89.10—*144-45*
121—*80*

Proverbs
18:16—*152*
22:22-23—*261, 262*

Daniel
5:8—*124*

Nehemiah
13:31—*21*

2 Ezra
3:1—*205*
3:1b-2—*205*
3:2—*205, 208*

3:29-30—*206*
4:12—*206*
4:13—*206*
4:21—*206*
4:22—*207*
4:23-25—*207*
5:29-30—*206*
6:19—*205*
7:62-68—*207*
7:116—*207*
8:36—*207*
8:41—*207*
8:43-45—*208*
8:47—*208*
8:51—*208*
8:55—*209*
8:56—*208*
8:57—*208*
8:59—*209*
9:14—*207*
10:48—*205*

4 Ezra—*210*

Christian Scriptures

Matthew
1:16—*221*
5—*24*
5:20—*188*
5:31-32—*234*
5:32—*233*
5:48—*188*
6:9-13—*185*

13:11—*186*
13:23—*186*
13:31-32—*187*
13:33—*187*
13:35—*187*
13:41—*186*
13:43—*187*
13:44—*151–53, 187*

13:45-46—*187*
13:47-50—*188*
13:58—*186*
16:4—*212*
16:12—*187*
19:21—*147*
19:3-12—*234*
19:9—*233*

Noncanonical Christian Sources

Rabbinic Literature

Other Ancient Sources

AUTHOR AND SUBJECT INDEX

FILM INDEX